RETIREMENT ISSUES, PLANS AND LIFESTYLES

PENSIONS: BACKGROUNDS, TRENDS AND ISSUES

RETIREMENT ISSUES, PLANS AND LIFESTYLES

Challenges Women Face In Retirement Security
Jean B. Larou (Editor)
2009. ISBN: 978-1-60741-747-7

Social Security Reform
Aaron P. Nazario (Editor)
2009. ISBN: 978-1-60692-275-0

Social Security Solvency
Jeffrey K. Bain (Editor)
2009. ISBN: 978-1-60692-833-2

Financial Asset Management and Wealth in Retirement
Terrance G. Waverly (Editor)
2010. ISBN: 978-1-60741-696-8

Impact of Financial Crisis on Retirement Security
John J. Turner (Editor)
2010: ISBN: 978-1-60692-960-5

Impact of Financial Crisis on Retirement Security
John J. Turner (Editor)
2010. ISBN: 978-1-61668-777-9
(E-book)

Pensions: Backgrounds, Trends and Issues
Henry J. Mullen (Editor)
2010. ISBN: 978-1-60876-840-0

Social Security Solvency: Issues and Projections
Martin G. Roth (Editor)
2010. ISBN: 978-1-60876-877-6

Social Security Reform: Disability, Indexing and Financing
Janet U. Burlington (Editor)
2010. ISBN: 978-1-61668-354-2

Social Security Reform: Disability, Indexing and Financing
Janet U. Burlington (Editor)
2010. ISBN: 978-1-61668-523-2 (E-book)

When to Retire: Issues in Working and Saving for a Secure Retirement
Maurice R. Davenworth (Editors)
2010. ISBN: 978-1-60876-982-7

Strengthening the Retirement System Beyond Social Security
Kala E. Upshaw (Editor)
2010. ISBN: 978-1-60741-752-1

The Role of Savings and Other Issues in Retirement Readiness
Joel K. Harris (Editor)
2010. ISBN: 978-1-60741-446-9

Overview of the Employee Retirement Income Security Act (ERISA) - Protecting Employee Benefit Plan
Terrence D. Anderson (Editor)
2010. ISBN: 978-1-60741-757-6

RETIREMENT ISSUES, PLANS AND LIFESTYLES

PENSIONS: BACKGROUNDS, TRENDS AND ISSUES

HENRY J. MULLEN
EDITOR

Nova Science Publishers, Inc.

New York

For permission to use material from this book please contact us:
Telephone 631-231-7269; Fax 631-231-8175
Web Site: http://www.novapublishers.com

LIBRARY OF CONGRESS CATALOGING-IN-PUBLICATION DATA

Pensions : backgrounds, trends, and issues / editor, Henry J. Mullen.
p. cm.
Includes index.
ISBN 978-1-60876-840-0 (hardcover)
1. Pensions. 2. Pension trusts. I. Mullen, Henry J.
HD7105.4.P47 2009
331.25'2--dc22

2009046488

Published by Nova Science Publishers, Inc. ✢ New York

CONTENTS

PREFACE

Millions of retired Americans rely on defined benefit pension plans for their financial well-being. Recent reports have noted that some plans are investing in 'alternative' investments such as hedge funds and private equity funds. To better understand this trend and its implications, this book examines the extent to which plans invest in hedge funds and private equity, the potential benefits and challenges of hedge fund investments, the potential benefits and challenges of private equity investments and what mechanisms regulate and monitor pension plan investments in hedge funds and private equity. Moreover, this book examines common 401(k) plan features and challenges sponsors face in fulfilling their fiduciary obligations when overseeing plan operations. In addition, the aging of the American population has made retirement income an issue of increasing concern to the Congress and the public. This book summarizes recent trends in pension sponsorship, labor force participation and social security issues. This book consists of public documents which have been located, gathered, combined, reformatted, and enhanced with a subject index, selectively edited and bound to provide easy access.

Chapter 1 - Millions of retired Americans rely on defined benefit pension plans for their financial well-being. Recent reports have noted that some plans are investing in 'alternative' investments such as hedge funds and private equity funds. This has raised concerns, given that these two types of investments have qualified for exemptions from federal regulations, and could present more risk to retirement assets than traditional investments.

To better understand this trend and its implications, GAO was asked to examine (1) the extent to which plans invest in hedge funds and private equity; (2) the potential benefits and challenges of hedge fund investments; (3) the potential benefits and challenges of private equity investments; and (4) what mechanisms regulate and monitor pension plan investments in hedge funds and private equity.

To answer these questions GAO interviewed relevant federal agencies, public and private pension plans, industry groups and investment professionals, and analyzed available survey data.

Chapter 2 - Private defined benefit (DB) pension plans are an important source of retirement income for millions of Americans. However, from 1990 to 2006, plan sponsors have voluntarily terminated over 61,000 sufficiently funded single-employer DB plans. An event preceding at least some of these terminations was a so-called plan "freeze"—an amendment to the plan to limit some or all future pension accruals for some or all plan participants. Available information that the government collects about frozen plans is limited in scope and may not be recent. GAO conducted a stratified probability sample survey of 471 single-employer DB plan sponsors out of a population of 7,804 (with 100 or more total plan participants) to gather more timely and detailed information about frozen plans. This report has been prepared under the Comptroller General's authority as part of our ongoing reassessment of risks associated with the Pension Benefit Guaranty Corporation's (PBGC) single-employer pension insurance program, which, in 2003, we placed on our high-risk list of programs that need broad-based transformations and warrant the attention of Congress and the executive branch. Frozen DB plans have possible implications for PBGC's long-term financial position. This report examines (1) the extent to which DB pension plans are frozen and the characteristics of frozen plans; and (2) the implications of these freezes for plan participants, plan sponsors, and the PBGC.

To view the full product, including the scope and methodology, click on GAO-08-817. To view the survey results click on GAO 08-818SP. For more information, contact Barbara Bovbjerg, at (202) 512-7215 or bovbjergb@gao.gov.

Chapter 3 - According to the Census Bureau's *Current Population Survey (CPS)*, the number of private-sector workers between the ages of 25 and 64 whose employer sponsored a retirement plan rose from 51.2 million in 2006 to 53.5 million in 2007. The number of private-sector workers who participated in employer-sponsored retirement plans rose from 42.0 million in 2006 to 44.1 million in 2007. The proportion of 25 to 64 year-old workers in the private sector who participated in employer-sponsored retirement plans increased from 43.2% in 2006 to 45.1% in 2007. Between 2000 and 2007, the number of private-sector workers between the ages of 25 and 64 who participated in employer-sponsored retirement plans fell from 46 million to 44 million. The percentage of workers who participated in an employer- sponsored plan fell from 50.3% in 2000 to 45.1% in 2007.

A CRS analysis of the *Current Population Survey* indicates that, among private-sector workers aged 25 to 64 who were employed *year-round, full-time*:

The percentage of workers whose employer sponsored a retirement plan rose from 57.2% in 2006 to 59.9% in 2007.

The percentage of workers who participated in employer-sponsored retirement plans rose from 49.2% in 2006 to 52.0% in 2007.

Only 25.5% of workers at firms with fewer than 25 employees participated in an employer-sponsored retirement plan in 2007, compared to 45.5% of workers at firms with 25 to 99 employees and 65.4% of workers at firms with 100 or more employees.

Among men and women who were employed year-round, full-time, 51.6% of men and 52.6% of women participated in an employer-sponsored retirement plan in 2007.

Only 43.0% of private-sector workers aged 25 to 34 and employed year- round, full-time participated in an employer-sponsored retirement plan in 2007, compared to 5 1.8% of workers aged 35 to 44, 57.4% of those aged 45 to 54, and 57.6% of those aged 55 to 64.

Black, Hispanic, and other non-white workers were less likely to have participated in an employer-sponsored retirement plan. Fifty-eight percent of white workers participated in a company-sponsored retirement plan in 2007, compared to 47.1% of black non-Hispanic workers, 30.6% of Hispanic workers, and 48.5% of other non-white workers (mainly Asian- American and Native American workers).

Only 27.7% of workers whose earnings were in the lowest quartile in 2007 (under $27,000) participated in a retirement plan at work, compared to 69.2% of workers whose earnings were in the top quartile (above $63,000).

The percentage of part-time workers in the private sector whose employer sponsored a retirement plan rose from 37.8% in 2006 to 38.3% in 2007. Twenty-three percent of part-year or part-time workers in the private sector participated in an employer sponsored retirement plan in 2007, essentially unchanged from 2006.

Chapter 4 - Conflicts of interest typically exist when someone in a position of trust, such as a pension consultant, has competing professional or personal issues. Such competing interests can make it difficult for pension plan fiduciaries and others, in general, to fulfill their duties impartially and could cause them to breach their duty to act solely in the interest of plan participants and beneficiaries. The proliferation of consulting work and the complexity of business arrangements among investment advisors, plan consultants, and others have increased the likelihood of conflicts of interests for both defined benefit (DB) plans, where investment risk is largely borne by the plan sponsor and defined contribution (DC) plans, where such risk is largely borne by the participant. Given the potential financial harm conflicts of interest may pose to DB and DC plans, GAO was asked to report on (1) the effects undisclosed conflicts of interest may have on the financial performance of DB plans, and (2) the vulnerabilities that conflicts of interest may pose for DC plan participants. GAO interviewed a variety of experts, reviewed the Department of Labor's (Labor) legal and regulatory authority and analyzed government and industry data associated with terminated plans.

Chapter 5 - American workers increasingly rely on 401(k) plans for their retirement security, and sponsors of 401(k) plans—typically employers—have critical obligations under the Employee Retirement Income Security Act of 1974 (ERISA). When acting as fiduciaries, they must act prudently and solely in the interest of plan participants and beneficiaries. The Department of Labor (Labor) is responsible for protecting private pension plan participants and beneficiaries by enforcing ERISA. GAO examined: (1) common 401(k) plan features, which typically have important fiduciary implications, and factors affecting these decisions; (2) challenges sponsors face in fulfilling their fiduciary obligations when overseeing plan operations; and (3) actions Labor takes to ensure that sponsors fulfill their fiduciary obligations, and the progress Labor has made on its regulatory initiatives. To address these objectives, GAO administered a survey asking sponsors how they select plan features and oversee operations, reviewed industry research, conducted interviews, and reviewed related documents.

In: Pensions: Backgrounds, Trends and Issues
Editor: Henry J. Mullen

ISBN: 978-1-60876-840-0

Chapter 1

GUIDANCE NEEDED TO BETTER INFORM PLANS OF THE CHALLENGES AND RISKS OF INVESTING IN HEDGE FUNDS AND PRIVATE EQUITY

United States Government Accountability Office

WHY GAO DID THIS STUDY

Millions of retired Americans rely on defined benefit pension plans for their financial well-being. Recent reports have noted that some plans are investing in 'alternative' investments such as hedge funds and private equity funds. This has raised concerns, given that these two types of investments have qualified for exemptions from federal regulations, and could present more risk to retirement assets than traditional investments.

To better understand this trend and its implications, GAO was asked to examine (1) the extent to which plans invest in hedge funds and private equity; (2) the potential benefits and challenges of hedge fund investments; (3) the potential benefits and challenges of private equity investments; and (4) what mechanisms regulate and monitor pension plan investments in hedge funds and private equity.

To answer these questions GAO interviewed relevant federal agencies, public and private pension plans, industry groups and investment professionals, and analyzed available survey data.

WHAT GAO RECOMMENDS

GAO recommends that the Secretary of Labor provide guidance on investing in hedge funds and private equity that describes steps plans should take to address the challenges and risks of these investments. Labor generally agreed with our findings and recommendation.

WHAT GAO FOUND

According to several recent surveys of private and public sector plans, investments in hedge funds and private equity generally comprise a small share of total plan assets, but a considerable and growing number of plans have such investments. Available survey data of mid to large-size plans indicate that between 21 and 27 percent invest in hedge funds while over 40 percent invest in private equity; such investments are more prevalent among larger plans, as shown below. The extent of investment in hedge funds and private equity by plans with less than $200 million in total assets is unknown.

Pension plans invest in hedge funds to obtain a number of potential benefits, such as returns greater than the stock market and stable returns on investment. However, hedge funds also pose challenges and risks beyond those posed by traditional investments. For example, some investors may have little information on funds' underlying assets and their values, which limits the opportunity for oversight. Plan representatives they take steps to mitigate these and other challenges, but doing so requires resources beyond the means of some plans.

Pension plans primarily invest in private equity funds to attain returns superior to the stock market. Pension plan officials GAO spoke with generally had a long history of investing in private equity and said such investments have met expectations for returns. However, these investments present several challenges, such as wide variation in performance among funds, and the resources required to mitigate these challenges may be too substantial for some plans.

The federal government does not specifically limit or monitor private sector plan investment in hedge funds or private equity, and state approaches to public plans vary. Under federal law, fiduciaries must comply with a standard of prudence, but no explicit restrictions on hedge funds or private equity exist. Although a federal advisory council recommended that the Department of Labor (Labor) develop guidance for plans to use in investing in hedge funds, Labor has not yet done so. While most states also rely on a standard of investor prudence, some also have legislation that restricts or prohibits plan investment in hedge funds or private equity. For example, one state prohibits plans below a certain size from investing directly in hedge funds.

ABBREVIATIONS

DB	defined benefit
DC	defined contribution
EBSA	Employee Benefits Security Administration
ERISA	Employee Retirement Income Security Act of 1974
NASRA	National Association of State Retirement Administrators
PBGC	Pension Benefit Guaranty Corporation
PERAC	Public Employee Retirement Administration Commission
SEC	U.S. Securities and Exchange Commission
SFAS	Statement of Financial Accounting Standards
S&P	Standard and Poor's
TRS	Teacher Retirement System of Texas

August 14, 2008

Congressional Requesters

Millions of Americans rely on defined benefit pension plans for their financial well-being after their working years.[1] In order to pay promised retirement benefits when due at an acceptable cost, employers must make adequate contributions to these funds and plan fiduciaries must invest the fund balance in assets that yield an adequate rate of return over time. Historically, public and private sector pension plans have primarily invested in traditional investments such as stocks and bonds; however, recent press reports indicate that plans are increasingly investing in "alternative" investments such as hedge funds and private equity funds.

While there is no statutory definition of hedge funds, the phrase "hedge fund" is commonly used to refer to a pooled investment vehicle that is privately organized and administered by professional managers, and that often engages in active trading of various types of securities and commodity futures and options contracts.[2] Similarly, private equity funds are not statutorily defined, but are generally considered privately managed investment pools administered by professional managers, who typically make long-term investments in private companies, taking a controlling interest with the aim of increasing the value of these companies through such strategies as improved operations or developing new products. Both hedge funds and private equity funds may be managed so as to be exempt from certain aspects of federal securities law and regulation that apply to other investment pools such as mutual funds.

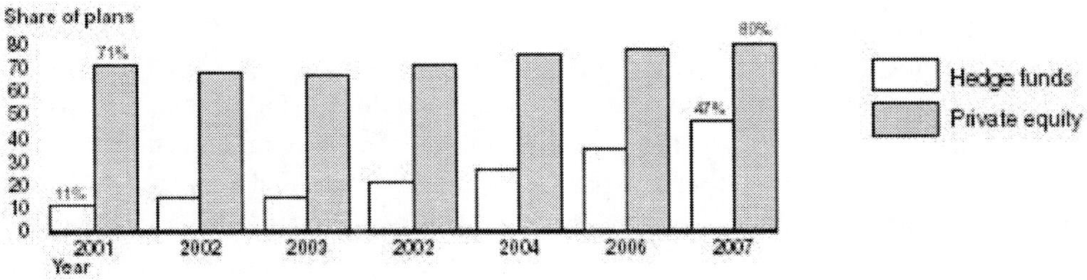

Source: *Pensions & Investments*' 2007 annual survey.

Share of Large Plans Investing in Hedge Funds and Private Equity

Pension plan investments in hedge funds and private equity have been controversial for a number of reasons. While hedge funds investments are made mainly by relatively wealthy individuals and institutional investors, the recent increase in pension plan investments in hedge funds indirectly exposes people of modest incomes to the risks of hedge fund investing. This has been cited as a concern because a pension plan that experiences substantial losses as a result of a hedge fund investment may be unable to meet its obligations to pensioners. The perceived riskiness of hedge funds and the collapse of some of these funds in recent years have led some industry experts and union officials to express concern about plan investments in such vehicles, including the appropriate steps plan officials should take in conducting proper due diligence. A further cause for their concern is the ability of hedge funds and private equity funds to qualify for exemptions from certain aspects of federal securities law and regulations that apply to other investment pools.

In order to better understand the extent to which defined benefit pension plans invest in hedge funds and private equity and the implications of such investments for the security of pension plan assets, you asked us to examine the extent and nature of defined benefit pension plans' investments in these alternative investments. Specifically, you asked us to address the following questions:

1. To what extent do public and private sector pension plans invest in hedge funds and private equity funds?
2. What are the potential benefits, risks, and challenges pension plans face in making hedge fund investments, and how do plans address the risks and challenges?
3. What are the potential benefits, risks, and challenges pension plans face in making private equity fund investments, and how do plans address the risks and challenges?
4. What mechanisms regulate and monitor pension plan investments in hedge funds and private equity funds?

To answer these questions, this report was reviewed with relevant literature and survey data and conducted in-depth interviews with pension plan representatives and industry experts. We obtained and analyzed data on the extent of pension plan investments in hedge funds and private equity from private organizations such as Greenwich Associates, *Pensions & Investments*, and Pyramis Global Advisors. Although these surveys had several limitations— for example, the survey data generally represent the holdings of larger pension plans—we determined they were sufficiently reliable for purposes of our study. To answer the second and third questions, we conducted in-depth interviews with representatives of 26 public and private sector DB pension plans and, where possible, obtained and reviewed supporting documentation. These plans were selected based on several criteria, including the range of investment in hedge funds and private equity and the amount of total plan assets. We also interviewed officials of regulatory agencies, relevant industry organizations, investment consulting firms, and other national experts. To identify state and federal regulatory and monitoring policies, we interviewed officials at the Department of Labor (Labor) and representatives of relevant agencies in selected states, and reviewed relevant policy documents. We contacted regulators in 11 states, including the 10 states with the largest amount of public pension assets according to the National Association of State Retirement Administrators (NASRA) Public Funds Survey data.[3]

We conducted this performance audit from June 2007 to July 2008, in accordance with generally accepted government auditing standards. Those standards require that we plan and perform the audit to obtain sufficient, appropriate evidence to provide a reasonable basis for our findings and conclusions based on our audit objectives. We believe that the evidence obtained provides a reasonable basis for our findings and conclusions based on our audit objectives.

RESULTS IN BRIEF

While hedge fund and private equity fund investments generally comprise a limited share of total plan assets, a considerable and growing number of private and public DB plans make such investments. According to available survey data, which generally reflect the holdings of larger DB plans, average allocations to hedge funds and private equity in 2007 were around 4 percent and 5 percent of total plan assets, respectively. However, according to one survey, a few pension plans had relatively large allocations of about 30 percent to hedge funds, while one public plan had an allocation of about 20 percent to private equity. Available survey data indicate that from about 21 to 27 percent of mid- to large-size pension plans invested in hedge funds in 2006, while just over 40 percent invested in private equity. Although investments in private equity remain more prevalent than hedge fund investments among both private and public pension plans surveyed, the number of plans investing in hedge funds has increased in recent years more than for private equity funds. Investments in hedge funds and private equity are more common among large pension plans, measured by assets under management, compared to mid-size plans. For example, about 16 percent of plans with $250 to $500 million were invested in hedge funds, while 29 percent of plans with $1 billion or more had such investments, according to a 2006 survey. Similarly, for private equity, 16 percent of plans with $250 - $500 million had such investments compared to 77 percent of plans with $1 billion or more in 2006. Survey data on plans with less than $200 million in assets are unavailable and, in their absence, the extent to which these plans invest in hedge funds or private equity is unknown.

Pension plans invest in hedge funds to obtain various benefits, but some characteristics of hedge funds also pose challenges that demand greater expertise and effort than more traditional investments, which some plans may not be able to fully address. Pension plans told us that they invest in hedge funds in order to achieve one or more of several goals, including steadier, less volatile returns, obtaining returns greater than those expected in the stock market, or diversification of portfolio investments. Pension plan officials we spoke with about hedge fund investments all said these investments had generally met or exceeded expectations. However, at the time of our contact in 2007, several plan officials noted that their hedge fund investments had not yet been tested under stressful economic conditions, such as a significant stock market decline. Further, some indicated mixed experiences with hedge fund investments. At the time of our discussions, however, officials of each plan interviewed indicated that they expected to maintain or increase the share of assets invested in hedge funds. Nonetheless, hedge fund investments pose investment challenges beyond those posed by traditional investments in stocks and bonds. These additional challenges include: (1) the inherent risks of relying on the skill and techniques of the hedge fund manager; (2) limited information on a hedge fund's underlying assets and valuation (limited transparency); (3) contract provisions which limit an investor's ability to redeem an investment in a hedge fund for a defined period of time (limited liquidity); and 4) the possibility that a hedge fund's active or risky trading activity will result in losses due to operational failure such as trading errors or outright fraud (operational risk). Although there are challenges of hedge fund investing, plan officials and others described steps to address these and other challenges. For example, plan officials and others told us that it is important to negotiate key investment terms and conduct a thorough "due diligence" review of prospective hedge funds, including review of a hedge fund's operational structure. Further, pension plans can invest in funds of hedge funds, which charge additional fees but provide diversification and the additional skill of the fund of funds manager. According to plan officials and others, some of these steps require considerably greater effort and expertise from fiduciaries than is required for more traditional investments, and such steps may be beyond the capabilities of some pension plans, particularly smaller ones.

Pension plans invest in private equity primarily in expectation of higher rates of return than traditional investments, but these investments too pose challenges that require substantial effort and expertise to address. The major benefits pension plans seek from private equity investments are long-term returns in excess of stocks and, to a lesser degree, to further diversify the plan's portfolio. Pension plan officials we spoke with generally had longer experience investing in private equity than in hedge funds—in some cases over 20 years—and each plan's representatives indicated these investments have met expectations and most expressed plans to maintain or increase their allocations. Nevertheless, investments in private equity present distinct challenges and risks beyond those faced with traditional investments. These include: (1) the variation of performance among private equity funds, which is greater than for other asset classes, and the difficulty of gaining access to recognized top-performing funds; (2) longer-term commitments of 10 years or more, during which the pension plan may not be able to redeem its investment; and (3) valuation of the investment, which is difficult to assess prior to the sale of underlying holdings. As with hedge funds, taking steps to mitigate the challenges of investing in private equity funds requires greater expertise and effort than making traditional investments. Plans told us that, as a part of their due diligence and ongoing monitoring efforts, they regularly reviewed reports on the performance of the underlying investments of the private equity fund and held periodic meetings with fund managers. As with hedge funds, the extensive amount of monitoring required for private equity investments may be impractical for pension plans that have more limited resources, such as smaller plans.

The federal government does not specifically limit or monitor private sector pension investment in hedge funds or private equity and, while some states do so for public plans, their approaches vary. Under the Employee Retirement and Income Security Act (ERISA), plan fiduciaries are expected to meet general standards of prudent investing and no specific restrictions on investments in hedge funds or private equity have been established. Labor is tasked with helping to ensure plan sponsors meet their fiduciary duties; however, it does not currently provide any guidance specific to pension plan investments in hedge funds or private equity. Conversely, some states do specifically regulate and monitor public sector pension investment in hedge funds and private equity, but these approaches vary from state to state. While states generally have adopted a "prudent man" standard similar to that in ERISA, some states also explicitly restrict or prohibit pension plan investment in hedge funds or private equity. For instance, in Massachusetts, the agency overseeing public plans will not permit plans with less than $250 million in total assets to invest directly in hedge funds. Some states have detailed lists of authorized investments that exclude hedge funds and/or private equity. Other states may limit investment in certain investment vehicles or trading strategies employed by hedge fund or private equity fund managers. While some guidance exists for hedge fund investors, specific guidance aimed at pension plans could serve as an additional tool for plan fiduciaries when assessing whether and to what degree hedge funds would be a prudent investment.

To ensure that all plan fiduciaries can better assess their ability to invest in hedge funds and private equity, and to ensure that those that choose to make such investments are better prepared to meet these challenges, we recommend that the Secretary of Labor provide guidance on investing in hedge funds and private equity specifically designed for qualified plans under ERISA. In responding to a draft of this report, Labor generally agreed with our findings and recommendation.

Labor and other federal agencies also provided technical comments on the draft report, which we have incorporated where appropriate.

BACKGROUND

Millions of current and future retirees rely on private or public DB pension plans, which promise to pay retirement benefits that are generally based on an employee's salary and years of service. The financial condition of these plans—and hence their ability to pay promised retirement benefits when such benefits are due—depends on adequate contributions from employers and, in some cases, employees, as well as prudent investments that preserve principal and yield an adequate rate of return over time. The plan sponsor must make required contributions to the plan that are intended to ensure it is adequately funded to pay promised benefits. To maintain and increase plan assets, fiduciaries of public and private sector pension plans invest in assets that are expected to grow in value or yield income. In making investments, DB plan managers consider a plan's benefit payment requirements and balance the desire to maximize return on investment and the desire to limit the overall risk to the investment portfolio to an acceptable level. In doing so, plan fiduciaries invest in various categories of assets classes, which traditionally have consisted mainly of stocks and bonds. Stocks offer relatively high expected longterm returns at the risk of considerable volatility, that is, the likelihood of significant short-term losses or gains. On the other hand, bonds and other fixed income investments offer a steady income stream and relatively low volatility, but lower expected long-term returns. Different proportions of these two asset classes will, therefore, provide different degrees of risk and expected return on investment. Pension fiduciaries may also invest in other asset classes or trading strategies, such as hedge funds and private equity, which are generally considered to be riskier investments, so long as such investments are prudent.

Private sector pension plan investment decisions must comply with the provisions of ERISA, which stipulates fiduciary standards based on the principle of a prudent man standard. Under ERISA, plan sponsors and other fiduciaries must (1) act solely in the interest of the plan participants and beneficiaries and in accordance with plan documents; (2) invest with the care, skill, and diligence of a prudent person with knowledge of such matters; and (3) diversify plan investments to minimize the risk of large losses. Under ERISA, the prudence of any individual investment is considered in the context of the total plan portfolio, rather than in isolation.[4] Hence, a relatively risky investment may be considered prudent, if it is part of a broader strategy to balance the risk and expected return to the portfolio. In addition to plan sponsors, under the ERISA definition of a fiduciary, any other person that has discretionary authority or control over a plan asset is subject to ERISA's fiduciary standards.[5] The Employee Benefit Security Administration (EBSA) at Labor is responsible for enforcing these provisions of ERISA, as well as educating and assisting retired workers and plan sponsors. Another federal agency, the Pension Benefit Guaranty Corporation (PBGC), collects premiums from federally insured plans in order to insure the benefits of retirees if a plan terminates without sufficient assets to pay promised benefits.

In the public sector, governments have established pension plans at state, county, and municipal levels, as well as for particular categories of employees, such as police officers, fire fighters, and teachers. The structure of public pension plan systems can differ considerably from state to state. In some states, most or all public employees are covered by a single consolidated DB retirement plan, while in other states many retirement plans exist for various units of government and employee groups. Public sector DB plans are not subject to funding, vesting and most other requirements applicable to private sector DB plans under ERISA, but must follow requirements established for them under applicable state law. While states generally have adopted standards essentially identical to the ERISA prudent man standard, specific provisions of law and regulation vary from state to state. Public plans are also not insured by the PBGC, but could call upon state or local taxpayers in the event of a funding shortfall.

Hedge Funds Use Broad Range of Investment Strategies to Achieve Desired Return

Although there is no statutory or universally accepted definition of hedge funds, the term is commonly used to describe pooled investment vehicles that are privately organized and administered by professional managers and that often engage in active trading of various types of securities, commodity futures, options contracts, and other investment vehicles. In recent years, hedge funds have grown rapidly. As we reported in January 2008, according to industry estimates, from 1998 to early 2007, the number of funds grew from more than 3,000 to more than 9,000 and assets under management from more than $200 billion to more than $2 trillion globally.[6]

Hedge funds also have received considerable media attention as a result of the high-profile collapse of several hedge funds, and consequent losses suffered by investors in these funds. Although hedge funds have the reputation of being risky investment vehicles that seek exceptional returns on investment, this was not their original purpose, and is not true of all hedge funds today. Founded in the 1940s, one of the first hedge funds invested in equities and used leverage and short selling to protect or "hedge" the portfolio from its exposure to movements in the stock market.[7] Over time, hedge funds diversified their investment portfolios and engaged in a wider variety of investment strategies. Because hedge funds are typically exempt from registration under the Investment Company Act of 1940, they are generally not subject to the same federal securities regulations as mutual funds. They may invest in a wide variety of financial instruments, including stocks and bonds, currencies, futures contracts, and other assets. Hedge funds tend to be opportunistic in seeking positive returns while avoiding loss of principal, and retaining considerable strategic flexibility. Unlike a mutual fund, which must strictly abide by the detailed investment policy and other limitations specified in its prospectus, most hedge funds specify broad objectives and authorize multiple strategies. As a result, most hedge fund trading strategies are dynamic, often changing rapidly to adjust to market conditions.

Hedge funds are typically structured and operated as limited partnerships or limited liability companies exempt from certain registration, disclosure and other requirements under the Securities Act of 1933,[8] Securities Exchange Act of 1934,[9] Investment Company Act of

1940,[10] and Investment Advisers Act of 1940[11] that apply in connection to other investment pools, such as mutual funds. For example, to allow them to qualify for various exemptions under such laws, hedge funds usually limit the number of investors, refrain from advertising to the general public, and solicit fund participation only from large institutions and wealthy individuals. The presumption is that investors in hedge funds have the sophistication to understand the risks involved in investing in them and the resources to absorb any losses they may suffer. Although many workers may be impacted by any losses resulting from pension fund investment in hedge funds, a pension plan counts as a single investor that does not prevent a hedge fund from qualifying for the various statutory exemptions.

Individuals and institutions may also invest in hedge funds through funds of hedge funds, which are investment funds that buy shares of multiple underlying hedge funds. Fund of funds managers invest in other hedge funds rather than trade directly in the financial markets, and thus offer investors broader exposure to different hedge fund managers and strategies. Like hedge funds, funds of funds may be exempt from various aspects of federal securities and investment law and regulation.

Private Equity Funds Obtain Returns from Manager Skill and Investing Capital in a Limited Number of Private Firms

Like hedge funds, there is no legal or commonly accepted definition of private equity funds, but the term generally includes privately managed pools of capital that invest in companies, many of which are not listed on a stock exchange. Although there are some similarities in the structure of hedge funds and private equity funds, the investment strategies employed are different. Unlike many hedge funds, private equity funds typically make longer-term investments in private companies and seek to obtain financial returns not through particular trading strategies and techniques, but through long-term appreciation based on corporate stewardship, improved operating processes and financial restructuring of those companies, which may involve a merger or acquisition of companies. Private equity is generally considered to involve a substantially higher degree of risk than traditional investments, such as stocks and bonds, for a higher return.[12]

While strategies of private equity funds vary, most funds target either venture capital or buy-out opportunities. Venture capital funds invest in young companies often developing a new product or technology. Private equity fund managers may provide expertise to a fledgling company to help it advance toward a position suitable for an initial public offering. Buyout funds generally invest in larger established companies in order to add value, in part, by increasing efficiencies and, in some cases, consolidating resources by merging complementary businesses or technologies. For both venture capital and buy-out strategies, investors hope to profit when the company is eventually sold, either when offered to the public or when sold to another investor or company. Each private equity fund generally focuses on only one type of investment opportunity, usually specializing in either venture capital or buyout and often specializing further in terms of industry or geographical area.[13] Investment in private equity has grown considerably over recent decades. According to a venture capital industry organization, the amount of capital raised by private equity funds grew from just over $2 billion in 1980 to about $207 billion in 2007; while the number of private equity funds grew from 56 to 432 funds over the same time period.

As with hedge funds, private equity funds operate as privately managed investment pools and have generally not been subject to Securities and Exchange Commission (SEC) examinations. Pension plans typically invest in private equity through limited partnerships in which the general partner develops an investment strategy and limited partners provide the large majority of the capital. After creating a new fund and raising capital from the limited partners, the general partner begins to invest in companies that will make up the fund portfolio (see figure 1). Limited partners have both limited control over the underlying investments and also limited liability for potential debts incurred by the general partners through the fund.

Similar to hedge funds, private equity funds may be structured to qualify for exemptions from certain registration and disclosure requirements of federal securities laws; for example, by refraining from advertising to the general public. The majority of investments in private equity funds come from wealthy individuals and institutional investors, such as endowments, banks, corporations, and pension plans.

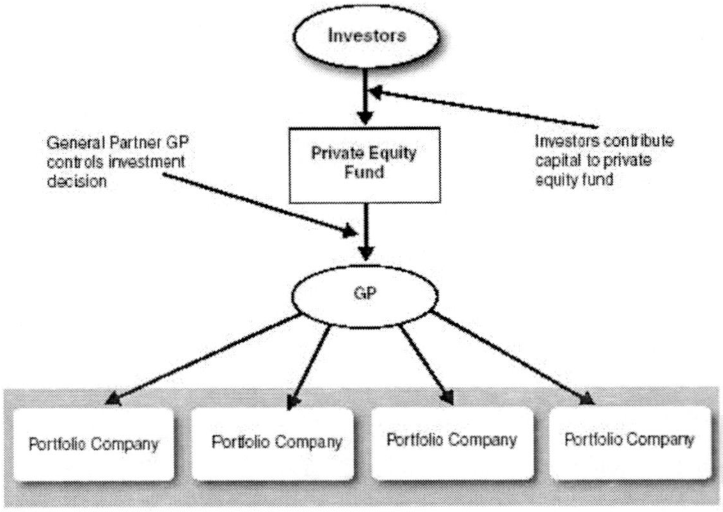

Source: New York State Common Retirement Fund Division of Pension Investment and Case Management.

Figure 1. Structure of Private Equity Investing

A GROWING NUMBER OF PENSION PLANS ARE INVESTING IN HEDGE FUNDS OR PRIVATE EQUITY, BUT SUCH INVESTMENTS ARE GENERALLY A SMALL PORTION OF PLAN ASSETS

According to several recent surveys, investments in hedge funds and private equity are typically a small portion of total plan assets—about 4 to 5 percent on average—but a considerable and growing number of plans invest in them. While investment in hedge funds is less common than private equity, the number of plans with investments in hedge funds has experienced greater growth in recent years. Furthermore, survey data show that larger plans, measured by total plan assets, are more likely to invest in hedge funds and private equity compared to mid-size plans. Survey data on plans with less than $200 million in assets are unavailable and, thus, the extent to which small plans invest in hedge funds and private equity is unknown.

Investments in Hedge Funds and Private Equity Typically Comprise a Small Share of Total Plan Assets

Individual plans' hedge fund or private equity investments typically comprise a small share of total plan assets. According to a *Pensions & Investments* survey of large plans (as measured by total plan assets), the average allocation to hedge funds among plans with such investments was about 4 percent in 2007.[14] Similarly, among plans with investments in private equity, the average allocation was about 5 percent. An earlier survey by Pyramis Global Advisors, which included mid- to large-size plans, found an average allocation of 7 percent for hedge funds and 5 percent for private equity in 2006.

Although the majority of plans with investments in hedge funds or private equity have small allocations to these assets, a few plans have relatively large allocations, according to the *Pensions & Investments* survey (see figure 2).[15] Of the 62 plans that reported investments in hedge funds in 2007, 12 plans had allocations of 10 percent or more and, of those, 3 plans had allocations of 20 percent or more. The highest reported hedge fund allocation was 30 percent of total assets. Large allocations to private equity were even less common. A total of 106 surveyed plans reported investments in private equity in 2007, of which 11 plans had allocations of 10 percent or more and, of those, 1 plan had an allocation of about 20 percent.

While More Pension Plans Invest in Private Equity, the Number of Plans with Investments in Hedge Funds Has Experienced Greater Growth in Recent Years

Two recent surveys of pension plans indicate that a considerable number of plans invest in hedge funds or private equity. As seen in table 1, from about 21 to 27 percent of all plans surveyed, which included mid- to large- size plans, held investments in hedge funds as of 2006, according to data from Greenwich Associates and Pyramis.[16] Both surveys reveal that a greater share of private sector plans invested in hedge funds compared to public sector plans. The Greenwich survey also found that hedge fund investment was most common among collectively bargained plans, although the number of these plans surveyed was substantially smaller as there are relatively few of these plans in operation.[17] Nearly half—8 out of 17—of collectively bargained plans surveyed invested in hedge funds.

Investment in private equity is much more prevalent than investment in hedge funds, among plans surveyed. The Greenwich survey found that about 43 percent of plans held investments in private equity in 2006, while the Pyramis survey found that 41 percent of plans had such investments. Both surveys also show that a larger percentage of public sector plans are invested in private equity compared to private sector plans. As with hedge funds, the Greenwich survey found that investment in private equity was most common among collectively bargained plans. More than two-thirds— 12 out of 17—of collectively bargained plans surveyed invested in private equity.

While pension plan investment in hedge funds is less prevalent than investment in private equity, hedge fund investment has increased much more in recent years. According to Greenwich Associates, from 2004 to 2006, the percent of plans with investments in hedge funds grew from just under 20 percent to almost 27 percent. Meanwhile, the percent of plans with investments in private equity increased at a lesser rate, from about 39 percent in 2004 to 43 percent in 2006. A survey by *Pensions & Investments* found that this comparison was more pronounced over a 6-year period (see figure 3). Among larger plans surveyed by Pensions & Investments, the percent of plans with investments in hedge funds grew from about 11 percent in 2001 to nearly 47 percent in 2007. Over the same time period, investments in private equity remained more prevalent, but grew much more slowly.

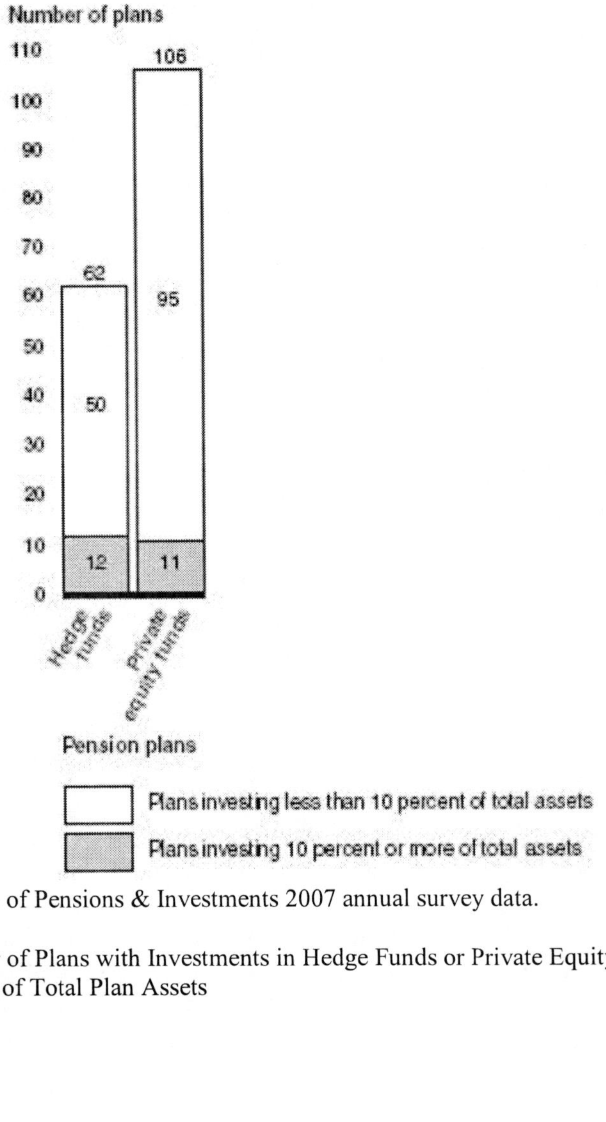

Source: GAO analysis of Pensions & Investments 2007 annual survey data.

Figure 2. The Number of Plans with Investments in Hedge Funds or Private Equity by Size of Investment as a Share of Total Plan Assets

Table 1. Extent of DB Plan Investments in Hedge Funds and Private Equity

	Greenwich Associates (2006)	Pyramis Global Advisors (2006)
Sample	164 public sector plans; 420 private sector plans, including 17 collectively bargained plans (all plans had $250 million or more in total assets)	90 public sector plans; 124 private sector plans (all plans had greater than $200 million in total assets)
Share of plans that invest in hedge funds:		
All plans	27%	21%
Public sector	24%	17%
Private sector	28%	25%
Private sector: collectively bargained	47%	n/a
Share of plans that invest in private equity:		
All plans	43%	41%
Public sector	51%	44%
Private sector	40%	38%
Private sector: collectively bargained	71%	n/a

Source: Greenwich Associates and Pyramis Global Advisors, 2006.
Note: The total assets of plans surveyed by Greenwich Associates was $3.6 trillion.

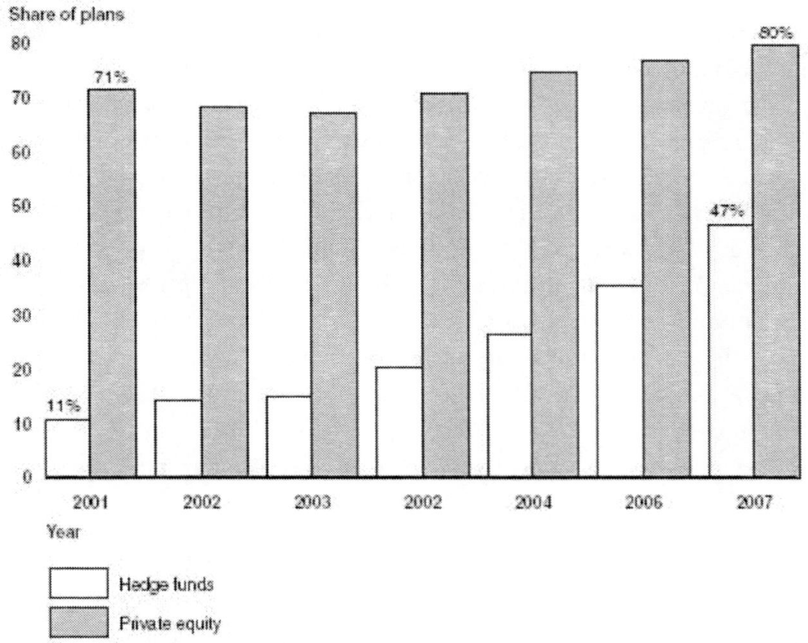

Source: *Pensions & Investments'* 2007 annual survey.

Figure 3. Share of Large DB Plans Investing in Hedge Funds and Private Equity

While pension plan investment in hedge funds has experienced greater growth in recent years, pension plan investment in private equity increased markedly following a 1979 Labor clarification that plans may make some investments in riskier assets, such as venture capital and buyout funds.[18] Prior to 1979, such investments were generally viewed as a potential violation of ERISA. Labor clarified that ERISA's prudent man standard applies to investment decisions in the context of the entire portfolio rather than in isolation. Following the Labor guidance, pension plan investments in venture capital and buy-out funds experienced rapid growth. One study reported that pension plans' share of venture capital investments grew from 15 percent in 1978 to 50 percent in 1986, during which time overall investment in venture capital increased more than 10-fold from $427 million to $4.4 billion.[19] More recently, the National Venture Capital Association estimates that pension plans held 42 percent of the approximately $20 billion invested in domestic venture capital funds in 2004.

Investments in Hedge Funds and Private Equity Are More Commonplace among Larger Pension Plans

Survey data show that larger plans, measured by total plan assets, are more likely to invest in hedge funds and private equity compared to midsize plans. Greenwich found that only 16 percent of mid-size plans—those with $250 to $500 million in total assets—were invested in hedge funds, compared to about 31 percent of the largest plans—those with $5 billion or more in assets (see figure 4). Similarly, only about 16 percent of mid-size plans held investments in private equity, whereas slightly over 71 percent of the largest plans held such investments. *Pensions & Investments* survey of large plans corroborates this pattern—about 47 percent of plans held investments in hedge funds and nearly 80 percent held investments in private equity in 2007 (see figure 3).

Survey data on plans with less than $200 million in assets are unavailable and, in the absence of this information, it is unclear to what extent these plans invest in hedge funds and private equity.[20] Representatives of investment consulting firms and industry experts told us that they suspect few small plans have such investments, but they could not provide data to confirm this. A representative of a large investment consulting firm explained that smaller plans face inherent restrictions on investing in hedge funds and private equity funds because the required minimum investments for these funds are often too high to allow small plans to make such investments while remaining sufficiently diversified.

Pension Plans Seek Various Investment Objectives through Hedge Funds, and Such Investments Pose Challenges That Require Considerable Effort and Expertise to Address

While pension plans seek important benefits through investments in hedge funds, hedge funds also pose challenges that demand greater expertise and effort than investments in more traditional assets. Pension plans told us that they invest in hedge funds to achieve one or more of several goals, including lessening the volatility of returns, obtaining returns greater than those expected in the stock market, and/or diversifying the portfolio by investing in a vehicle that will not be correlated with other asset classes in the portfolio. While all the pension plans we contacted that had invested in hedge funds expressed general satisfaction with these investments, hedge fund investments nonetheless pose significant challenges to pension plan fiduciaries, beyond the inherent challenges of investing in more familiar asset classes such as stocks and bonds. Plan officials and others outlined steps to limit these and other challenges, such as conducting in-depth due diligence reviews or investing through funds of funds, which can mitigate some of the main difficulties of hedge funds. Such steps entail greater expense, effort, or expertise than is required for more traditional investments, and some pension plans may not be equipped to meet these demands.

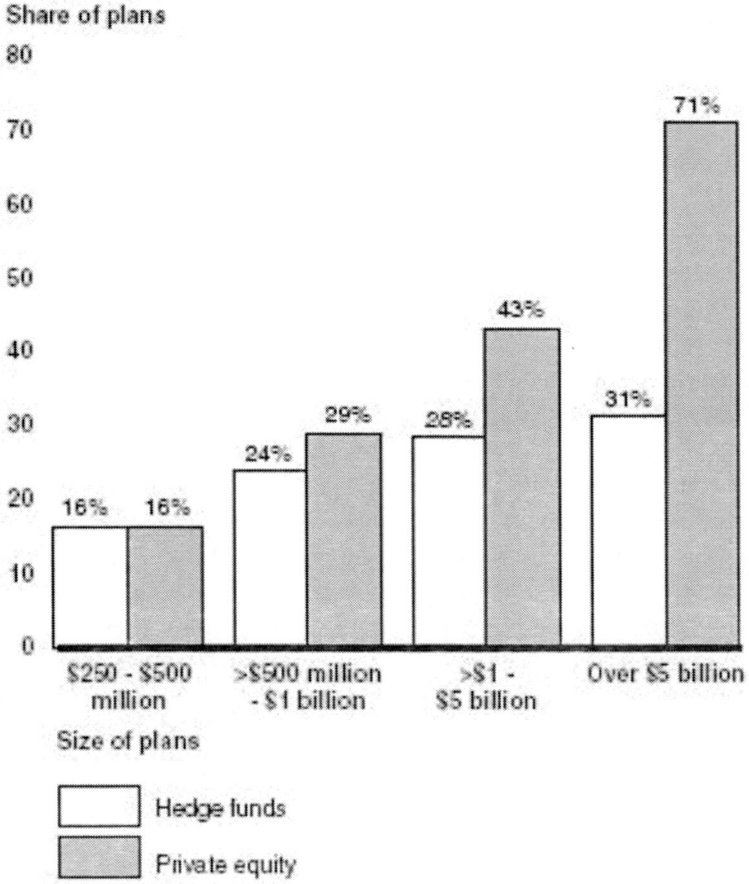

Source: Greenwich Associates, 2006.

Note: The figures above include public and private sector plans (excluding collectively bargained plans). Information on the investments of collectively bargained plans by size of total assets was not available. Data reported in figures 3 and 4 differ because these data are based on different surveys.

Figure 4. Pension Plans with Investments in Hedge Funds and Private Equity by Size of Total Plan Assets Share of plans.

Broad Market Events and a Desire for Specific Benefits Have Driven Pension Plans' Allocations to Hedge Funds

Pension plans' investments in hedge funds resulted in part from stock market declines and disenchantment with traditional investment management in recent years. Most pension plan officials we contacted cited the steep declines in the public equity market early in this decade as a reason for initiating or expanding hedge fund investments. From August 2000 to February 2003, the stock market, as measured by the Standard and Poor's 500 index, declined in value by about 45 percent, and according to plan sponsors and others, this massive market decline severely affected pension plans that were deeply invested in the U.S. stock market. For example, representatives of one public pension plan told us that this market decline led to largest annual loss in its history and resulted in the plan's first hedge fund investments 2003. A representative of another large public pension plan told us that the main motive for initially investing in hedge funds was the weak equity markets early in this decade, and the perceived need for greater exposure to alternative assets that relied less on the stock market for returns. At the same time, some plan officials also cited disenchantment with traditional "long-only" investment managers, and questioned whether such managers delivered returns that justified the fees the managers' charge.[21]

Officials with most of the plans we contacted indicated that they invested in hedge funds, at least in part, to reduce the volatility of returns.[22] According to a representative of an investment consulting firm, this is a common objective of pension plans that invest in hedge funds. One plan official explained the importance of reducing volatility by noting that even in periods of relatively good stock returns, volatility can eat away at the compounding effect of returns over time, and substantially reduce longterm growth. Another plan official said that in trying to reduce volatility through hedge funds, the plan expected that certain hedge fund returns may lag behind stock market indices during bull (rising) markets, but also expected that it would not suffer nearly the same declines during bear (falling) markets.

Officials of several pension plans told us that they sought to obtain returns greater than the returns of the overall stock market through at least some of their hedge fund investments. For example, officials of one pension plan explained that one of the overall goals of its hedge fund portfolio strategy was to obtain an annual return of 2.5 percentage points greater than returns in the stock market, as measured by the S&P 500 stock index.

Officials of pension plans that we contacted also stated that hedge funds are used to help diversify their overall portfolio and provide a vehicle that will, to some degree, be uncorrelated with the other investments in their portfolio. This reduced correlation has a number of benefits, including reduction in overall portfolio volatility and risk. For example, officials of one pension plan told us that hedge funds are attractive because they are not solely dependent on equity and fixed income markets for their returns, thus reduce the overall risk of the investment portfolio.

At the time of our contacts with pension plans in 2007, the 15 pension plans with hedge fund investments indicated mixed but generally positive results.[23] Among officials of these plans, all said that their hedge fund investments had generally met or exceeded expectations, although some noted mixed experiences. For example, one plan explained that it had dropped some hedge fund investments because they had not performed at or above the S&P 500 benchmark. Also, this plan redeemed its investment from other funds because they began to deviate from their initial trading strategy. Further, officials of several plans noted that their venture into hedge funds was only a few years old, and, at the time of our contact, their investment had not yet been tested by trying economic conditions or financial events, such as a significant stock market decline. Nonetheless, representatives of all of the plans with hedge fund investments indicated that they planned to maintain or increase their portfolio allocation to hedge funds in the foreseeable future.

Hedge Funds Pose Significant Challenges and Risks, Beyond Those Posed by Traditional Investments

Pension plans face a number of challenges in hedge fund investing beyond those of more traditional investing, including specific investment risks, limited transparency and liquidity, and risks related to the operations of the hedge fund.

Investment Risks

While any plan investment may fail to deliver expected returns over time, hedge fund investments pose investment challenges beyond those posed by traditional investments. These include (1) reliance on the skill of hedge fund managers, who often have broad latitude to engage in complex investment techniques that can involve various financial instruments in various financial markets; (2) use of leverage, which amplifies both potential gains and losses; and (3) higher fees, which require a plan to earn a higher gross return to achieve a higher net return.

Hedge funds are among the most actively managed investments, and thus returns are often dependent not on broad market movements, but on smaller moves in the markets they invest in and the skills and abilities of the hedge fund manager.[24] For example, hedge fund managers may seek to profit through complex and simultaneous positions in stocks, bonds, options contracts, futures contracts, currencies, and other vehicles, and can abruptly change their positions and trading tactics in order to achieve desired return as changing market conditions warrant. Representatives of some pension plans that had not invested in hedge funds, cited concerns about the ability of hedge fund managers to accomplish this over the longterm. One plan official said the plan had avoided hedge funds in part because of doubt that the managers' skills could generate an acceptable return over time. Instead, this plan seeks to capture the increase in the overall stock market. Regulatory officials and plan sponsors also said that, given the growth of the hedge fund industry in recent years, the market inefficiencies from which hedge funds profit may diminish. For example, SEC noted in a 2004 regulatory proposal that the capacity of hedge fund advisers to generate large returns is limited because the use of similar financial strategies by other hedge funds narrows spreads and decreases profitability.[25]

Hedge fund managers may use leverage—that is, use borrowed money or other techniques—to potentially increase an investments value or return without increasing the amount invested.[26] While registered investment companies are subject to leverage limits, hedge funds can make relatively unrestricted use of leverage to magnify the expected returns of an investment.[27] At the same time that leverage can magnify profits, it can also magnify losses to the hedge fund if the market goes against the fund's expectations.[28] Concerns about leverage were cited by several pension plans either as an important consideration in selecting a hedge fund, or as a reason for avoiding them altogether. For example, one public pension plan told us that it has avoided hedge funds because when hedge funds hit "potholes," the potholes are deep because of high amounts of leverage used.

The challenge of relying on manager skill for a desired rate of return is compounded by the costly fee structure that is typical of the hedge fund industry. Whereas mutual fund managers reportedly charge a fee of about 1 percent of assets under management, hedge fund managers often charge a flat fee of 2 percent of total assets under management, plus a performance fee, of about 20 percent of the fund's annual profits.[29]

The impact of such fees can be considerable. As figure 5 illustrates, an annual return of 12 percent falls to about 7.6 percent after fees are deducted. Several pension plans cited the costly fee structure fees as a major drawback to hedge fund investing. For example, representatives of one plan that had not invested in hedge funds said that they are focused on minimizing transaction costs of their investment program, and the hedge fund fee structure would likely not be worth the expense. On the other hand, an official of another plan noted that, as long as hedge funds add value net of fees, they found the higher fees acceptable.

Lack of Transparency

Because many hedge funds may own thinly traded securities and derivatives whose valuation can be complex, and in some cases subjective, a plan may not be able to obtain timely information on the value of assets owned by a hedge fund.[30] Further, hedge fund managers may decline to disclose information on asset holdings and the net value of individual assets largely because release of such information could compromise their trading advantage. In addition, even if hedge fund managers were to provide detailed positions, plan sponsors might be unable to fully analyze and assess the prospective return and risk of a hedge fund. As a consequence, a plan may not be able to independently ascertain the value of its hedge fund investment or fully assess the degree of investment risk posed by its hedge fund investment. Although we noted in January 2008 that hedge funds have improved disclosure and transparency about their operations due to the demands of institutional investors, several pension plans cited limited transparency as a prime reason they had chosen not to invest in hedge funds.[31] For example, representatives of one plan told us that they had considered investing in hedge funds several years ago, but that most of the hedge funds it contacted would not provide position-level information, and that they were reluctant to make such an investment without this information.

Liquidity Limitations

Hedge funds offer investors relatively limited liquidity, that is, investors may not be able to redeem a hedge fund investment on demand because of a hedge fund's redemption policy. Hedge funds often require an initial "lockup" of a year or more, during which an investor cannot cash out of the hedge fund. After the initial lockup period, hedge funds offer only occasional liquidity, sometimes with a pre-notification requirement.[32]

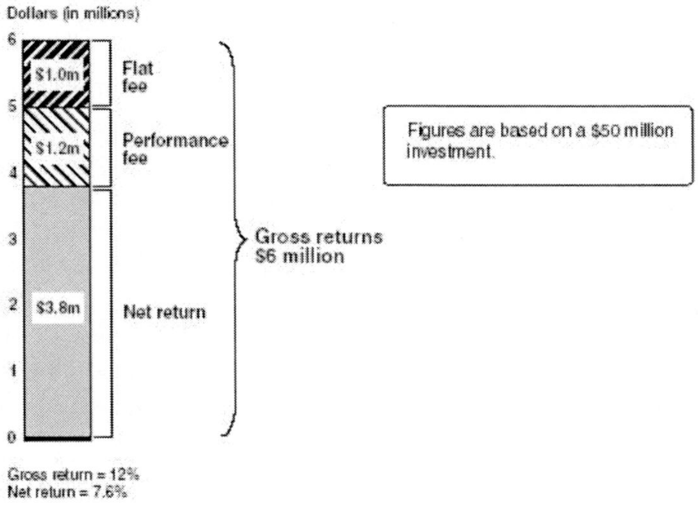

Source: GAO analysis.

Note: This example assumes a fee structure of 2 percent of assets under management and 20 percent of profits.

Figure 5. Effect of Hedge Fund Fee Structure on the Returns of an Investment of $50 Million

While some pension plans told us that liquidity limitations are not a significant concern because the plan has other liquid assets to pay benefits, they nonetheless can pose certain disadvantages. For example, liquidity limitations can inhibit a plan's ability to minimize a hedge fund investment loss. As one state official noted after a state fund had suffered losses in the wake of the 2006 collapse of Amaranth, even when a plan learns that a hedge fund is losing value, various lockup provisions often make it difficult to promptly withdraw from the investment.[33] Further, an investor's rights with regard to cashing out may not be entirely clear from the written contract. According to an investigative study by a Grand Jury of one pension plan's experience with a failed hedge fund, the contracts can be dense with legal language, which may make understanding of basic terms and conditions difficult, especially with regard to withdrawal provisions.[34] Further, the study noted that contracts can delegate immense discretionary authority to the hedge fund manager to change conditions and rules.

Operational Risk

Pension plans investing in hedge funds are also exposed to operational risk—that is, the risk of investment loss due not to a faulty investment strategy, but from inadequate or failed internal processes, people, and systems, or problems with external service providers. Operational problems can arise from a number of sources, including inexperienced operations personnel, inadequate internal controls, lack of compliance standards and enforcement, errors in analyzing, trading, or recording positions, or outright fraud. According to a report by an investment consulting firm, because many hedge funds engage in active, complex, and sometimes heavily leveraged trading, a failure of operational functions such as processing or clearing one or more trades may have grave consequences for the overall position of the hedge fund. Concerns about some operational issues were noted by SEC in a 2003 report on the implications of the growth of hedge funds. For example, the 2003 report noted that SEC had instituted a significant and growing number of enforcement actions involving hedge fund fraud in the preceding 5 years.[35] Further, SEC noted that while some hedge funds had adopted sound internal controls and compliance practices, in many other cases, controls may be very informal, and may not be adequate for the amount of assets under management. Similarly, a recent Bank of New York paper noted that the type and quality of operational environments can vary widely among hedge funds, and investors cannot simply assume that a hedge fund has an operational infrastructure sufficient to protect shareholder assets.[36]

Several pension plans we contacted also expressed concerns about operational risk. For example, one plan official noted that the consequences of operational failure are larger in hedge fund investing than in conventional investing. For example, the official said a failed long trade in conventional investing has relatively limited consequences, but a failed trade that is leveraged five times is much more consequential. Representatives of another plan noted that back office and operational issues became deal breakers in some cases. For example, they said one fund of funds looked like a very good investment, but concerns were raised during the due diligence process. These officials noted, for example, the importance of a clear separation of the investment functions and the operations and compliance functions of the fund. One official added that some hedge funds and funds of funds are focused on investment ideas at the expense of important operations components of the fund.

Addressing the Challenges and Risks of Hedge Fund Investing Requires Considerable Effort and Expertise

Pension plans that invest in hedge funds take various steps to mitigate the risks and challenges posed by hedge fund investing, including developing a specific investment purpose and strategy, negotiating important investment terms, conducting due diligence, and investing through funds of funds. Such steps require greater effort, expertise and expense than required for more traditional investments. As a result, some plans, especially smaller plans, may not have the resources to take the steps necessary to address these challenges.

Clear Investment Purpose and Strategy

Discussions with pension plan officials revealed the importance of defining a clear purpose and strategy for their hedge fund investments. As one pension fiduciary noted, plan managers should define exactly why they want to invest in hedge funds. He added that there are many different possible hedge fund strategies, and wanting to invest in hedge funds to obtain the large returns that other investors have reportedly obtained is not a sufficient reason. Most of the 15 pension plans with hedge fund investments that we contacted described one or more strategies for their hedge funds investments. For example, an official of one state plan told us that the plan invested only in long-short hedge fund strategies while other plans use multiple strategies.[37]

Our contacts with plan officials and others also highlighted the importance of diversification. All of the plans having hedge fund investments that we contacted invested in either multiple individual hedge funds, or through funds of funds, which are designed to provide diversification across many underlying funds. Some plans described specific diversification requirements, and spread their hedge fund investment across many funds to limit exposure to one or a small number of hedge funds. For example, one plan determined that no more than 15 percent of its hedge fund portfolio would be with a single hedge fund manager and that no more than 40 percent in a particular hedge fund investment strategy.

Identification and Negotiation of Important Investment Terms

Our contacts with plan officials and others also highlighted the importance of identifying specific investment terms to guide hedge fund investing and ensuring that the hedge fund investment contract complies with these criteria. These can include fee structure and conditions, degree of transparency, valuation procedures, redemption provisions, and degree of leverage employed. For example, pension plans may want to ensure that they will not pay a performance fee unless the value of the investment passes a previous peak value of the fund shares—known as a high water mark. Some plans we contacted also specified leverage limits for their hedge funds. For example, one public plan that we contacted has established specific leverage limits for each of 10 hedge fund strategies employed by its funds of funds—ranging from an upper limit of 2 times invested capital for one strategy, to 20 times invested capital for another. Once decided upon, these and other terms of the investment can be used as criteria in the hedge fund search, and if necessary, negotiated with the hedge fund or fund of funds manager.

Due Diligence and Monitoring

Pension plans take steps to mitigate the challenges of hedge fund investing through an in-depth due diligence and ongoing monitoring process. While plans conduct due diligence reviews of other investments as well, such reviews are especially important when making hedge fund investments, because of hedge funds' complex investment strategies, the often small size of hedge funds, and their more lightly regulated nature, among other reasons. Due diligence can be a wide-ranging process that includes a review and study of the hedge fund's investment process, valuation, and risk management. The due diligence process can also include a review of back office operations, including a review of key staff roles and responsibilities, the background of operations staff, the adequacy of computer and telecommunications systems, and a review of compliance policies and procedures.

Investing via Funds of Hedge Funds

Representatives of several plans told us they mitigate several of the major hedge fund challenges by investing through funds of funds, which are investment funds that buy shares of multiple underlying hedge funds. Funds of hedge funds provide plan investors diversification across multiple hedge funds, thereby having the potential to mitigate investment risk. For example, one plan fiduciary told us the plan reduces investment risk by investing in a fund of funds that diversifies their hedge fund investments into at least 40 underlying hedge funds. Further, by investing in a fund of funds, a pension plan relies on the fund of funds' manager to conduct negotiations, due diligence, and monitoring of the underlying hedge funds. According to pension plan officials, funds of funds can be appropriate if a plan does not have the necessary skills to manage its own portfolio of hedge funds. According to a hedge fund industry organization, investing through a fund of funds may provide a plan better access to hedge funds than a plan would be able to obtain directly.[38] Nonetheless, investing through funds of funds has some drawbacks. Funds of funds' managers also charge fees—for example, they may charge a 1 percent flat fee and a performance fee of between 5 and 10 percent of profits—on top of the substantial fees that the fund of funds manager pays to the underlying hedge funds. Funds of funds also pose some of the same challenges as hedge funds, such as limited transparency and liquidity, and the need for a due diligence review of the fund of funds firm.

Some Pension Plans May Not Be Able to Meet the Demands of Hedge Fund Investing

According to plan officials, state and federal regulators, and others, some pension plans, especially smaller plans, may not be equipped to address the various demands of hedge fund investing. For example, an official of a national organization representing state securities regulators told us that medium- and small-size plans are probably not equipped with the expertise to oversee the trading and investment practices of hedge funds. This official said that smaller plans may have only one or two person staff, or may lack the resources to hire outside consulting expertise. A labor union official made similar comments, noting that smaller pension plans lack the internal capacity to assess hedge fund investments, and noted that such plans may be locked out of top-performing hedge funds.

Some plans may also lack the ability to conduct the necessary due diligence and monitoring of hedge fund investments. One hedge fund consultant told us that certain types of plans, such as plans that are not actively overseen by an investment committee and plans that do not have a sufficient in-house dedicated staff, should not invest in hedge funds. Similarly, a representative of a firm specializing in fiduciary education and support noted the special relationship of trust and legal responsibility that plan fiduciaries carry and concluded that the challenges of hedge fund investing are too high for most pension plans. While such plans might often be smaller plans, larger plans may also lack sufficient expertise. A representative of one pension plan with more than $32 billion in total assets noted that before investing in hedge funds, the plan would have to build up its staff in order to conduct the necessary due diligence during the fund selection process.

Private Equity Investments May Provide Important Benefits, but Pension Plans Face Limited Access to Top-Performing Funds and Other Challenges

According to plan representatives, investment consultants, and other experts we interviewed, pension plans invest in private equity primarily to attain returns superior to those attained in the stock market in exchange for greater risk, but such investments pose several distinct challenges. Generally, these plan representatives based their comments on significant experience investing in private equity—in some cases over 20 years—and said they had experienced returns in excess of the stock market. Nonetheless, private equity funds can require longer-term commitments of 10 years or more, and during that time, a plan may not be able to redeem its investments. In addition, plan representatives described extensive and ongoing management of private equity investments beyond that required for traditional investments and that, like hedge fund investments, may be difficult for plans with relatively limited resources.

Plans Have Long Investment History in Private Equity and Primarily Seek Returns Superior to Those Attained in the Stock Market

Unlike hedge funds, pension plan investment in private equity is not a recent phenomenon. The majority of plans included in our review began investing in private equity more than 5 years before the economic downturn of 2000 to 2001, and some of these plans have been investing in private equity for 20 years or more.[39] According to a pension investment consultant we interviewed, due to the longer history of pensions' investment in private equity, it is generally regarded as a more well-established and proven asset class compared to other alternative investments, such as hedge funds.

Pension plans invest in private equity primarily to attain returns in excess of returns from the stock market over time in exchange for the greater risk associated with these investments. Officials of each plan we interviewed said these investments had provided the expected returns. Plan representatives and investment consultants said that attaining returns superior to stocks was a primary reason for investing in private equity.[40]

Among the plan representatives we interviewed the most commonly reported benchmark for private equity funds ranged from 3 to 5 percentage points above the S&P 500 stock index, net of fees. At the time of our interviews with plans about private equity investments, between October 2007 and January 2008, plan representatives indicated their private equity investments had met their expectations for relatively high returns and many said they planned to maintain or increase their allocation in the future.[41] Further, representatives of some plans told us that private equity has been their best performing asset class over time despite some individual investments that resulted in considerable losses. For example, according to documentation provided by one private sector plan, the plan had earned a net return of slightly more than 16 percent on its private equity investments over the 10-year period ending September 30, 2007, which was their highest return for any asset class over that time period.[42]

To a lesser degree, pension plans also invest in private equity to further diversify their portfolios. To the extent that private equity is not closely correlated with the stock market, these investments can reduce the volatility of the overall portfolio. However, some plan representatives cautioned that the diversification benefits are limited because the performance of private equity funds is still strongly, although not perfectly, linked to the stock market.[43]

Pension Plans Face Several Challenges and Risks When Investing in Private Equity

Pension plans investing in private equity face several challenges and risks, which include the concentration of underlying holdings, use of leverage, and wide variation in performance among funds. In addition, the value of the underlying holdings is difficult to estimate prior to their sale and private equity investments entail long-term commitments, often of 10 years or more.

Investment Risk

Pension plans that invest in private equity funds face a number of investment risks, beyond the risks of traditional investments. Unlike a traditional fund manager who diversifies by investing in many stocks or bonds, a private equity fund manager's strategy typically involves holding a limited number of underlying companies in their portfolio. A single private equity fund generally invests in only about 10 to 15 companies, often in the same sector.[44] The risks associated with such concentrated, undiversified funds may be compounded by particular aspects of the buyout and venture capital sectors. Fund managers in the buyout sector generally invest using leverage to seek greater returns but such investments also increase investment risks. In the venture capital sector, fund managers typically make smaller investments in companies that may have a limited track record and rely on technological development and growing the company's commercial capacity for success. In light of this, some plan officials noted that some of these companies will fail, but the success of one or more of the portfolio firms is often large enough to more than compensate for the losses of other investments.

Like other investments, the returns to private equity funds are susceptible to market conditions when investments are bought or sold. When competition among private equity fund managers is intense, research has shown that a fund manager may pay more for an investment opportunity that leads to lower net returns.[45] In addition, the returns of a private equity fund are also affected by the condition of the market when the underlying investments are sold. For example, a private equity fund may have lower returns if its underlying holdings are sold through an initial public offering made during a period of low stock values. An official from one plan told us that private equity funds that sold investments around 2000 had lower returns because of the overall decline in the stock market. However, a representative of another plan noted that, while market conditions have some effect on the performance of a private equity fund, the effect may be mitigated by the ability of the fund managers to enact sound business plans and thereby add value to the underlying companies.

Further, the challenge of meeting the high performance goals for private equity investments is compounded by the relatively high fees that private equity funds charge. Similar to hedge funds, private equity funds typically charge an annual fee of 2 percent of invested capital and 20 percent of returns, whereas mutual fund managers typically charge a fee of about 1 percent or less of assets under management. If the gross returns from a private equity fund are not sufficiently high, net returns to investors will not meet the commonly cited goal of exceeding the return of the stock market.

Variation of Performance among Private Equity Funds

Another risk from investing in private equity is the variation of performance among private equity funds. Officials of an investment consulting firm, a state regulatory agency, and several pension plans noted that, compared to other asset classes, private equity has greater variation in performance among funds and cited research to support this view. For example, one study found that the difference in returns between the median and top quartile funds is much greater for private equity, particularly among venture capital investments, than it is for domestic stocks.[46] Another study found that returns of private equity funds at the 75th percentile were more than seven times greater than the returns of funds at the 25th percentile.[47]

Long-Term Commitment of Private Equity Funds

A further challenge of investing with private equity funds—regardless of how they perform—is that they often require commitments of 10 years or more during which a plan may not be able to redeem its investment. The longer-term commitment of private equity funds contrasts with stock and bond investments, which can be bought and sold daily, and hedge fund investments, which can be redeemed episodically. Plans must provide committed capital when called upon by the fund manager, and may not redeem invested capital or typically see any return on the investment, for at least several years.[48] However, several plan representatives and other experts we interviewed stated that the nature of private equity funds necessitates long commitments as returns are generated through longer-term growth strategies, rather than short-term gains. A private equity fund cycle typically follows a pattern known as the "J-curve," which reflects an initial period of negative returns during which investors provide the fund with capital and then obtain returns over time as investments mature (see figure 6). Representatives of several plans noted that they expect higher returns from private equity in exchange for the long-term commitment.

Valuation of Private Equity Fund Investments

An additional challenge of private equity investments is the uncertain valuation during the fund cycle. Unlike stocks and bonds, which are traded and priced in public markets, plans have limited information on the value of private equity investments until the underlying holdings are sold. Some plan representatives we interviewed explained that fund managers often value underlying holdings at their initial cost until they are sold through an initial public offering or other type of sale.[49] In some cases private equity funds estimate the value of the fund by comparing companies in their portfolio to the value of comparable publicly-traded assets. However, an investment consultant explained that such periodic valuations have limited utility. Prior to the sale of underlying investments, it is difficult to assess the value a private equity fund manager has generated. While plan officials we interviewed acknowledged the difficulty of valuing private equity investments, they generally accepted it as a trade-off for the potential benefits of the investment.

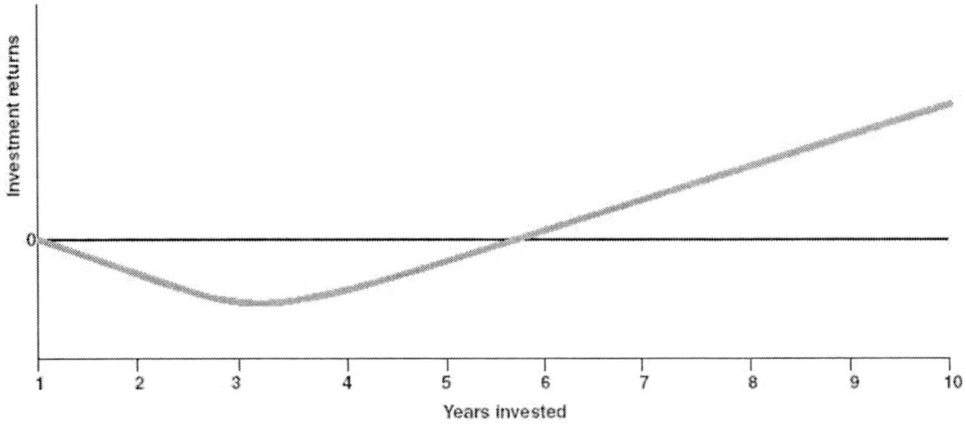

Source: CalPERS.

Figure 6. Returns from a Private Equity Fund Generally Follow a J-Curve Trend over the 10-Year Fund Cycle.

Taking Steps to Address the Challenges and Risks of Investing in Private Equity May Be Too Costly and Complex for Some Plans

Plan representatives said that they take several key steps to address the challenges of investing in private equity funds. Plan representatives and industry experts emphasized the importance of investing with top- performing funds to mitigate the wide variation in fund performance; however, they noted that access to these top-performing funds is very limited, particularly for new investors.[50] Furthermore, due diligence and ongoing monitoring of private equity investments requires substantial effort and expertise, which may be too complex or costly for plans with more limited resources.

Selection of Private Equity Fund Investments

The majority of plan representatives we interviewed told us that, because of the wide variation in performance among private equity funds, they must invest with top-performing funds in order to achieve long-term returns in excess of the stock market. In addition to identifying the top-performing fund managers, plan officials explained that the selection process involves a thorough assessment of the fund manager's investment strategy. For example, an official from one state plan told us that their assessment includes a review of a fund manager's strategy for improving the operations and efficiency of its proposed investments and they invest with managers that have a persuasive business model. Plan officials stressed the importance of these steps, and some noted that investing in private equity is only worthwhile if they can invest with funds in the top quartile of performance. For example, one plan official said that if a plan does not invest with a top quartile fund, it may not obtain returns in excess of stock market returns and, thus, will not have earned a premium for assuming the risks and fees inherent in private equity fund investments.

While many plans we interviewed noted the importance of investing with top-performing funds, the competition to gain access to these funds may make it difficult or impossible for some plans, especially smaller plans, to do so. Several of the plan representatives we interviewed noted that investment opportunities with top-performing funds are limited, and the demand for such opportunities is high. According to representatives of a venture capital trade association, there is greater demand to invest in venture capital funds than can be absorbed, because the venture capital sector is relatively small in size.[51] Plan officials also noted that access to private equity funds can be limited, because fund managers prefer to deal with larger, more sophisticated investors or investors who have invested in the fund manager's previous private equity funds. For example, one state official told us that the largest public plan in the state has the clout to gain access to top-performing funds, but smaller public funds in the state do not. He added that top-performing funds are very selective, and generally will not respond to solicitation by smaller public funds.

Diversification

Plan representatives told us they further mitigate the challenges of investing in private equity funds by diversifying their investments. Plan representatives we interviewed said they invest with multiple fund managers to mitigate the risk that some managers may have mediocre or poor performance. For example, a representative of one plan said they would be comfortable investing about 5 percent of their private equity allocation with one carefully vetted fund manager, but investing 20 percent with one manager would be overly risky. The director of another plan told us the plan aims to ensure diversification by investing with over 130 different private equity funds, encompassing more than 80 fund managers. Plans also stagger investments over several years to ensure their private equity fund investments are ready to sell their underlying investments at different times. Staggering investments over time helps mitigate the risk of fund managers selling funds' underlying holdings during a time of poor market conditions, which may reduce the funds' returns to investors. For example, one plan official noted they have investments in funds that were established in many different years, dating back to 1994. In addition, some plan officials told us they further diversify their private equity investments among funds concentrated in different industries and regions.

Planning for Liquidity Needs

Plan representatives said that they mitigate the long-term commitments of private equity investments by limiting the size their allocation. Officials we interviewed at several plans noted that their allocation to private equity is only about 5 percent of the portfolio and benefit obligations can be paid from more liquid assets. They said it is important to estimate a plan's benefit obligations and determine the need for liquid investments to ensure the plan can pay benefits when they are due. They also noted that once liquidity needs are determined, a plan can more safely invest in an illiquid asset that cannot be used to pay benefits in the near term.

Negotiation of Key Terms of the Investment Contract

Plans attempt to negotiate key terms of the investment contract to further manage the risks of investing in private equity, but, as one large public plan noted, their ability to negotiate favorable contract provisions is limited when investing with top-performing funds because investing in these funds is highly competitive. Like hedge fund investments, these contract terms may include the fee structure and valuation procedures of the fund. In addition, many plan representatives we interviewed said they can redeem their investments before the end of the originally agreed investment period if staff that are considered key to the success of the fund leave prematurely.

Due Diligence and Ongoing Monitoring

Similar to hedge fund investments, plans take additional steps to mitigate challenges of investing in private equity through extensive and ongoing management, beyond those required for traditional investments. Plan representatives we interviewed said these steps include regularly reviewing reports on the performance of the underlying investments of the private equity fund and having periodic meetings with fund managers. In some cases, plans participate on the advisory board of a private equity fund, which provides a greater opportunity for oversight of the fund's operations and new investments; however this involves a significant time commitment and may not be feasible for every private equity fund investment.[52] Plan representatives and investment consultants noted that, as with hedge funds, private equity investments entail considerably greater due diligence and ongoing monitoring than traditional investments and some plan representatives said they needed to hire an external investment consultant because the plan lacked sufficient internal resources.

Funds of Private Equity Funds

Funds of private equity funds, like funds of hedge funds, enable plans to address several challenges of investing in private equity, for an additional cost. Benefits of investing in funds of funds can include diversification across fund managers, industry, geographic region, and year of initial investment. Through funds of funds, plans can also gain access to top-performing fund managers that may otherwise be unavailable to them. One plan representative stated that, due to the competition among investors, funds of funds are their best option for accessing top-performing funds. In addition, several plan representatives said that they invest in funds of funds to benefit from the expertise of the fund manager. For example, officials of two large plans said they generally limit their use of funds of funds to private equity investments in emerging markets and small funds because the plan prefers not to devote resources to maintaining expertise in these areas. Nonetheless, fund of funds' managers charge their own fees in addition to the fees the fund of funds pays the underlying private equity fund managers. According to a plan official and an investment consulting firm, a fund of funds manager typically charges a fee of 1 percent of invested capital over the fees it pays to the underlying funds.

THE FEDERAL GOVERNMENT DOES NOT SPECIFICALLY LIMIT OR MONITOR PRIVATE SECTOR PLANS' INVESTMENTS IN HEDGE FUNDS AND PRIVATE EQUITY, BUT SOME STATES DO SO FOR PUBLIC SECTOR PLANS THROUGH VARIOUS APPROACHES

The federal government does not specifically limit or monitor private sector pension investments in hedge funds or private equity, and state approaches for public plans vary. ERISA requires that plan fiduciaries meet general standards of prudent investing but does not impose specific limits on investments in hedge funds or private equity. Further, while Labor has conducted enforcement actions that have involved hedge fund or private equity funds, it does not specifically monitor these investments. While states generally impose a prudent man standard, similar to ERISA's, on plan fiduciaries, some states still have policies that restrict or prohibit pension plan investment in hedge funds or private equity.

The Federal Government Does Not Specifically Limit or Monitor Pension Plans' Investments in Hedge Funds or Private Equity nor Has It Provided Recommended Guidance

Although ERISA governs the investment practices of private sector pension plans, neither federal law nor regulation specifically limit pension investment in hedge funds or private equity. Instead, ERISA requires that plan fiduciaries apply a prudent man standard, including diversifying assets and minimizing the risk of large losses. The prudent man standard does not explicitly prohibit investment in any specific category of investment.[53] Further, an unsuccessful individual investment is not considered a per se violation of the prudent man standard, as it is the plan fiduciary's overall management of the plan's portfolio that is evaluated under the standard.[54] In addition, the standard focuses on the process for making investment decisions, requiring documentation of the investment decisions, due diligence, and ongoing monitoring of any managers hired to invest plan assets.

Although there are no specific federal limitations on pension plan investments in hedge funds, two federal advisory committees have, in recent years, highlighted the importance of developing best practices in hedge fund investing. In November 2006, the ERISA Advisory Council recommended that Labor publish guidance describing the unique features of hedge funds, and matters for consideration in their adoption for use by qualified pension plans.[55] To date, Labor has not acted on this recommendation. According to Labor officials, an effort to address these recommendations was postponed while Labor focused on implementing various aspects of the Pension Protection Act of 2006.[56] However, in April 2008, the Investors' Committee established by the President's Working Group on Financial Markets, composed of representatives of public and private pension plans, endowments and foundations, organized labor, nonU.S. institutions, funds of hedge funds, and the consulting community, released draft best practices for investors in hedge funds.[57] These best practices discuss the major challenges of hedge fund investing, and provide an in-depth discussion of specific considerations and practices that investors in hedge funds should take. While this guidance should serve as an additional tool for pension plan fiduciaries and investors to use when assessing whether and to what degree hedge funds would be a wise investment, it may not fully address the investing challenges unique to pension plans leaving some vulnerable to inappropriate investments in hedge funds. Although many private sector plans are insured by the PBGC, which guarantees most benefits when an underfunded plan terminates, public sector plans are not insured and may call upon state or local taxpayers to overcome funding shortfalls.[58]

Labor does not specifically monitor pension investment in hedge funds or private equity. Labor annually collects information on private sector pension plan investments via the Form 5500, on which plan sponsors report information such as the plan's operation, funding, assets, and investments. However, the Form 5500 includes no category for hedge funds or private equity funds, and plan sponsors may record these investments in various categories on the form's Schedule H. In addition, because there is no universal definition of hedge funds or private equity and their strategies vary, their holdings can fall within many asset classes. While EBSA officials analyze Form 5500 data for reporting compliance issues—including looking for assets that are "hard to value"—they have not focused on hedge fund or private equity investments specifically.[59] According to EBSA officials, there have been several investigations and enforcement actions in recent years that involved investments in hedge funds and private equity, but these investments have not raised significant concerns.

Some Selected States Regulate and Monitor Investments of Public Sector Plans Using Varying Approaches

Our state pension plan contacts indicated that, in recent years, state regulation of public pension plan investments has become generally more flexible. According to a NASRA official, state regulation of public pension plan investments has gradually become less restrictive and more reliant on fiduciary prudence standards.[60] This official noted that, for example, blanket prohibitions on investments such as international stocks or real estate have given way to permission for a wider range of investments. Some of our state contacts described this shift over time from a prescriptive list of authorized investments ("legal lists") and asset allocation limits to a more flexible approach, such as adoption of the prudent man standard.

Of the state pension plan officials we contacted in 11 states, officials in 7 states indicated that applicable state law imposes restrictions on the ability of public pension plans to invest in hedge funds and/or private equity, as seen in table 2.[61] Among these seven states, the restriction may be in the form of (i) a provision applicable to investments in hedge funds or private equity funds specifically, (ii) an exclusive list of permissible of investments that is not likely to capture hedge funds or private equity investments, or (iii) a provision that restricts investments in certain categories of assets that, because of the typical structure or investment strategy of hedge funds or private equity funds, are likely to apply to investments in such funds.[62]

Some of the selected states have, through statute or regulation, established explicit limitations on the amount that pension plans can invest in hedge funds or private equity. For example, under Texas law, the Teacher Retirement System of Texas (TRS)—the largest public pension plan in Texas—is statutorily limited to investing no more than 5 percent of the plan's total assets in hedge funds.[63] According to a Texas Pension Review Board official, the statute codified TRS's ability to invest in hedge funds while at the same time limiting the amount TRS can invest in hedge funds. According to a TRS official, this law was a compromise between TRS's desire to invest more broadly in hedge funds and some state legislators who were concerned about the possible risks of hedge funds.[64] Other states we reviewed have comparable limitations for public plans.

Table 2. Restrictions on Pension Investments in Hedge Funds and Private Equity Identified by Plan Officials in 11 Selected States

State	Hedge funds	Private equity
California		
Florida	X	X
Illinois	X	X
Massachusetts[a]	X	X
New Jersey	X	X
New York	X	X
North Carolina	X	X
Ohio		
Pennsylvania		
Texas	X	
Wisconsin		

Source: GAO analysis based on information provided by state officials.

[a] Restrictions identified in Massachusetts are based on administrative policy adopted by its Public Employees Retirement Administration Commission, which is generally responsible for oversight of public pension systems in the state, rather than on statute or regulation.

Table 3. Massachusetts Policies on Public Plan Investments in Hedge Funds

Plans with less than $250 million	Plans with greater than $250 million
• May invest in hedge funds only through the state's common hedge fund vehicle • May not invest more than 10 percent of assets in hedge funds	• May not invest more than 10 percent of assets in hedge funds • May only invest in hedge funds through funds of funds • May only invest in hedge fund products whose performance is not influenced by market movements • No single fund of funds may account for more than 2 percent of assets • Hedge fund investments should be invested through a minimum of 75 separate underlying hedge funds • The market value of any single underlying hedge fund investment should not exceed 2.5 percent of the total hedge fund investment • A fund of hedge funds' volatility should not be greater than 7.5 percent • Funds of hedge funds must provide reasonable transparency and disclosure • Funds registered with SEC are to be preferred

Source: Commonwealth of Massachusetts Public Employee Retirement Administration Commission Guidelines for Hedge Fund Investment.

The Commonwealth of Massachusetts' Public Employee Retirement Administration Commission (PERAC) has established a detailed set of limitations and guidance, with particular limitations on smaller public plans. In Massachusetts, public plans with less than $250 million in assets may not invest in hedge funds directly, but they may invest through a state- managed hedge fund investment pool (see table 3). According to a PERAC official, this limitation exists because hedge funds are relatively new investments for pension plans and because they require high levels of due diligence and expertise that may be excessive for smaller plans. PERAC also limits and offers guidance to larger public plans, emphasizing diversification, to help limit a plan's exposure to potential losses from hedge fund failures. According to a PERAC official, the group is less strict about private equity investments because private equity is a more familiar asset class among the state's public plans. Public plans with less than $25 million in assets may invest up to three percent of assets in private equity and plans with more than $25 million may invest up to 5 percent of assets in private equity. PERAC requires plans of either size to obtain PERAC permission before investing in private equity above those levels.

Some of the selected states have instituted "legal lists" of authorized investments for pension plans that do not specifically include investments in hedge funds or private equity funds as authorized assets. According to a NASRA official, this was the dominant regulatory approach of state pension investment 40 years ago, and while some states have moved away from this approach, others have continued to maintain legal lists. Illinois has established a legal list of assets that does not include interests in hedge funds or private equity funds, in which certain smaller plans that cover police officers and fire fighters are authorized to invest.[65] Large statewide plans, such those managed by the Illinois State Board of Investment, are governed by a prudent man standard, which does not explicitly restrict investment of pension assets in any particular investment. In some instances, states allow a certain percentage of plan assets to be invested in assets that do not qualify under one of the authorized categories on the legal list. For example, the New York State Common Retirement Fund is governed by a legal list, but the state allows the plan to invest up to 25 percent of its assets in investments not otherwise permitted by the legal list.[66]

Finally, public pension plan investments in hedge funds are prohibited or limited in some states by laws restricting pension plan investment in certain investment vehicles or trading strategies. For example, the North Carolina Retirement system can not invest more than 10 percent of plan assets in limited partnerships or limited liability corporations. Similarly, before new legislation broadening investment authority went into effect in April 2008, the Wisconsin Retirement System could not invest assets in vehicles that trade options or engage in short selling, two techniques commonly used by hedge funds.[67] However, with the new statutory authority, the Wisconsin Retirement System may use any investment strategy that meets its prudent investor standard.[68]

States we contacted take a variety of approaches to overseeing and monitoring public pension plan investment. In Massachusetts, before conducting a hedge fund manager search, public plans must first obtain PERAC approval and provide the agency with a summary of the plan's objectives, strategies, and goals in hedge fund investing. PERAC requires pension plans to document the major due diligence steps taken in the hedge fund manager selection process. In addition, prospective hedge fund managers must submit detailed information to PERAC regarding their key personnel, assets under management, investment strategy and process, risk controls, past performance, and organizational structure. Finally, hedge fund managers must also submit quarterly performance and strategy review reports directly to PERAC. Officials in other states we contacted may review hedge fund and private equity investments as part of a broader oversight approach. For example, the Ohio Retirement Study Council reviews the five large statewide public retirement funds semiannually to evaluate a plan's investment policies and objectives, asset allocations decisions, and risk and return assumptions. In California, individual pension boards have sole and exclusive authority over investment decisions; however, they ensure public information on investment decisions and fund performance, including detailed reports of alternative investments, are publicly available.

CONCLUSIONS

Available data indicate that pension plans have increasingly invested in hedge funds and have continued to invest in private equity to complement their traditional investments in stocks and bonds. Further, these data indicate that individual plans' hedge fund or private equity investments typically comprise a small share of total plan assets. However, data are generally not available on the extent to which smaller pension plans have made such investments. Because such investments require a degree of fiduciary effort well beyond that required by more traditional investments, this can be a difficult challenge for plans, especially smaller plans. Smaller plans may not have the expertise or financial resources to be fully aware of these challenges, or have the ability to address them through negotiations, due diligence, and monitoring. In light of this, such investments may not be appropriate for some pension plans.

Although plans are responsible for making prudent choices when investing in any asset, EBSA also has a role in helping to ensure that pension plan sponsors fulfill their fiduciary duties in managing pension plans that are subject to ERISA. This can include educating employers and service providers about their fiduciary responsibilities under ERISA. Many private sector plans are insured by the PBGC, which guarantees most benefits when an underfunded plan terminates; however, public sector plans are not insured and may call upon state or local taxpayers to overcome funding shortfalls.

The importance of educating investors about the special challenges presented by hedge funds has been recognized by a number of organizations. For example, in 2006, the ERISA Advisory Council recommended that Labor publish guidance about the unique features of hedge funds and matters for consideration in their use by qualified plans. To date, EBSA has not acted on this recommendation. More recently, in April 2008, the Investors' Committee formed by the President's Working Group on Financial Markets published draft best practices for investors in hedge funds. This guidance will be applicable to a broad range of investors, such as public and private pension plans, endowments, foundations, and wealthy individuals. EBSA can further enhance the usefulness of this document by ensuring that the guidance is interpreted in light of the fiduciary responsibilities that ERISA places on private sector plans. For example, EBSA could outline the implications of a hedge fund's or fund of funds' limited transparency on the fiduciary duty of prudent oversight. EBSA can also reflect on the implications of these best practices for some plans—especially smaller plans—that might not have the resources to take actions consistent with the best practices, and thus would be at risk of making imprudent investments in hedge funds. While EBSA is not tasked with offering guidance to public sector plans, such plans may nonetheless benefit from such guidance.

RECOMMENDATION FOR EXECUTIVE ACTION

To ensure that all plan fiduciaries can better assess their ability to invest in hedge funds and private equity, and to ensure that those that choose to make such investments are better prepared to meet these challenges, we recommend that the Secretary of Labor provide guidance specifically designed for qualified plans under ERISA. This guidance should include such things as (1) an outline of the unique challenges of investing in hedge funds and private equity; (2) a description of steps that plans should take to address these challenges and help meet ERISA requirements; and (3) an explanation of the implications of these challenges and steps for smaller plans. In doing so, the Secretary may be able to draw extensively from existing sources, such as the finalized best practices document that will be published in 2008 by the Investors' Committee formed by the President's Working Group on Financial Markets.[69]

Agency Comments and Our Evaluation

We provided a draft copy of this report to the Department of Labor, PBGC, the Department of the Treasury, the SEC, and the Federal Reserve Bank for their review and comment. Labor generally agreed with our findings and recommendation. With regard to our recommendation, Labor stated that providing more specific guidance on investments in hedge funds and private equity may present challenges. Specifically, Labor noted that given the lack of uniformity among hedge funds, private equity funds, and their underlying investments, it may prove difficult to develop comprehensive and useful guidance for plan fiduciaries. Nonetheless, Labor agreed to consider the feasibility of developing such guidance. Labor's formal comments are reproduced in appendix III.

We agree that the lack of uniformity among hedge funds or private equity funds may pose challenges to Labor. However, we do not believe it will be an insurmountable obstacle to developing guidance for plan sponsors. Indeed, the lack of uniformity among hedge funds and private equity funds is itself an important issue to convey to fiduciaries, and highlights the need for an extensive due diligence process preceding any investment. Additionally, as we state in the recommendation, Labor's efforts can be facilitated through use of existing best practices documents, such as the best practices for investors in hedge funds document that will be published in the summer of 2008 by the Investors' Committee formed by the President's Working Group on Financial Markets.

The PBGC also provided formal comments, which are reproduced in appendix IV. PBGC generally concurred with our findings. Labor, PBGC, the Department of the Treasury, and the Federal Reserve Bank also provided technical comments and corrections, which we have incorporated where appropriate.

As arranged with your offices, unless you publicly announce its contents earlier, we plan no further distribution of this report until 30 days from the date of this letter. At that time, we will send copies of this report to interested congressional committees and members, federal agencies, and other interested parties. We will also make copies available to others upon request.

If you or your staff has any questions concerning this report, please contact Barbara Bovbjerg on (202) 512-7215 or Orice Williams on (202) 512-8678. Contact points for our Office of Congressional Relations and Office of Public Affairs can be found on the last page of this report. Key

Barbara D. Bovbjerg
Director, Education, Workforce and Income Security

Orice M. Williams
Director, Financial Markets and Community Investment

List of Congressional Requesters

The Honorable Max Baucus
Chairman
The Honorable Charles E. Grassley
Ranking Member
Committee on Finance
United States Senate

The Honorable Charles B. Rangel
Chairman
The Honorable Jim McCrery
Ranking Member
Committee on Ways and Means
House of Representatives

The Honorable Barney Frank
Chairman
Committee on Financial Services
House of Representatives

The Honorable Michael E. Capuano
House of Representatives

The Honorable Paul E. Kanjorski
House of Representatives

APPENDIX I : OBJECTIVES, SCOPE, AND METHODOLOGY

Our objectives were to address the following questions:

1. To what extent do public and private sector pension plans invest in hedge funds and private equity funds?
2. What are the potential benefits, risks, and challenges pension plans face in making hedge fund investments, and how do plans address the risks and challenges?
3. What are the potential benefits, risks, and challenges pension plans face in making private equity fund investments, and how do plans address the risks and challenges?
4. What mechanisms regulate and monitor pension plan investments in hedge funds and private equity funds?

To answer the first question, we obtained and analyzed survey data of private and public sector defined benefit (DB) plans on the extent of plan investments in hedge funds and private equity from three private organizations: Greenwich Associates, *Pensions & Investments*, and Pyramis Global Advisors.[70]

We identified the three surveys through our literature review and interviews with plan representatives and industry experts. As seen in table 4, the surveys varied in the number and size of plans surveyed. Using the available survey data, we determined the percentage of plans surveyed that reported investments in hedge funds or private equity. Using data from Greenwich Associates, we also determined the percentage of plans surveyed that invested in hedge funds or private equity by category of plan size, measured by total plan assets. We further examined data from each survey on the size of allocations to hedge funds or private equity as a share of total plan assets. Using the *Pensions & Investments* data, we analyzed allocations to these investments for individual plans and calculated the average allocation for hedge funds and private equity, separately, among all plans surveyed that reported these investments. The Greenwich Associates and Pyramis data reported the size of allocations to hedge funds or private equity as an average for all plans surveyed. Through our research and interviews, we were not able to identify any relevant surveys that included plans with less than $200 million in total assets.

Table 4. Number and Size of DB Plans Observed in Recent Surveys.

	Greenwich Associates (2006)	Pensions & Investments (2007)	Pyramis Global Advisors (2006)
Sample size	584 DB plans	133 DB plans	214 DB plans
Total assets of plans in survey	$3.649 trillion	$4.4 trillion	n/a
Range of total plan assets	$250 million or more	>$1 billion or more	>$200 million

Source: GAO analysis.

Note: Pensions & Investments surveyed the largest 200 plans, ranked by combined DB and defined contribution (DC) plan assets. With one exception, all DB plans ranked in the top 200 plans had more than $1 billion in total assets. Of the top 200 plans, 133 were DB plans that completed the survey and provided asset allocation information.

While the information collected by each of the surveys is limited in some ways, we conducted a data reliability assessment of each survey and determined that the data were sufficiently reliable for purposes of this study. These surveys did not specifically define the terms hedge fund and private equity; rather, respondents reported allocations based on their own classifications. *Pensions & Investments* reported private equity in three mutually-exclusive categories—buyout, venture capital, and an "other" private equity category, which includes investments such as mezzanine financing and private equity investments traded on the secondary market. Data from all three surveys are reflective only of the plans surveyed and cannot be generalized to all plans.

To answer the second and third questions, we conducted in-depth interviews with representatives of 26 private and public sector DB plans, listed in table 5, from June 2007 to January 2008 and, where possible, obtained and reviewed supporting documentation.

Table 5. List of DB Plans for In-Depth Interviews

	Hedge fund interview	Privateequity interview
Private sector plans:		
American Airlines	√	
Boeing	√	
Exxon Mobil	√	
GE Asset Management	√	
International Association of Machinists National Pension Fund	√	
John Deere		√
Macy's	√	
Northrop Grumman		√
Prudential	√	
Target		√
United Mine Workers of America Health and Retirement Funds	√	√
United Technologies	√	
Walt Disney	√	√
Public sector plans:		
California Public Employees' Retirement System	√	√
California State Teachers' Retirement System	√	√
Illinois State Board of Investments	√	
Los Angeles County Employee Retirement Administration	√	
Massachusetts Pension Reserves Investment Management Board	√	
Missouri State Employees' Retirement System	√	
National Railroad Retirement Trust Fund		√
New York State Common Retirement Fund	√	√
Pennsylvania Public School Employees' Retirement System	√	√
Pennsylvania State Employees' Retirement System	√	√
San Diego County Employees' Retirement System	√	
South Dakota Retirement System		√
Washington State Investment Board		√

Source: GAO.

Note: Five of the plans interviewed about hedge funds did not invest in hedge funds.

Interviews related to hedge fund investments were conducted from June 2007 to December 2007. Interviews related to private equity investments were conducted from October 2007 to January 2008. The interviews with plan representatives were conducted using a semi-structured interview format, which included open-ended questions on the following topics, asked separately about hedge funds or private equity: the plan's history of investment in hedge funds or private equity; the plan's experiences with these investments to date; the plan's expected benefits from these investments; challenges the plan has faced with these investments; and steps the plan has taken to mitigate these challenges, including due diligence and ongoing monitoring. We interviewed five plans that did not invest in hedge funds to discuss the reasons the plan decided not have such investments. We also interviewed officials of government agencies, relevant industry organizations, investment consulting firms, and other national experts listed in appendix II. In addition, we interviewed officials from the Arizona State Retirement System and Missouri Local Government Employees' Retirement System to discuss the recent decision of these plans to invest in private equity.

The plans we interviewed were selected based on several criteria. We attempted to select plans that varied in the size of allocations to hedge funds and private equity as a share of total plan assets. We also attempted to select plans with a range of total plan assets, as outlined in table 6. We identified these plans using data from the *Pensions & Investments* 2006 survey and through our interviews with industry experts.

Table 6. Criteria Used in Selection of Plans for In-Depth Interviews

	Number of plans interviewed – hedge funds	Number of plans interviewed – private equity
Size of allocation to hedge funds or private equity:		
None	5	
5% or less	10	5
>5 to 10%	3	6
>10%	2	2
Total plan assets:		
$10 billion or less	8	5
>$10 to $100 billion	9	5
>$100 billion	3	3

Source: GAO analysis of Pension & Investments 2006 survey.

Table 7. Ten States with the Largest Total Public DB Pension Plan Assets (Dollars in billions)

Rank	State	Sum of market value for state's public
1	California	$417.4
2	New York	301.9
3	Texas	156.3
4	Ohio	147.3
5	Florida	116.3
6	Illinois	96.0
7	Pennsylvania	90.1
8	New Jersey	79.3
9	Wisconsin	67.9
10	North Carolina	66.7

Source: GAO analysis of NASRA Public Funds Survey 2007 data.

APPENDIX II : COMMENTS FROM THE DEPARTMENT OF LABOR

U.S. Department of Labor

Assistant Secretary for
Employee Benefits Security Administration
Washington, D.C. 20210

July 16, 2008

Ms. Barbara D. Bovbjerg
Director, Education, Workforce, and
Income Security Issues
United States Government Accountability Office
Washington, DC 20548

Dear Ms. Bovbjerg:

We have reviewed the Government Accountability Office's (GAO) draft report entitled "DEFINED BENEFIT PENSION PLANS: Guidance Needed to Better Inform Plans of the Challenges and Risks of Investing in Hedge Funds and Private Equity" (GAO-08-692). Based upon our review of the report, below are the comments and observations.

As recognized in the draft report, ERISA requires, among other things, that in making plan investment decisions, an ERISA fiduciary must act prudently, solely in the interest of the plan and its participants and beneficiaries, and to diversify plan investments so as to minimize the risk of large losses. Under the framework set out in the Department of Labor's regulations,[1] a fiduciary's investment decision is considered prudent, if the fiduciary gives appropriate consideration to all those facts and circumstances that the fiduciary knows or should know are relevant to the particular investment decision involved, including the role the investment plays in the plan's investment portfolio and acts accordingly. With respect to any plan investment, including an investment in a hedge fund or private equity fund, a plan fiduciary must gather sufficient information to understand the nature of the investment, make a determination as to its prudence, and periodically monitor the investment to evaluate whether it remains a prudent plan investment.

We appreciate GAO's interest in helping plan fiduciaries understand the challenges of investing in hedge funds and private equity and their attendant obligations under ERISA. The Department shares this interest and carries out an extensive outreach program to assist plan fiduciaries, service providers, and others in understanding their responsibilities under ERISA. The program addresses investment decisions and the importance of selecting and monitoring plan service providers. However, providing more specific guidance on investments in hedge funds and private equity funds, as recommended by the draft report, may present challenges. In this regard, we note that

[1] 29 CFR § 2550.404a-1.

the draft report indicates there is no statutory definition of hedge fund or private equity fund, and investment objectives and strategies may vary greatly among these funds. Given this apparent lack of uniformity in describing hedge funds, private equity funds, and their investments and operations, it may prove difficult to develop comprehensive and useful guidance for plan fiduciaries. Nonetheless, we will consider the feasibility of developing the type of specific guidance regarding investments in hedge funds and private equity funds as recommended in the draft report.

EBSA is committed to protecting the employer-sponsored benefits of American workers, retirees, and their families. We appreciate having had the opportunity to review and comment on the draft report. Please do not hesitate to contact us if you have questions concerning this response or if we can be of further assistance.

Sincerely,

Bradford P. Campbell
Assistant Secretary

To identify and analyze the regulation of public DB pension investments by states we consulted officials at the Department of Labor and representatives of relevant agencies in selected states, and reviewed relevant policy documents. The states we selected included the 10 states with the largest public pension assets according to our review of the National Association of State Retirement Administrators (NASRA) Public Funds Survey data listed in table 7. We also included Massachusetts because our previous contact with that state produced valuable information for this objective.[71] Those states chosen based on the size of plan assets were: California, New York, Texas, Ohio, Florida, Illinois, Pennsylvania, New Jersey, Wisconsin, and North Carolina. In 9 of 10 states we spoke with the offices of the State Auditor, the State Treasurer, and the State Comptroller or equivalent offices. North Carolina's Chief Investment Officer of the State Treasurer's Office affirmed our analysis through email. Finally we informed each of these states of our analysis and gave them the opportunity to comment on our description of regulations in their state.

We conducted this performance audit from June 2007 to July 2008, in accordance with generally accepted government auditing standards. Those standards require that we plan and perform the audit to obtain sufficient, appropriate evidence to provide a reasonable basis for our findings and conclusions based on our audit objectives. We believe that the evidence obtained provides a reasonable basis for our findings and conclusions based on our audit objectives.

APPENDIX III : COMMENTS FROM THE PENSION BENEFIT GUARANTY CORPORATION

PBGC
Protecting America's Pensions

Pension Benefit Guaranty Corporation
1200 K Street, N.W., Washington, D.C. 20005-4026

Office of the Director

July 11, 2008

Ms. Barbara Bovbjerg, Director
Education, Workforce, and Income Security Issues
Mr. Orice M. Williams, Director,
Financial Markets and Community Investment
Government Accountability Office
441 G Street, N.W.
Washington, D.C. 20548

Dear Ms. Bovbjerg and Mr. Williams:

Thank you for the opportunity to comment on the draft report entitled, "DEFINED BENEFIT PENSION PLANS: Guidance Needed to Better Inform Plans of the Challenges and Risks of Investing in Hedge Funds and Private Equity" (GAO-08-692).

In our role as an insurer, PBGC has an interest in the transparency of the investments made by plans it insures. Existing disclosure requirements provide only a limited window on hedge funds and private equity investments. However, to date, defined benefit pension plans that have been terminated and trusteed by PBGC have not had significant amounts invested in either hedge funds or private equity investments.

The draft report notably acknowledges that, within the wide and growing array of hedge funds, despite having a reputation of being "risky" investment vehicles, "this was not their original purpose, and is not true of all hedge funds today." In addition, the draft report underscores ERISA's notion of the prudence of an individual investment being considered within the context of the total plan portfolio.

As there are risks involved with all investments, we certainly agree with the principle enunciated in ERISA, that plan trustees should exercise due diligence in making prudent investment decisions solely for the benefit of the plan and its participants and beneficiaries, and closely monitor investment performance on an on-going basis. In seeking to fully meet the obligations of the plan under ERISA, plan trustees must fully understand the potential benefits and risks and the relative performance of all of its investments, including hedge funds and private equity investments.

With nearly 44 million workers and retirees relying on PBGC's insurance programs, we appreciate GAO's work in highlighting issues that relate to pensions, including those raised in this report and look forward to continuing to work with GAO. Again, thank you for the opportunity to comment.

Sincerely,

Charles E.F. Millard

End Notes

[1] A defined benefit (DB) pension plan generally provides benefits in the form of a guaranteed retirement benefit, the value of which is typically determined by a formula based on salary and years of service.

[2] A futures contract is an agreement to buy or sell a specific amount of a commodity or financial instrument at a particular price on a stipulated future date. An option is a securities transaction agreement tied to stocks, commodities, or stock indexes.

[3] We contacted the following states: California, Florida, Illinois, Massachusetts, New Jersey, New York, North Carolina, Pennsylvania, Ohio, Texas, and Wisconsin.

[4] ERISA's prudent man standard is satisfied if the fiduciary has given appropriate consideration to the following factors (1) the composition of the plan portfolio with regard to diversification of risk; (2) the volatility of the plan investment portfolio with regard to general movements of investment prices; (3) the liquidity of the plan investment portfolio relative to the funding objectives of the plan; (4) the projected return of the plan investment portfolio relative to the funding objectives of the plan; and (5) the prevailing and projected economic conditions of the entities in which the plan has invested and proposes to invest. 29 C.F.R. § 2550.404a-1(b) (2007).

[5] Under ERISA, a fiduciary is a person who (1) exercises discretionary authority or control over plan management or any authority or control over plan assets; (2) renders investment advice regarding plan moneys or property for direct or indirect compensation; or (3) has discretionary authority or responsibility for plan administration. 29 U.S.C. § 1002(21).

[6] For additional information about hedge funds, see GAO, *Hedge Funds: Regulators and Market Participants Are Taking Steps to Strengthen Market Discipline, but Continued Attention Is Needed*, GAO-08-200 (Washington, D.C.: Jan. 24, 2008).

[7] Leverage involves the use of borrowed money or other techniques to potentially increase an investment's value or return without increasing the amount invested. A short sale is the sale of a security that the seller does not own or a sale that is consummated by the delivery of a security borrowed by, or for, the account of the seller. Short selling is used to profit by a decline in the price of the security.

[8] Ch. 38, tit. I, 48 Stat. 74 (codified at 15 U.S.C. § 77a et seq.).

[9] Ch. 404, 48 Stat. 881 (codified at 15 U.S.C. § 78a et seq.).

[10] Ch. 686, tit. I, 54 Stat. 797 (codified as amended at 15 U.S.C. § 80a-1 et seq.).

[11] Ch. 686, tit. II, 54 Stat. 847 (codified as amended at 15 U.S.C. § 80b-1 et seq.).

[12] GAO is issuing a forthcoming report on leveraged buyouts by private equity funds.

[13] Other less common types of private equity include mezzanine financing, in which investors provide a final round of financing to help carry the company through its initial public offering, and distressed debt investments, in which firms buy companies that have filed for bankruptcy or may do so and then typically liquidate the company.

[14] We reviewed data from surveys of DB pension plans conducted by three organizations—Greenwich Associates (covering mid- to large-size pension plans, with $250 million or more in total assets), Pyramis Global Advisors (covering mid- to large-size pension plans, with $200 million or more in total assets), and *Pensions & Investments* (limited to large plans, which generally had $1 billion or more in total assets). Greenwich Associates is an institutional financial services consulting and research firm; Pyramis Global Advisors, a division of Fidelity Investments, is an institutional asset management firm; and *Pensions & Investments* is a money management industry publication. These data cannot be generalized to all plans. See appendix I for more information on these surveys.

[15] *Pensions & Investments* was the only survey we reviewed that reported the allocations of individual plans to hedge funds and private equity. Among the top 200 pension plans, ranked by combined assets in DB and defined contribution plans, 133 were DB plans that completed the survey and provided asset allocation information in 2007.

[16] The figures reported by these surveys differ somewhat because, as described in table 1, they are based on different samples. Comprehensive data on plan investments in hedge funds and private equity are not available. The federal government collects information on investment allocations but does not require plan sponsors to report information on hedge funds or private equity as separate asset classes. Existing data may not include plans that engage in hedge fund-like activities outside of a formal hedge fund partnership structure.

[17] Collectively bargained plans are arrangements between a labor union and an employer. These plans may cover workers at a single employer or multiple employers and are jointly governed by management and labor representatives.

[18] 44 Fed. Reg. 37, 221.

[19] Paul Gompers, J. Lerner. M. M. Blair, and T. Hellmann, "What Drives Venture Capital Fundraising," *Brookings Papers: Microeconomics*, pp. 149–204 (1998).

[20] According to the PBGC, individual DB plans with less than $200 million in total assets comprised about 15 percent of the total assets of all DB plans in 2005.

[21] "Long only" investment managers can generally be defined as those whose strategies are limited to buying assets whose value is expected to increase. That is, they cannot "short" or sell borrowed securities.

[22] Volatility refers to the propensity of a security to move up or down over time; if a security moves up or down rapidly over a short period of time, it is considered to have high volatility.

[23] Our discussions with pension plan officials about their hedge fund investments occurred in 2007. Consequently, we have no information about how their investments might have been affected by the financial market turbulence that occurred since that time.

[24] In contrast, mutual fund managers must comply with various aspects of federal securities law, and operate in a much more constrained manner.

[25] 69 Fed. Reg. 45,172, 45,178.

[26] Historically, leverage is the use of various financial instruments or borrowed capital to increase the potential return of an investment. As we reported in January 2008 (GAO-08-200), since the near collapse of the Long Term Capital Management fund in 1998, investors, creditors, and counterparties have increased efforts to impose market discipline on hedge funds, including tightening credit standards for hedge funds. However, we also noted that no one entity may have all the necessary data to assess the total leverage used by a hedge fund.

[27] According to the SEC, a hedge fund's use of leverage is limited by margin or collateral requirements imposed by lenders and others. In contrast, registered investment companies are subject to specific statutory limitations.

[28] For example, a 15 percent decline in an investment of $50 with no leverage is exactly a 15 percent loss—a loss of $7.50—and the investor still has $42.50 and can hope for a rebound. On the other hand, an investment of $50 leveraged 10 times exposes the investor to an investment of $500, and a 15 percent decline in value will result in a loss of $75. The added risk of leverage can be seen in the fact that this 15 percent decline in such a leveraged position leads to not only a total loss of the original $50 investment, but a remaining debt of $25—half of the initial investment.

[29] Fees can vary somewhat among hedge funds.

[30] A security is described as thinly traded when traded infrequently and/or in low volumes.

[31] See GAO-08-200.

[32] Lock-ups can be important to hedge funds because sudden liquidations could disrupt a carefully calibrated investment strategy and because some of the hedge fund's underlying assets may themselves be illiquid.

[33] The $9 billion fund operated by Amaranth Advisors, LLC, collapsed in the fall of 2006 as a result of natural gas derivatives trading.

[34] "San Diego County Employees Retirement Association - The Quest for 'Alpha,'" San Diego County Grand Jury 2006-2007, Online: http://www.co.sandiego.ca.us/grandjury/report06_07.html, accessed June 18, 2008.

[35] *Implication of the Growth of Hedge Funds,* Staff Report to the United States Securities and Exchange Commission, September 2003. Although hedge funds are substantially unregulated, they are nonetheless subject to anti-fraud, and some other provisions of federal securities law.

[36] *Hedge Fund Operational Risk: Meeting the Demand for Higher Transparency and Best Practice*, Bank of New York/Amber Partners White Paper, June 2006.

[37] A long-short strategy exploits perceived anomalies in the price of securities. For example, a hedge fund may buy bonds that it believes to be under-priced, and sell short bonds that it believes to be overpriced.

[38] "Funds of Hedge Funds FAQs: MFA's Concise Guide to Hedge Funds," Managed Funds Association.

[39] As described in the first section, pension investment in private equity increased markedly following publication of guidance by Labor in 1979 clarifying that private sector plans may make some investments in riskier assets, such as venture capital and buy-out funds.

[40] Several plans cited research which shows that the average performance of top-quartile private equity funds exceeds the stock market. See, for example: Steven Kaplan and Antoinette Schoar, "PE Performance: Returns, Persistence, and Capital Flows," *Journal of Finance*, VOL. LX, No.4, (August 2005); Alexander Ljungquist and Matthew Richardson, "The Cash Flow, Return and Risk Characteristics of Private Equity." *National Bureau Economic Research, Working Paper*, #9454, (January 2003); and David Swensen, *Pioneering Portfolio Management: An Unconventional Approach to Institutional Investment*. The Free Press: New York (2000).

[41] We conducted our interviews on plans' private equity investments from October 2007 to January 2008; therefore, their comments may not reflect more recent changes to market conditions.

[42] Some public plans also invest in private equity, in part, to promote local economic development in accordance with state policy. According to plan representatives and an industry organization, venture capital investments have, in some cases, been viewed as a way to promote local economic growth, while at the same time, providing returns that bolster retirement income for plan beneficiaries. Most public plan officials we interviewed, however, did not cite promoting local economic development as an explicit goal for their private equity investments.

[43] Several studies show a range of correlation between private equity and the stock market. Correlations cited range from the low, 30 percent, to the very high, 95 percent.

[44] One study shows that, on average, funds in the study invested close to 40 percent of capital in a single industry. Alexander Ljungquist and Matthew Richardson, "The Cash Flow, Return and Risk Characteristics of Private Equity," *National Bureau Economic Research, Working Paper*, No. 9454 (January 2003).

[45] See, for example: Paul Gompers and Josh Lerner, "Money chasing deals? The impact of fund inflows on private equity valuations," *Journal of Financial Economics,* vol 55. (2000); and Alexander Ljungquist and Matthew Richardson, "The Cash Flow, Return and Risk Characteristics of Private Equity." *National Bureau Economic Research, Working Paper,* #9454, Jan. 2003; and David Swensen, *Pioneering Portfolio Management: An Unconventional Approach to Institutional Investment,* The Free Press: New York (2000).

[46] David Swensen, *Pioneering Portfolio Management: An Unconventional Approach to Institutional Investment*, The Free Press: New York (2000).

[47] Steven Kaplan and Antoinette Schoar, "Private Equity Performance: Returns, Persistence, and Capital Flows." *Journal of Finance,* vol. LX, No. 4 (August 2005).

[48] Officials with some plans explained that an investor might sell its stake in a private equity fund on a secondary market; however, interests in a private equity fund are typically sold at a discount. One plan also noted that selling a stake on the secondary market would also jeopardize their reputation as an investor with private equity funds since the fund managers look unfavorably on such transactions.

[49] Plan officials we interviewed also noted that they expect private equity valuation to become more frequent and market-based following recent changes to accounting standards. In September 2006, the Financial Accounting Standards Board issued Statement of Financial Accounting Standards (SFAS) No.157, "Fair Value Measurements." This standard defines fair value as the price that would be received to sell an asset or paid to transfer a liability in an orderly transaction between market participants at the measurement date. As discussed in SFAS No. 157, the changes to current practice resulting from the application of this standard relate to the definition of fair value, the methods used to measure fair value, and the expanded disclosures about fair value measurements. The new definition of fair value may change the manner in which some entities, such as private equity funds, determine fair value.

[50] Plan officials noted that top-performing private equity fund managers tend to consistently perform well over time and some plans cited research in support of this view. See, for example, Steven Kaplan and Antoinette Schoar, "Private Equity Performance: Returns, Persistence, and Capital Flows." Journal of Finance, vol. LX, No. 4 (August 2005).

[51] According to the National Venture Capital Association, more than half of venture capital funds manage $100 million or less in capital.

[52] While the advisory board of a private equity fund may allow investors some degree of oversight, it does not provide investors with an active role in the management of the fund.

[53] However, ERISA may indirectly limit a pension plan's ability to invest in specific hedge funds or private equity funds. Under Labor's plan asset regulation, if the aggregate investment by benefit plan investors in the equity interest of a particular entity is "significant," and that equity interest is not (i) a publicly-offered security, (ii) issued by a registered investment company, such as a mutual fund, nor (iii) issued by an operating company, then the assets of that entity are deemed assets of each benefit plan investor (i.e., plan assets). See 29 C.F.R. § 2510.3-101 (2007). As a result, any person who exercises management authority over the entity now deemed to hold plan assets will become subject to ERISA's fiduciary standards. The equity investments by benefit plan investors are considered "significant" if at any time the aggregate investment of the benefit plan investors represents 25 percent or more of the value of any class of equity in the entity. According to one industry expert, in order to avoid being deemed a plan fiduciary (and assuming all of the liabilities that accompany that status), many managers of hedge funds, which generally are not publicly-traded, not registered investment companies, nor operating companies, carefully monitor the level of investments in the hedge fund by benefit plan investors to ensure that their aggregate investment remains below the 25 percent threshold. Prior to the Pension Protection Act of 2006 (PPA), the calculation of the 25 percent threshold pertained to investments by ERISA plans and certain non-ERISA covered plans, such as public sector and foreign retirement plans. However, in accordance with section 611(f) of the PPA, investments by certain plans, including public sector and foreign retirement plans, are now excluded from the calculation. Pub. L. No.109-280, § 611(f), 120 Stat. 780, 972 (codified at 29 U.S.C. § 1002(42)). This modification may facilitate an increase in the level of investments by pension plans in hedge funds and private equity funds.

[54] With some exceptions, ERISA does prohibit plans from investing more than 10 percent of plan assets in the sponsoring company's stock. See 29 U.S.C. § 1107. In addition to requiring plan fiduciaries to adhere to certain standards of conduct, ERISA also prohibits plan fiduciaries from engaging in specified transactions. See 29 U.S.C. § 1106.

[55] The ERISA Advisory Council was created by ERISA to provide advice to the Secretary of Labor. 29 U.S.C. § 1142.

[56] The PPA is the most recent comprehensive reform of federal pension laws since the enactment of ERISA. It establishes new funding requirements for DB pensions and includes reforms that will affect cash balance pension plans, defined contribution plans, and deferred compensation plans for executives and highly compensated employees.

[57] *Principles and Best Practices for Hedge Fund Investors: Report of the Investors' Committee to the President's Working Group on Financial Markets*, April 15, 2008. The President's Working Group on Financial Markets includes the heads of the U.S. Treasury Department, the Federal Reserve, the SEC, and the Commodity Futures Trading Commission.

[58] Plan underfunding can occur for several reasons, including poor investment performance and insufficient contributions.

[59] "Hard to value" assets are those that are not traded on an exchange. "Hard to value" assets may include hedge funds, private equity funds, and real estate. It is difficult to distinguish the type of investment with the information provided. Federal agency officials use the Form 5500 report data to enforce ERISA pension requirements, monitor plan compliance, develop aggregate pension statistics, and conduct policy and economic research.

[60] NASRA is a non-profit association whose members are the directors of the nation's state and territorial public retirement systems.

[61] We contacted the 10 states with the largest amount of public pension assets under management, as well as Massachusetts, because that state provided valuable information during our initial work. Our methodology is discussed in greater detail in appendix I.

[62] Restrictions applicable across various plans were identified through conversations with relevant officials in each state, except North Carolina. In addition, individual plans may have their own restrictions adopted by plan boards or staff. In some states, state restrictions apply quite broadly, and in others, the restrictions apply to a more narrow range of plans or public plan assets, therefore the existence of a restriction in a state does not necessarily indicate that the restriction exists for every public plan in the state.

[63] See Tex. Gov. Code Ann. § 825.3012. For purposes of this Texas state law restriction, "hedge fund" is defined as a private investment vehicle that (i) is not registered under an investment company act, (ii) issues securities only to accredited investors or qualified purchasers under an exemption from registration, and (iii) engages primarily in the strategic trading of securities and other financial instruments.

[64] According to TRS officials, no other public funds in Texas are, by state law, under explicit restrictions regarding hedge fund or private equity investments.

[65] See Ill. Comp. Stat. Ann. 5/1-113.1.

[66] Assets invested under the basket provision are still subject to the prudent investor standard.

[67] The Wisconsin Retirement System is a consolidated system that covers all state, local, and school district employees, with the exception of the city and county of Milwaukee. Short selling is the selling of a security that the seller does not own, or any sale that is completed by the delivery of a security borrowed by the seller. Short sellers assume that they will be able to buy the stock at a lower amount than the price at which they sold

short. Selling short is the opposite of going long. That is, short sellers make money if the stock goes down in price.

[68] 2008 Wis. Sess. Laws. 212.

[69] A draft version of this report, *Principles and Best Practices for Hedge Fund Investors: Report of the Investors' Committee to the President's Working Group on Financial Markets*, was published on April 15, 2008.

[70] Greenwich Associates is an institutional financial services consulting and research firm; Pyramis Global Advisors, a division of Fidelity Investments, is an institutional asset management firm; and *Pensions & Investments* is a money management industry publication.

[71] Massachusetts ranks 20th with $32.4 billion in public pension plan assets, according to the 2007 Public Funds Survey.

In: Pensions: Backgrounds, Trends and Issues
Editor: Henry J. Mullen
ISBN: 978-1-60876-840-0

Chapter 2

PLAN FREEZES AFFECT MILLIONS OF PARTICIPANTS AND MAY POSE RETIREMENT INCOME CHALLENGES

United States Government Accountability Office

WHY GAO DID THIS STUDY

Private defined benefit (DB) pension plans are an important source of retirement income for millions of Americans. However, from 1990 to 2006, plan sponsors have voluntarily terminated over 61,000 sufficiently funded single-employer DB plans. An event preceding at least some of these terminations was a so-called plan "freeze"—an amendment to the plan to limit some or all future pension accruals for some or all plan participants. Available information that the government collects about frozen plans is limited in scope and may not be recent. GAO conducted a stratified probability sample survey of 471 single-employer DB plan sponsors out of a population of 7,804 (with 100 or more total plan participants) to gather more timely and detailed information about frozen plans. We have prepared this report under the Comptroller General's authority as part of our ongoing reassessment of risks associated with the Pension Benefit Guaranty Corporation's (PBGC) single-employer pension insurance program, which, in 2003, we placed on our high-risk list of programs that need broad-based transformations and warrant the attention of Congress and the executive branch. Frozen DB plans have possible implications for PBGC's long-term financial position. This report examines (1) the extent to which DB pension plans are frozen and the characteristics of frozen plans; and (2) the implications of these freezes for plan participants, plan sponsors, and the PBGC.

To view the full product, including the scope and methodology, click on GAO-08-817. To view the survey results click on GAO 08-818SP. For more information, contact Barbara Bovbjerg, at (202) 512-7215 or bovbjergb@gao.gov.

WHAT GAO FOUND

Frozen plans are fairly common today, with about half of all sponsors in our study population having one or more frozen DB plans. Overall, about 3.3 million active participants in our study population, who represent about 21 percent of all active participants in the single-employer DB system, are affected by a freeze. The most common type of freeze is a hard freeze—a freeze in which all future benefit accruals cease—which accounts for 23 percent of plans in our study population; however, an additional 22 percent of plans are frozen in some other way. Larger sponsors (i.e. those with 10,000 or more total participants) are significantly less likely than smaller sponsors to have implemented a hard freeze, with only 9 percent of plans under a hard freeze among larger sponsors compared with 25 percent of plans under a hard freeze among smaller sponsors. The vast majority of sponsors with frozen plans in our study population, 83 percent, have alternative retirement savings arrangements for these affected participants, but 11 percent of sponsors do not. (An additional 6 percent of sponsors froze plans under circumstances that preclude a replacement plan.) Plan sponsors cited many reasons for freezing their largest plans but most often noted two: the impact of annual contributions on their firm's cash flows and the unpredictability of plan funding. Sponsors of frozen plans generally expressed a degree of uncertainty about the anticipated outcome for their largest plan, but sponsors whose largest plan was hard frozen were significantly more likely to anticipate plan termination as the likely plan outcome.

The implications of a freeze vary for sponsors, participants, and PBGC. For plan sponsors, while hard freezes appear to indicate an increased likelihood of plan termination, a rise in plan terminations has yet to materialize. For participants, a freeze generally implies a reduction in anticipated future retirement benefits, though this may be somewhat or entirely offset by increases in other benefits or a replacement retirement-savings plan. However, because the replacement plans offered to affected participants most frequently are defined contribution, the investment risk and responsibility for saving are shifted to employees. Finally, plan freezes may potentially improve PBGC's net financial position, but the degree to which it is accompanied by sponsor efforts to improve plan funding is unclear. In any event, the shrinking of the single-employer pension insurance program plan base seems likely to continue.

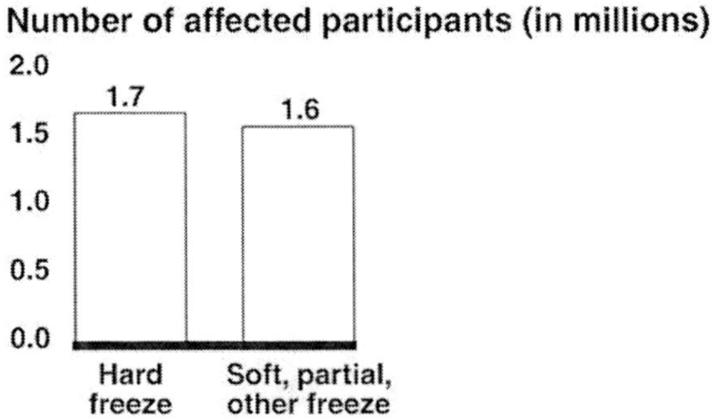

Source: GAO analysis of survey of DB pension plan sponsors regarding frozen plans.

Estimated Number of Active Participants Affected by Sponsors' Largest Plan Freeze, by Freeze Type

ABBREVIATIONS

CB	collective bargaining
CUSIP	Committee on Uniform Securities Identification Procedures
DB	defined benefit
DC	defined contribution
EIN	employee identification number
PBGC	Pension Benefit Guaranty Corporation

July 21, 2008

Congressional Addressees

The number of private defined-benefit (DB) plans, an important source of retirement income for millions of Americans, has declined substantially over the past two decades.[1] For example, plan sponsors voluntarily terminated over 61,000 sufficiently funded single-employer DB plans from 1990 to 2006.[2] An event preceding at least some of these terminations was a so-called plan "freeze"—an amendment to the plan to limit some or all future pension accruals for some or all plan participants. Over the last five years, a number of large, high profile employers have announced their intention to freeze one or more of their DB plans. These larger plans represent a significant portion of plan liabilities and participants in the private DB pension system.

In 2003, when asked to determine the number of frozen DB plans, we reported that reliable and timely data on DB plan freezes were not generally available.[3] Since that report, additional studies have been published, including two from the Pension Benefit Guaranty Corporation (PBGC), the federal corporation that insures private DB pension plans.[4] PBGC's studies analyze plan freezes using information submitted by DB pension plan sponsors on the Form 5500 Annual Return/Report of Employee Benefit Plan.[5] However, the data from the Form 5500, the primary source of information on DB plans, are limited to so-called "hard freezes." Under a hard freeze, all current employees who participate in the plan receive no additional benefit accruals after the effective date of the freeze, and employees hired after the freeze are ineligible to participate in the plan. The Form 5500 information on freezes does not include so-called "soft-freezes," which limit future benefit accruals based on a component of the benefit accrual formula (that is, the service or salary component). According to the most recent PBGC study, 14 percent of the single- employer plans it insures were hard frozen at the end of 2005, a 48 percent increase since 2003. The PBGC study also found that plans with 100 or fewer participants were generally more likely to be frozen than larger plans.

In addition to the informational limitations of the Form 5500, we have also noted that its data are not always available on a timely basis. For example, the Form 5500's most recently available and complete information on plan freezes is for calendar year 2005 and thus does not include recent plan freezes. Given these concerns and broader concerns about the implications of plan freezes for the retirement security of plan participants, GAO initiated a survey of frozen DB plans under the authority of the Comptroller General of the United States as part of our ongoing reassessment of risks associated with the PBGC's single-employer pension insurance program. In 2003, we placed this program on our high-risk list of programs that need broad-based transformations and warrant the attention of Congress and the executive branch. Frozen DB plans have possible implications for PBGC's long-term financial position.

Reporting Objectives

To better understand the current plan-freeze environment and its significance to the DB system going forward, we address the following questions:

1. To what extent are DB pension plans frozen, and what are the characteristics of such freezes?
2. What are the implications of such freezes for plan sponsors, participants, and the PBGC?

Scope and Methodology

To determine the extent and characteristics among plans that are currently frozen, we collected and analyzed original survey data. We also analyzed and reviewed recent studies of frozen DB plans, notably PBGC's studies of hard frozen DB plans. Appendix I contains revised slides that update the preliminary briefing information that we provided to interested congressional staffs and members, as well as officials from the Department of Labor, PBGC, and the Department of the Treasury from late-April to June 2008.

We conducted our work from April 2006 to July 2008, in accordance with generally accepted government auditing standards. Those standards require that we plan and perform our work to obtain sufficient, appropriate evidence to provide a reasonable basis for our findings and conclusions based on our research objectives. We believe that the evidence obtained provides a reasonable basis for our findings and conclusions based on our objectives.

To achieve our survey objectives, we surveyed a stratified probability sample of 471 DB pension sponsors from PBGC's 2004 Form 5500 Research Database. We limited our study population to 7,804 sponsors that had 100 or more total participants in sponsored plans, and our survey population results represent estimates for all sponsors with this characteristic. While they are a minority of sponsors (about 34 percent), sponsors whose plans have more than 100 participants represent about 99 percent of all DB plan participants in the single-employer DB system. Further, sponsors with more than 100 participants in participating plans also represent 99.1 percent of the total liabilities among single-employer plans. To deploy the survey, we mailed a questionnaire to DB pension plan sponsors in the three smallest strata we identified. In addition, as part of a longer questionnaire, we collected similar information via a web survey about plan freezes from the very largest strata of plan sponsors. The survey results can be reviewed in GAO-08-818SP. See appendix II for a more detailed discussion about our survey methodology.

FROZEN PLANS AFFECT ABOUT ONE-FIFTH OF ACTIVE DB PLAN PARTICIPANTS

Overall, an estimated 3.3 million active participants[6] in our study population—or 21 percent of all active participants in the private, single- employer DB system—are affected by reported freezes. (See app. I, slide 9 and slide 10.) Active participants are employees that are or may become eligible to accrue or receive additional benefits under a plan; if all participants in the DB system (that is, active participants, retirees, and separated vested participants) are considered, the proportion represented by active participants who are affected by plan freezes falls to 10 percent.[7] (See app. I, Slide 9.) We considered only those participants who are currently accruing benefits (that is, active participants) at the time of freeze implementation to be affected by a freeze. The above calculations, therefore, do not include sponsors whose largest frozen plans are under a new-employee-only soft freeze, where the plan is closed to new entrants and benefit accruals for active participants remain unchanged. The extent to which active participants are affected by a freeze depends on the type of freeze in place. Under hard freezes, future benefit accruals cease for active participants. In contrast, soft freezes may reduce future benefit accruals for some or all active participants. Soft freezes are distinct from hard freezes in that the restrictions on participants' future benefit accruals are less comprehensive than the total cessation of future accruals under hard freezes.[8]

Our survey shows that about half the sponsors in the study population have one or more frozen plans. (See app. I, slide 11.) Overall, about 51 percent of plans in the study population were reported as closed to new entrants, the basic requirement of a plan freeze. Nearly half of plans with a reported freeze, or 23 percent of all plans in the study population, were under a hard freeze. (See app. I, slide 12.)[9] In addition, 12 percent reported some type of soft freeze. About 6 percent reported a partial plan freeze, while 4 percent reported an "other" freeze, which include situations where plan participants are separated into plan tiers,[10] or freezes brought on by bankruptcy, plant closure, or plan merger.

The survey results suggest that two factors may influence the likelihood that sponsors will implement a hard freeze: sponsor size and the extent to which a sponsor's plans are subject to collective bargaining (CB) agreements. Larger sponsors, those with 10,000 or more total participants, are significantly less likely than smaller sponsors to have implemented a hard freeze, with only 9.4 percent of plans under a hard freeze among larger sponsors compared with 25.4 percent of plans under a hard freeze among smaller sponsors. (See app. I, slide 13.) Similarly, firms with some or all plans subject to CB are significantly less likely to implement hard freezes than sponsors with no plans subject to CB.[11] (See app. I, Slide 14.) However, these two factors may be related, as larger sponsors in our survey are generally more likely to have one or more plans subject to CB than smaller sponsors.[12]

About half of the freezes of sponsors' largest frozen plans have occurred since 2005. (See app. I, slide 16.) This figure includes only plans that are currently frozen, and it does not represent a longitudinal dataset of all plan freezes. Any plans frozen during the same time period and terminated prior to GAO's survey are not included. However, PBGC data shows us that there has been a recent decline in the number of plan terminations among plans with 100 or more participants. The number of standard terminations declined by two-thirds from 2001 to 2002 through 2005 to 2006, a period during which there was a significant increase in the number of current plan freezes. This may suggest possible growth in the number of frozen plans currently in the single-employer DB system.

Of sponsors in the study population with one or more frozen plans, 83 percent offered a replacement retirement savings vehicle to affected participants in their largest frozen plans. (See app. I, slide 18.) Eleven percent of sponsors did not offer any replacement plan to affected participants; however, this figure includes any sponsors who allowed affected participants to join or increase employee contributions to an existing but unchanged plan.[13] An additional 6 percent of sponsors froze plans under extenuating circumstances that preclude the offering of a replacement plan (such as, a firm merger, bankruptcy, plant closure, multiple employer plan, or new-employee-only soft freeze). Of those sponsors offering replacement plans, over 80 percent offered enhanced existing or new DC plans. (See app. I, slide 19.) About 5 percent of sponsors offered a new DB plan to affected participants.

Sponsors of frozen plans cited a number of reasons why they froze their largest plan. "Annual contributions needed to satisfy funding requirements and their impact on cash flows" was cited most often, with 72 percent of sponsors responding that this was a reason for freezing their largest frozen plans; "unpredictability/volatility of plan funding requirements" followed with 69 percent.[14] (See app. I, slide 21.) The remaining 13 reasons range in prevalence from 54 percent responding that "plan was frozen in anticipation of replacing it with an alternative retirement plan" to 12 percent for "other reason."[15]

About two-thirds of sponsors with frozen plans reported at least some level of confidence that their largest frozen plan was reasonably well-funded at the time of freeze. (See app. I, slide 22.) Further, 58 percent of sponsors were highly or moderately confident that their largest frozen plans could have undergone standard, fully-funded terminations instead of freezing. This is compared with 30 percent of sponsors who were not at all confident that their largest frozen plans could have undergone standard terminations. However, there are some limitations to these data. First, the survey asked about sponsor beliefs, not actual funding levels. Second, the data refer to when the freezes were implemented and may bear no relation to current funding levels. Third, the data only include each sponsor's largest frozen plan. Nevertheless, the data provide some insight into sponsors' state of mind when they chose to freeze their largest frozen plans.

For sponsors with plans that are already frozen, fewer than half reported having a firm idea of the anticipated outcome for their largest frozen plans. Among these sponsors, a very small number anticipate "thawing," or unfreezing, their plan, and about one-third said they will eventually terminate their largest frozen plans. (See app. I, slide 24.) In contrast, nearly half say they will keep the plan frozen indefinitely. Another 14 percent report that it is too early to make a decision or that they are uncertain what the outcome will be. The anticipated outcome for a sponsor's largest plan varies significantly by the type of frozen plan. Sponsors with frozen plans that were not under a hard freeze were significantly less likely to anticipate termination as the outcome for their largest frozen plan. (See app. I, slide 25.)[16] Among sponsors with one or more plans not currently frozen, only 10 percent have firmly decided to freeze, or not freeze, any plans in the future. (See app. I, slide 26.) Thirty-five percent of sponsors have considered freezing additional plans in the future but are uncertain if they will, while nearly 50 percent have not yet considered or discussed future freezes.

PLAN FREEZES HAVE VARIOUS IMPLICATIONS FOR KEY STAKEHOLDERS

The prevalence of frozen DB plans today has different implications for key stakeholders in the single-employer DB system—plan sponsors, participants, and the PBGC.

Our survey found that nearly a third of the sponsors ultimately expect to terminate their largest frozen plan. Further, we found that about half of all frozen plans were hard frozen and that sponsors of hard frozen plans appear more likely to anticipate termination as an eventual outcome. However, the number of plan terminations has not increased recently. For example, from 1990 to 2006, total annual standard terminations averaged about 7 percent of insured single-employer plans. However, from 2002 to 2006, this rate had been far lower. (See app. I, slide 28.) Further, larger plans, or those plans with 100 or more participants, which account for about 36 percent of plans but which account for the overwhelming number of the system's active participants, accounted for only about 9 percent of the terminations during the 2002 to 2006 period. This suggests that the single-employer DB system's decline does not appear to be accelerating, with many large plans continuing in operation.

Plans may freeze for many reasons, and our survey population of frozen plan sponsors cited cost of contributions and volatility of plan funding as the key reasons for freezing their largest plans. However, when we asked all sponsors, including those with no frozen plans, about the key challenges to the future health of the single-employer DB system generally, the very same issues of plan cost and volatility were listed most frequently. Given that these issues seem to be an inherent problem for all sponsors, it may be that each sponsor decision to freeze a plan has a firm-specific reason or is based on other factors not picked up in our survey. In any case, the current prevalence of plan freezes does not present an encouraging landscape for DB plan sponsorship.

For active plan participants, plan freezes imply a possible reduction in anticipated retirement income. In particular, a hard freeze, which ceases future benefit accruals, is especially likely to reduce anticipated retirement income—unless this income is made up through increased savings, possibly from such sources as higher wages or other nonwage benefit increases. Although a majority of the sponsors with frozen plans cited plan cost considerations as a key motivation for the freeze—suggesting that they may be somewhat reluctant to fully redirect any potential cost savings from the freeze to other areas of compensation or benefits—our survey did not collect information to fully address this issue. For example, while our survey indicated that sponsors most often do offer a replacement plan for frozen participants and this offering is most often a DC or 401(k)-type plan, we did not ask about the generosity of these replacement plans or of the previous frozen DB plan.

The offering of an alternative plan may have different consequences for employees in different stages of their career. Reductions to anticipated accruals for participants affected by a freeze will vary considerably depending on key plan features, participant demographic characteristics, and market interest rate factors.[17] However, for those participants with traditional pension plan formulas[18] that are hard frozen and replaced with a typical DC, or 401(k)-type plan, all else being equal, longer-tenured, midcareer workers are most likely to see the greatest reductions in anticipated retirement income. This effect occurs because older, longer- tenured employees generally have less time remaining in their careers to offset anticipated accrual losses through typical 401(k)-type plan contributions compared to younger workers. Alternatively, depending on the generosity of the frozen, pay-based pension plan, certain younger (or less well-tenured) and more mobile participants might actually see increases in their anticipated retirement incomes by moving to a typical, or average, 401(k)-type plan.

These concerns are not just relevant for the current active participants of a frozen plan. Our survey also shows that roughly a majority of sponsors in our study population have closed their plans to new employees, many of whom will also likely depend on a DC plan as a source of retirement income. Our survey did not collect information on the degree to which affected employees are participating in either the newly offered DC plans or any existing, but enhanced, DC plan. DC plans are increasingly the dominant retirement savings vehicle for private sector workers. Like DB plans, DC plans pose their own potential retirement-income challenges, including the need for employees to participate in the plan and to effectively manage the investment risk of their DC accounts if they are to have a secure retirement. Yet for some workers, especially for lower-income workers, this may be difficult to do as they are less likely to participate when offered the opportunity to do so and less able to make even limited contributions.[19]

The effect of plan freezes on PBGC's net financial position is not certain, but it could be modestly positive in both the immediate- and long-term; freezes generally reduce system liabilities and potentially minimize claims among financially weak plans.[20] The possible improvement in PBGC's net position, however, assumes that the aggregate effect of plan freezes does not significantly reduce the agency's premium income over time.[21] The reductions in flat-rate premium[22] income could come from a decline in participants, possibly from the considerable number of plans that we found that were closed to new employees or from terminations that may result from the freeze. Variable-rate premium income[23] could also be reduced to the degree that sponsors of underfunded plans improve funding as a result of a plan freeze.

PBGC's financial status is influenced not only by the number of freezes and terminations but also by the relative health and size of the plans and sponsors that decide to terminate. For example, PBGC finds that hard frozen plans are more likely to be underfunded and to terminate, which may highlight two other trends. Plan sponsors that initiate a standard termination must have sufficient assets in the plan to pay participants their accrued benefits and are unlikely to represent the very same plan sponsors that are also underfunded. If relatively well-funded and financially healthy sponsors are the ones who terminate their frozen plans, it may leave the underfunded, and potentially financially distressed, frozen plan sponsors under PBGC's insurance responsibility. Alternatively, data from PBGC shows that relatively large plans terminate at a much lower rate than smaller plans. This is possibly encouraging for PBGC's financial status, to the degree that these larger plans do not result in claims, because these plans represent the bulk of liabilities and participants.

Ultimately, no matter what the impact on its net financial position, the freezing of plans and the exiting from the single-employer DB system by sponsors do not indicate future plan growth for the PBGC. One part of its mission is to foster the continuation and maintenance of private-sector pension plans. PBGC's single-employer insurance program currently covers 28,800 plans, which is 65 percent fewer plans than it covered 15 years ago. Given the prevalence of plans that are currently frozen and the relationship between plan freezes and plan termination, the shrinking of the single-employer insurance program plan base seems likely to continue.

CONCLUDING OBSERVATIONS

The private DB pension system, a key source of retirement income for millions of Americans, continues to experience a slow decline. Plan freezes are a common phenomenon, affect a large number of participants, and have important implications for plan sponsors, participants, and the PBGC. While plan freezes are not as irrevocable as plan terminations, they are indicative of the system's continued erosion. Yet freezes are just one of the many developments now affecting the DB system. The broad ranging Pension Protection Act of 2006, changes in accounting rules, rising retiree health care costs and health care costs generally, a weak economy, and falling interest rates all represent challenges that DB plan sponsors may need to confront. How key stakeholders, plan sponsors, participants, the PBGC, other government agencies, and congressional policymakers respond to all of these challenges will shape the fortunes of the DB system and its future role in providing retirement security to American workers.

AGENCY COMMENTS AND OUR EVALUATION

We provided a draft of this report to the Department of Labor, the Department of the Treasury, and PBGC. The PBGC provided written comments, which appear in appendix III. PBGC generally agreed with the findings and conclusions of the report. However, PBGC did express some concerns about our survey methodology—especially with respect to the comparability of our estimates of hard frozen plans and affected active participants with their estimates, which are based on the Form 5500 filings for plan year 2006 received to date. PBGC notes that differences in results may be due to a variety of reasons, including that our survey data are more recent than the 2006 Form 5500 and the potential for some reporting errors on the Form 5500. Other explanations include the potential for response bias in the GAO survey, our use of a size variable that is sponsor-based rather than plan-based and the GAO survey's omission of newly formed pension plans since 2004.

We addressed many of PBGC's specific methodological concerns by providing additional information to our technical appendix. We note that the very different methodologies used by PBGC and GAO in estimating the number of hard plan freezes and the number of active participants affected by such freezes suggest that the studies' results should be compared with extreme caution. We do note that our survey questionnaire was pre-tested extensively. Further, regarding the issue of response bias, we considered this as we analyzed our survey's results. We do not believe response bias is a significant issue because we did not find significant differences when we analyzed a comparison of key characteristics of the survey respondents to all sponsors in the study population. We also did not include newly-formed DB plans other than those formed by survey respondents because such data were not available, and, in our view, would not have a significant effect on our estimates.

PBGC identified a number of explicit areas of agreement with our report. They noted that our finding with respect to the differences in prevalence of freezes between large and small plans is generally consistent with their estimates. They also mentioned that our report was consistent with their views on the effect that freezes may have on the future health of the DB system, the PBGC itself, as well as the impact of freezes on retirement incomes. Further, despite PBGC's concerns about the magnitude of certain estimates in our report, they generally found the relative estimates of alternative definitions of plan freezes to be new and important information. Lastly, PBGC noted that the comparison of our survey estimates to Form 5500 estimates highlights the delay that PBGC faces getting basic plan data. PBGC expects that plan data will become timelier in the near future, but some delay will still remain that may hinder PBGC's awareness of changing trends among plans that it insures.

The Department of Labor and Treasury provided technical comments, which we incorporated as appropriate.

We are sending copies of this report to the Secretary of Labor, the Secretary of the Treasury, and the Director of the PBGC, appropriate congressional committees, and other interested parties. We will also make copies available to others on request. In addition, the report will be available at no charge on GAO's Web site at http://www.gao.gov.

If you have any questions concerning this report, please contact me at (202) 512-7215 or bovbjergb@gao.gov. Contact points for our Office of Congressional Relations and Public Affairs may be found on the last page of this report. GAO staff who made contributions are listed in appendix V.

Barbara D. Bovbjerg
Director, Education, Workforce, and Income Security Issues

List of Addressees

The Honorable Max Baucus, Chairman
The Honorable Chuck Grassley, Ranking Member
Committee on Finance ,United States Senate

The Honorable Herb Kohl,Chairman
The Honorable Gordon Smith, Ranking Member
Special Committee on Aging, United States Senate

The Honorable George Miller, Chairman
The Honorable Buck McKeon, Ranking Member
Committee on Education and Labor, House of Representatives

The Honorable Charles B. Rangel, Chairman
The Honorable Jim McCrery, Ranking Member
Committee on Ways and Means, House of Representatives

The Honorable Earl Pomeroy, Member

APPENDIX I. FROZEN DB PLAN BRIEFING SLIDES

GAO
Accountability * Integrity * Reliability

Defined Benefit Pensions: Plan Freezes Affect Millions of Participants and May Pose Retirement Income Challenges

July 2008

1

Survey Objective

Assess the extent to which private, defined benefit (DB) plan sponsors are "freezing" (closing the plan and/or reducing future accruals in some manner) their plans
Results part of a broader survey focusing on how DB plan sponsors are responding to recent developments affecting the DB pension system

GAO Freeze Survey

A statistically representative, stratified survey of sponsors of private, single-employer DB plans with 100 or more total participants in all sponsored plans.
Survey administered via mail for smaller sponsors, and by web for certain larger sponsors (as part of a larger survey)

Of the original 471 sponsors in sample, 469 were deemed 'in scope.' 330 in-scope sponsors responded, resulting in a 70 percent raw response rate (or 78 percent weighted response rate)

Our study population represents all sponsors of single-employer plans with 100 or more total participants, which account for 7,804 sponsors and their 11,090 plans

These sponsors represent 34 percent of all sponsors and 42 percent of plans, but 99 percent of participants and 99 percent of liabilities

GAO Freeze Survey: Sampling Summary

Total Participant Category of Sponsor	Sponsors Sampled	Number of Sponsors	Percent of Sponsors	Number of Plans	Percent of Plans	Number of Participants	Percent of Participants	Liabilities (in billions)	Percent of Liabilities
less than 100	0	15,156	66.0%	15,344	58.0%	306,757	1.0%	$13	0.9%
100 - 999	126	5,010	21.8%	5,801	21.9%	1,730,589	5.4%	$53	3.5%
1,000 - 4,999	123	1,829	8.0%	2,711	10.3%	4,171,045	13.0%	$138	9.2%
5,000 - 49,999	117	858	3.7%	1,978	7.5%	12,442,522	38.6%	$506	33.8%
50,000 - plus	105	107	0.5%	600	2.3%	13,553,358	42.1%	$786	52.5%
Study Group Total	471	7,804	34.0%	11,090	42.0%	31,897,514	99.0%	$1,483	99.1%

Source: GAO analysis of 2004 PBGC Form 5500 Research Data

Note: sampling columns represent sponsor, participants and liabilities as of 2004

Background: What Is a Plan Freeze?

A plan freeze is a plan amendment that closes the plan to new entrants and may limit future benefit accruals for some or all active plan participants

General types include:

Hard Freeze – the plan is closed to new entrants and participants no longer accrue additional benefits

Soft Freeze – at a minimum the plan is closed to new entrants. The plan's prospective benefit formula may or may not be changed in such a way as to limit future benefit accruals for participants.

Partial Freeze – the plan is closed to new entrants and, for only a subset of active participants, the plan's prospective benefit formula is changed to limit or cease future benefit accruals.

Background: Freeze Data

- Most reports of pre-2003 freezes were based on:
  - limited data obtained from restricted/proprietary client bases of consulting firms and
  - survey questions on freezes that were often indirect or could be misconstrued
- The Pension Benefit Guaranty Corporation (PBGC) began analyzing generalizable information on single-employer, "hard frozen" plans in 2005 (using plan year 2003 data)
- Most recent PBGC data shows that:
  - 14 percent of plans were hard frozen as of 2005
  - There has been a nearly 50 percent increase in frozen plans since 2003
  - Hard freezes are generally more prevalent among smaller plans

Overview: Survey Findings

- Frozen plans are common—affecting roughly one-fifth of all active participants
- Most current freezes were recently implemented, with about half freezing between 2005 and the present
- Most sponsors offered some form of alternative retirement plan to affected participants
- Sponsors of frozen plans said cost (impact on cash flows) and funding volatility were key reasons in their decisions
- Sponsors of non-frozen plans are uncertain about future course of action
- Frozen plans have varied implications for key stakeholders

Finding: Plan Freezes Are a Common Occurrence

- About 3.3 million active participants (21 percent of all active participants in single employer DB plans) affected by a freeze
  - 51 percent of all plan *sponsors* with 100 or more total participants had one or more frozen plans
  - 44 percent of *plans* reported a specific freeze in some form
  - 51 percent of *plans* do not allow eligible, new hires to enter or accrue benefits in the plan
- Hard freezes are the most common occurrence, accounting for about half of all frozen plans
- Larger sponsors are significantly less likely to have plans that are hard frozen
- Sponsors with only collectively bargained (CB) plans froze plans at about the same rate as the overall study population, but have a lower proportion of hard freezes
- About half of plan freezes (among sponsors' largest frozen plans) were implemented after 2004

Note: The 95 percent confidence interval of the total participant estimate ranges from 2.25 to 4.34 million participants

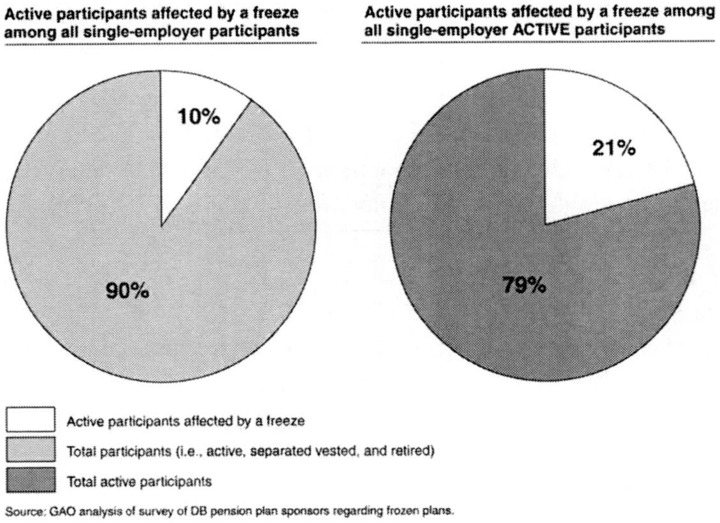

N=3,298,923 (Affected Parts.); 31,897,514 (Total Parts.); 15,598,254 (Active Parts.)

Note: Stratified survey results are weighted and represent the population of 'large' plan sponsors, or sponsors who had 100 or more participants in all plans reported in PBGC's 2004 Form 5500 Research Database.

Figure 1. Participants Affected by Freezes Comprise a Significant Number of All DB Plan Participants.

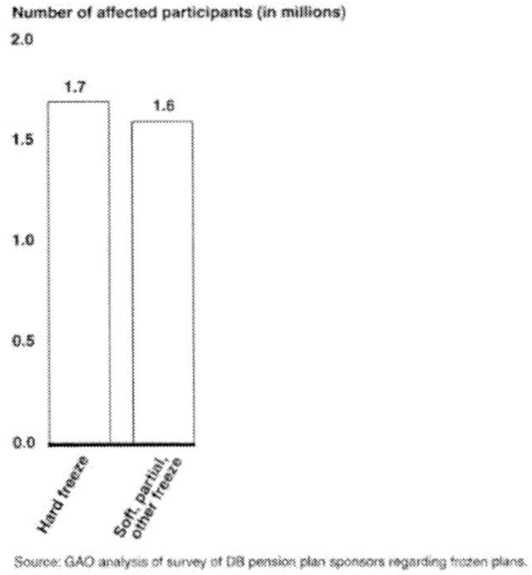

N=3,298,923 (Affected Parts.)

Note: The 95 percent confidence interval for participants affected by hard freeze is from 1.1 to 2.3 million. The 95 percent confidence interval for participants affected by soft, partial, or other freezes is from 0.7 to 2.5 million. Stratified survey results are weighted and represent the population of 'large' plan sponsors, or sponsors who had 100 or more participants in all plans reported in PBGC's 2004 Form 5500 Research Database.

Figure 2. About 3.3 Million Participants Are Currently Affected by a Freeze.

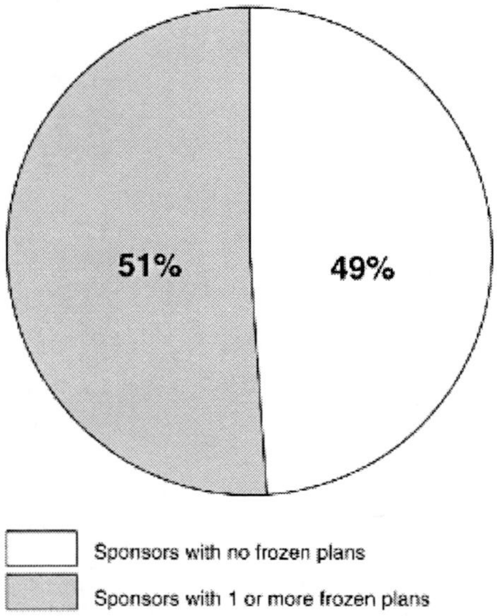

Source: GAO analysis of survey of DB pension plan sponsors regarding frozen plans.

N=7,804 (Sponsors)

Note: Stratified survey results are weighted and represent the population of 'large' plan sponsors, or sponsors who had 100 or more participants in all plans reported in PBGC's 2004 Form 5500 Research Database.

Figure 3. Around Half of All Survey Sponsors Have at Least One Frozen Plan

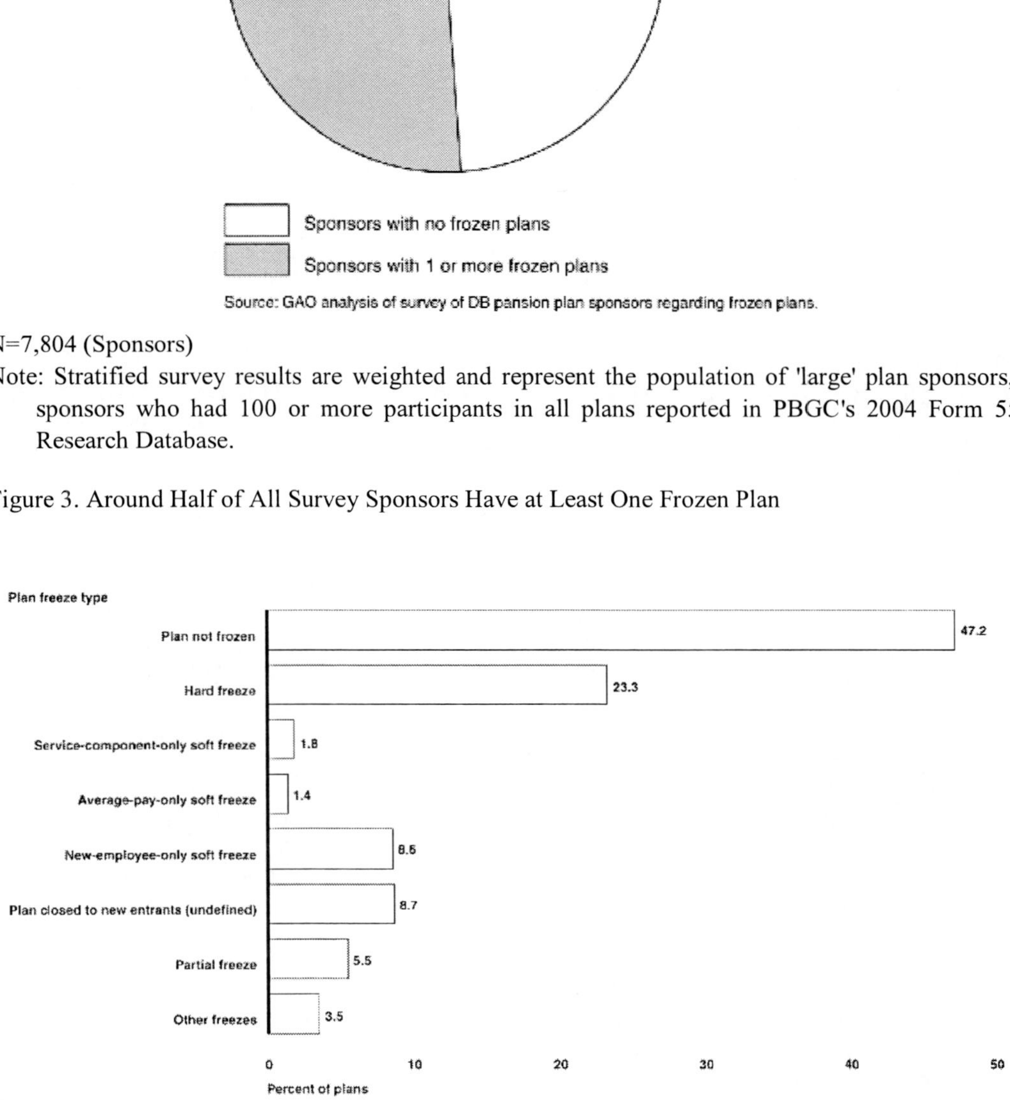

Source: GAO analysis of survey of DB pension plan sponsors regarding frozen plans.

Note: Stratified survey results are weighted and represent the population of 'large' plan sponsors, or sponsors who had 100 or more participants in all plans reported in PBGC's 2004 Form 5500 Research Database.

Figure 4. 53 Percent of All Plans in Study Population Are Frozen to Some Extent.

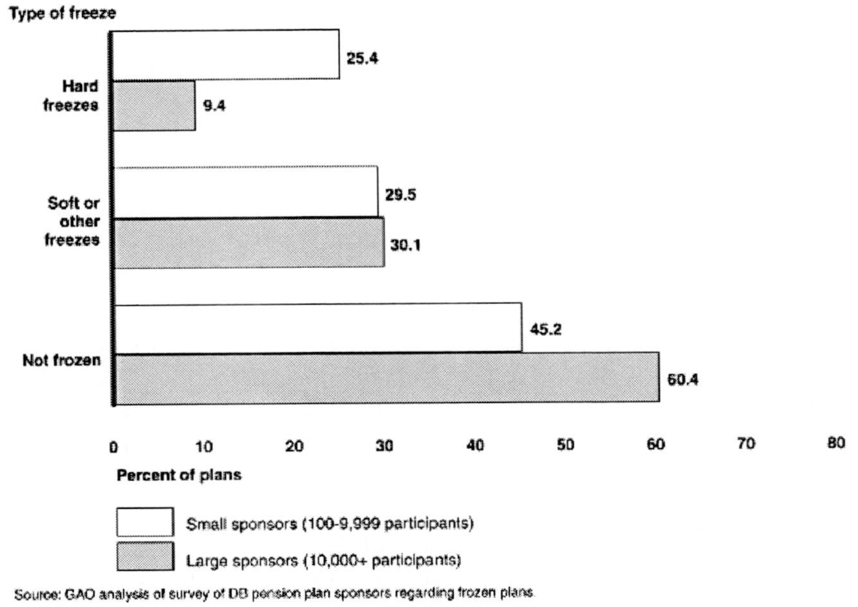

N=5,985 (Frozen), 11,341 (Total)

Note: Stratified survey results are weighted and represent the population of 'large' plan sponsors, or sponsors who had 100 or more participants in all plans reported in PBGC's 2004 Form 5500 Research Database.

Figure 5. Larger Sponsors are Significantly Less Likely to Have Hard Frozen Plans.

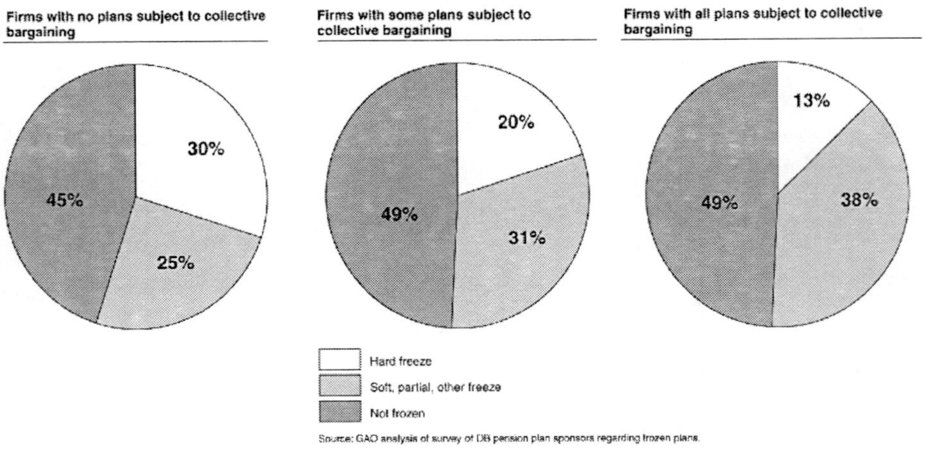

N=4,259 (CB Plans), 11,340 (Total Plans)

Note: Estimated percentages for sponsors with no CB or some CB have 95 percent confidence intervals of within +/- 11 percentage points of the estimates themselves. For sponsors with all plans subject to CB, the confidence intervals are within +/- 15 percentage points of the estimates themselves. Stratified survey results are weighted and represent the population of 'large' plan sponsors, or sponsors who had 100 or more participants in all plans reported in PBGC's 2004 Form 5500 Research Database.

Figure 6. Sponsors with Collectively Bargained Plans Are Less Likely to Have Hard Freezes.

For Sponsors' Largest Plans, Just Over Half Were Frozen during or after 2005

Just over half of sponsors froze their largest frozen plan between 2005 and the present

Because most sponsors have just one plan, distribution of freeze types among sponsors' largest plans is generally consistent with the overall plan population

Because our data are limited to currently frozen plans and exclude plans frozen in the past that have already terminated, identifying long term trends is difficult. However, based on data from 2003 to 2005, PBGC has found that:

hard frozen plans are more likely to terminate than non-hard frozen plans

there has been a general, recent decline in the number of plan terminations

plans frozen in earlier years seem no more likely to terminate than more recently frozen plans

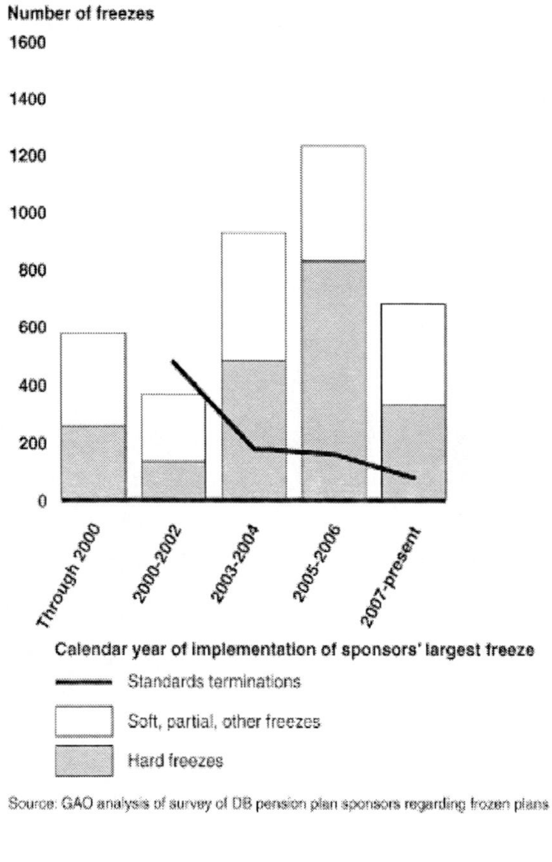

Source: GAO analysis of survey of DB pension plan sponsors regarding frozen plans and preliminary PBGC data.

Median=2005

Note: 2007-2008 freeze data represents 2008 data as of survey close. PBGC termination data for 2007-2008 includes terminations as of 2007 only. Also, PBGC termination data is at the plan level, while GAO data is at the sponsor level. This graphic represents the distribution of dates of currently implemented freezes only. Stratified survey results are weighted and represent the population of 'large' plan sponsors, or sponsors who had 100 or more participants in all plans reported in PBGC's 2004 Form 5500 Research Database.

Figure 7. Among Sponsors' Largest Frozen Plans, Many Freezes Have Been Recently Implemented

Finding: Most Sponsors Who Froze a Plan Made an Alternative Replacement Plan Available

83 percent of sponsors offered a replacement plan to participants affected by the plan freeze

an overwhelming majority offered enhanced contributions to an existing defined contribution (DC) plan or a new DC plan

about 5 percent offered a new DB plan

About 1 in 9 sponsors who froze a plan (11 percent) offered no new or replacement retirement plan of any type

Note that these sponsors may have offered an already existing plan, but did not replace or improve employer contributions in such a way as to 'replace' the frozen DB plan

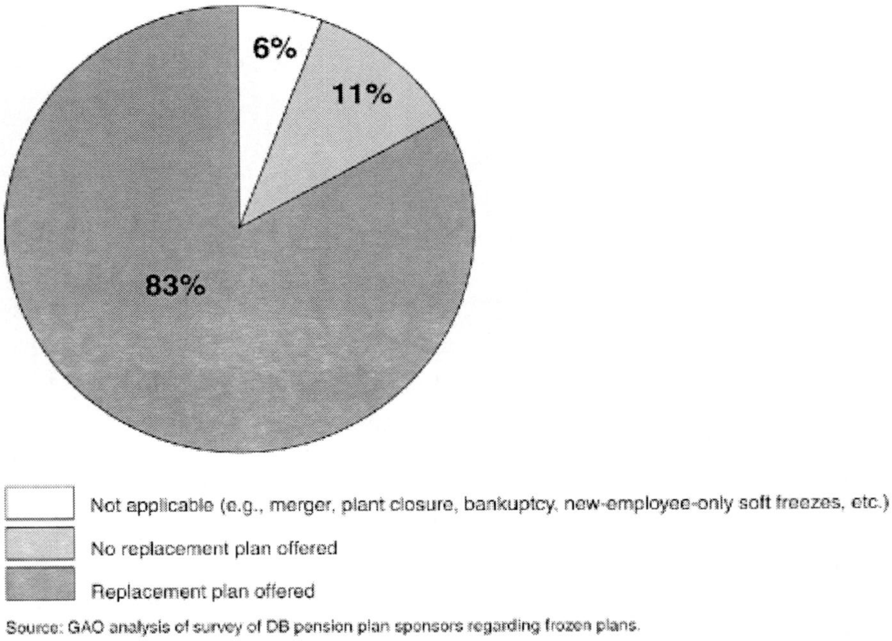

N=3,865

Note: Stratified survey results are weighted and represent the population of 'large' plan sponsors, or sponsors who had 100 or more participants in all plans reported in PBGC's 2004 Form 5500 Research Database.

Figure 8. 11 Percent of Sponsors with Frozen Plan(s) Did Not Offer Affected Participants a New or Enhanced Retirement Plan of Any Type.

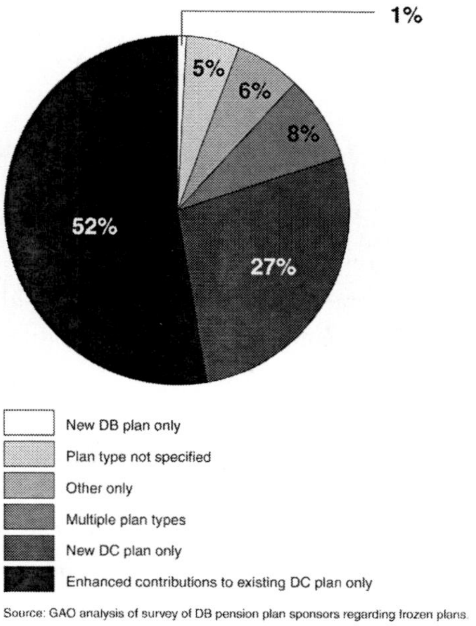

N=3,145

Note: Stratified survey results are weighted and represent the population of 'large' plan sponsors, or sponsors who had 100 or more participants in all plans reported in PBGC's 2004 Form 5500 Research Database.

Figure 9. About 83 Percent of Replacement Plans Offered Were New or Existing DC Plans

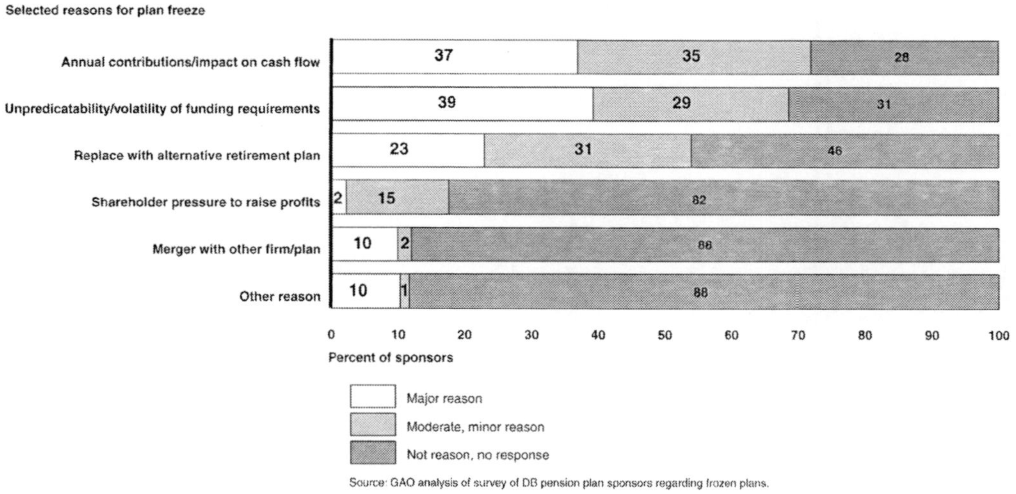

N= 3,865

Note: Stratified survey results are weighted and represent the population of 'large' plan sponsors, or sponsors who had 100 or more participants in all plans reported in PBGC's 2004 Form 5500 Research Database. Values may not sum to 100 percent due to rounding.

Figure 10. Funding Volatility, Effect on Cash Flows Key Reasons for Freezing Plans.

Finding: Sponsors Froze Plans for a Variety of Reasons

Top reasons sponsors reported for freezing a plan were:

- Cost of annual contributions needed to satisfy funding requirements and their impact on cash flow (72 percent)
- Unpredictability/volatility of plan funding requirements (69 percent)

Few plans were frozen because of mergers (12 percent)

Many sponsors (58 percent) were highly or moderately confident that their plan was sufficiently well-funded for a standard termination at time of freeze

Finding: Sponsors of DB Plans Uncertain About Future Course of Action

For those sponsors with frozen plans:

- About a third say that they will ultimately terminate the plan, but this varies by freeze type
- About 60 percent say that they will keep plan frozen indefinitely or were otherwise unsure

Many sponsors with at least one not frozen plan have considered or discussed a freeze (45 percent), but very few are certain they will freeze a plan in the future

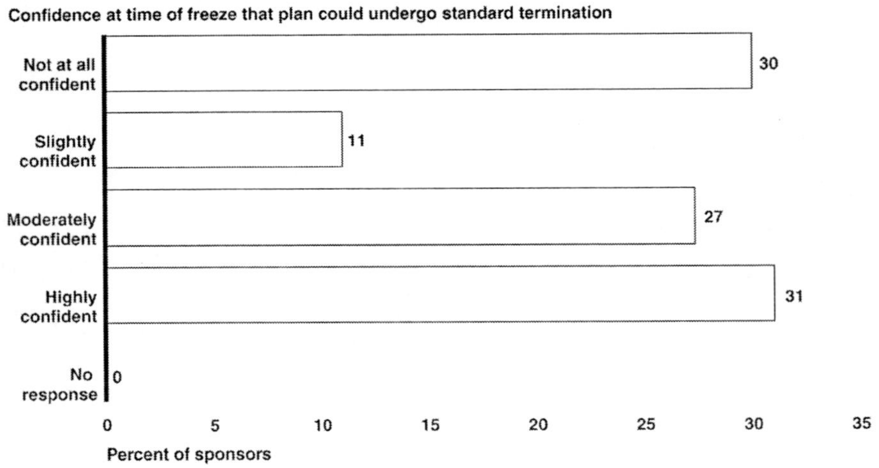

Source: GAO analysis of survey of DB pension plan sponsors regarding frozen plans.

N= 3,863

Note: Stratified survey results are weighted and represent the population of 'large' plan sponsors, or sponsors who had 100 or more participants in all plans reported in PBGC's 2004 Form 5500 Research Database.

Figure 11. About 30 Percent of Sponsors Did Not Believe Their Frozen Plan was Sufficiently Funded to Permit Termination at The Time Plan Was Frozen.

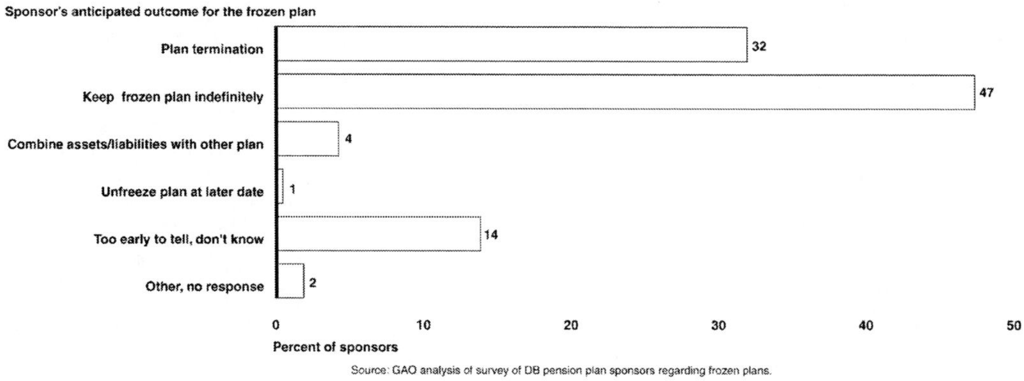

DateN= 3,863

Note: Stratified survey results are weighted and represent the population of 'large' plan sponsors, or sponsors who had 100 or more participants in all plans reported in PBGC's 2004 Form 5500 Research Database.

Figure 12. Few Sponsors Anticipate "Thawing" a Frozen Plan at a Later Date.

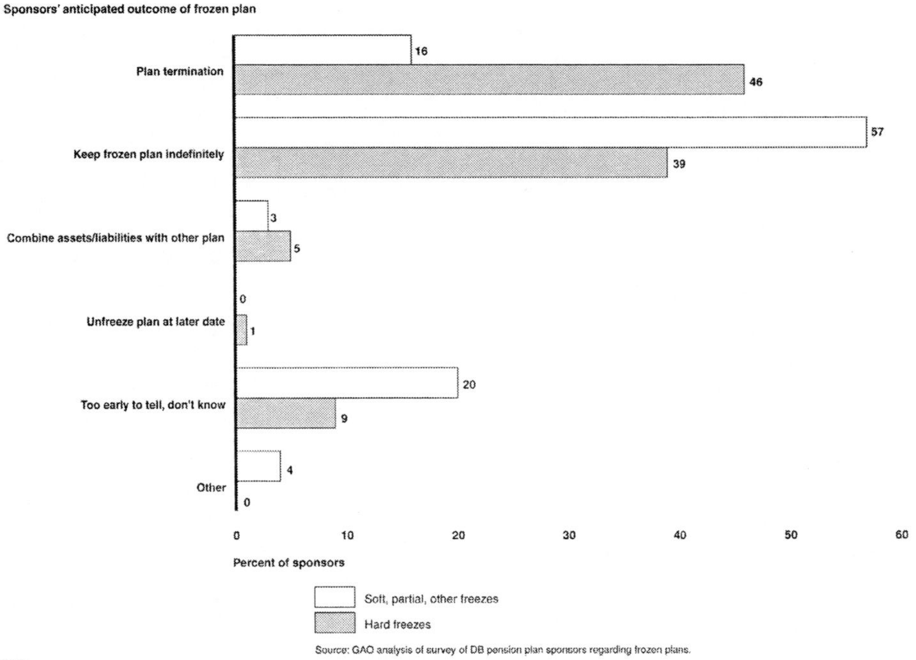

N= 3,863

Note: The 95 percent confidence intervals for percentage estimates by plan types are within +/- 14 percentage points of the estimates themselves. Stratified survey results are weighted and represent the population of 'large' plan sponsors, or sponsors who had 100 or more participants in all plans reported in PBGC's 2004 Form 5500 Research Database.

Figure 13. Sponsors of Soft Frozen Plan-Types Are Significantly Less Likely to Anticipate Termination as Outcome for Largest Frozen Plan.

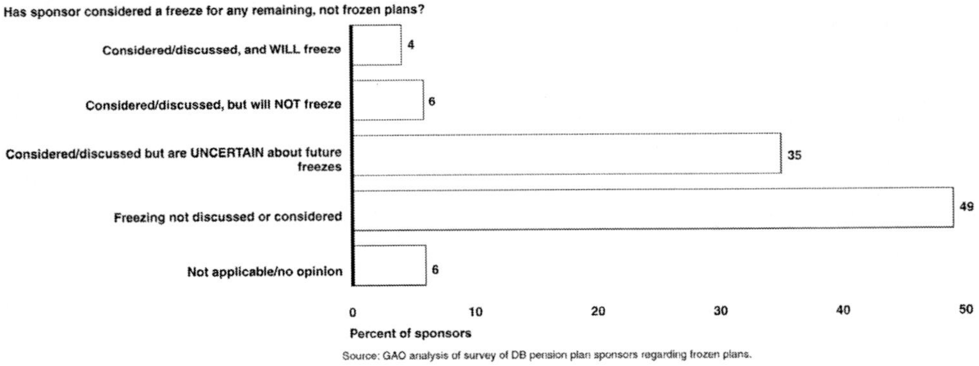

N=3,666

Note: Stratified survey results are weighted and represent the population of 'large' plan sponsors, or sponsors who had 100 or more participants in all plans reported in PBGCs 2004 Form 5500 Research Database.

Figure 14. 4 Percent of Sponsors with One or More Not Frozen Plans Have Decided to Freeze a Plan in the Future.

Implications for Sponsors

Despite the widespread prevalence of plan freezes, a rise in terminations has yet to materialize (notably among the largest plans)

Sponsor decision to freeze is either firm-specific reason or based on other factors not picked up in our survey

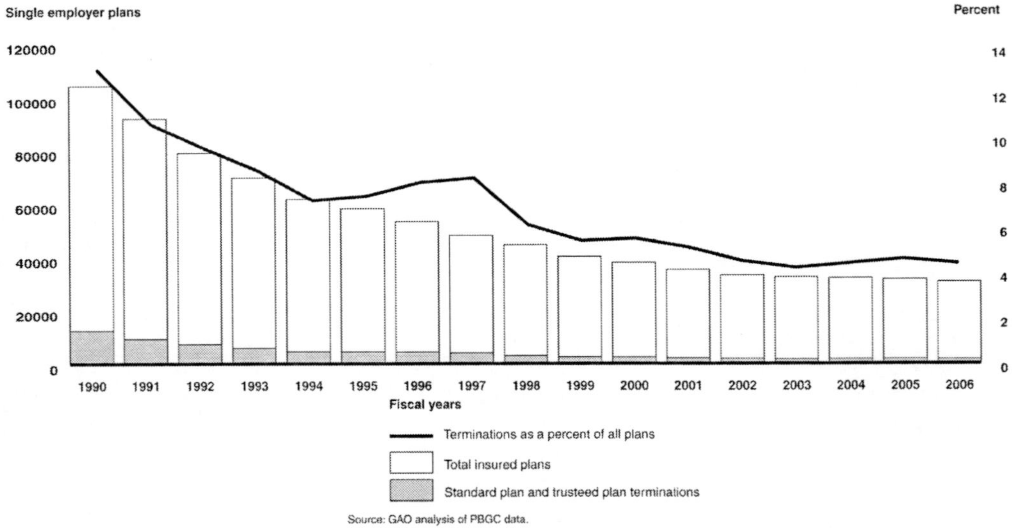

Figure 15. Sponsors of Frozen Plans May Terminate at Higher Rates, but the Number and Ratio of Terminations Are Currently Relatively Low.

Implications for Participants

A freeze may imply:

a reduction in anticipated future retirement income for currently active employees—especially for mid-career employees—depending on type of plan frozen and/or any replacement plan

a continued shift towards defined contribution plans, such as 401k-type plans, which tend to:

- shift the responsibility for saving and participating in in retirement plan, and,
- place investment risk with the participant

Implications for PBGC

Freezes likely to have a slightly positive effect on net financial position

However, how much frozen sponsors will improve funding is unclear

Freezes imply a continued decline in number of plans covered by PBGC single-employer insurance program

APPENDIX II. SCOPE AND METHODOLOGY

To achieve our objectives, we conducted a survey of sponsors of defined- benefit (DB) pension plans. For the purposes of our study, we defined "sponsors" as the listed sponsor on the 2004 Form 5500 for the largest sponsored plan (by total participants).[24] To identify all plans for a given sponsor we matched plans through unique sponsor identifiers.[25] See appendix I for further detail on how we defined a sponsor in the data.

Population and Sample Design

We constructed our population of DB plan sponsors from the 2004 Pension Benefit Guaranty Corporation's (PBGC) Form 5500 Research Database by identifying unique sponsors listed in this database and aggregating plan level data (for example, plan participants) for any plans associated with this sponsor. As a result of this process, we identified 22,960 plan sponsors. A summary of the number of sponsors and participants is shown in table 1.

As shown in table 1, sponsors having 100 or more participants accounted for about 99 percent of DB plan participants and about 99 percent of total liabilities in sponsored plans in 2004. We limited our study to this population of 7,804 larger sponsors (our study population)

because it would be informative about the vast majority of covered participants and we expected a higher success rate in locating, contacting, and obtaining responses from this group than would have been obtained from the smallest sponsors.

We drew a stratified probability sample of 471 DB plan sponsors, where the strata were based on the number of participants covered by the sponsor's plans. See table 2 for a summary of the study population, the selected sample, respondents, and out-of-scope sponsors by stratum.[26]

Table 1. Summary of Key Survey Sample Characteristics

Participant category of sponsor	Number sponsors	Percent of total sponsors	Number participants	Percent of total participants	Liabilities	Percent of liabilities
less than 100	15,156	66.0	306,757	1.0	13,369,579,852	0.9
100 - 999	5,010	21.8	1,730,589	5.4	53,057,015,994	3.5
1,000 - 4,999	1,829	8.0	4,171,045	13.0	137,965,716,185	9.2
5,000 - 49,999	858	3.7	12,442,522	38.6	506,194,771,738	33.8
50,000-plus	107	0.5	13,553,358	42.1	785,694,847,153	52.5
Total	**22,960**	**100.0**	**32,204,271**	**100.0**	**1,496,281,930,922**	**100.0**

Source: GAO analysis of 2004 PBGC Form 5500 research data.

Table 2. Summary of Study Population by Sampling Stratum

Stratum number	Sampling stratum	Sponsor population	Sample selected	Respondents	Out of scope	Response rate %
1	100 - 999	5010	126	99	1	79
2	1,000 - 4,999	1829	123	101	0	82
3	5,000 - 49,999	858	117	82	1	71
4	50,000 +	107	105	48	0	46
Total		**7804**	**471**	**330**	**2**	**78**

Source: GAO analysis of survey of DB pension plan sponsors regarding frozen plans and 2004 PBGC Form 5500 research data.

The sample was designed to provide acceptably precise estimates of the proportions of sponsors with at least one frozen plan. Further, sponsors in the larger sponsor strata are sampled at a higher rate than sponsors in the smaller strata to improve the precision of estimates of plan-level and participant-level estimates. As shown in table 2, response rates ranged from 46 percent to 82 percent, with an overall weighted response rate of 78 percent.

Administration of Survey

We developed two questionnaires to obtain information about the experiences of DB pension plan sponsors that have 100 or more participants. One questionnaire—with 18 questions—was mailed in November 2007 to a stratified random sample of 366 pension plan sponsors and asked questions about their experiences with DB plans, benefit freezes, if any, and factors that may have contributed to the decision to freeze. The strata were based on the size of the plan sponsor (as measured by number of participants) and were comprised of three categories. In the initial mailing, we sent a cover letter and questionnaire to pension plan sponsors. To encourage responses, we followed up with another mailing of a copy of the questionnaire in December 2007. In addition, to try to increase the response rate, we called all sponsors who had not responded to the mail survey.

A second, longer questionnaire was sent in December 2007, via the Internet, to the 105 largest pension plan sponsors who were part of the Fortune 500 or Global Fortune 500 and had 50,000 or more participants. This was preceded by an email to notify respondents of the survey and to test our email addresses for these respondents. This web questionnaire asked plan sponsors about their recent experiences with DB plans and benefit freezes. The first 17 questions and last question of this questionnaire mirrored the questions asked in the mail questionnaire about benefit freezes. We asked these plan sponsors additional questions about their reactions to the current environment for such plans and how the plan or plans may be a part of the firm's total compensation structure. To help increase our response rate, we sent four follow-up emails from January through April 2008. In addition, we also contacted some respondents by telephone to clarify unclear responses. We received responses from 48 respondents. For the 18 questions that asked about frozen pension plans in both the mail and web survey, we obtained an overall unweighted response rate of 70 percent and a weighted response rate of 78 percent.

To pretest the questionnaires, we conducted cognitive interviews and held debriefing sessions with 11 pension plan sponsors; three pretests were conducted in-person and focused on the web survey, and eight were conducted by telephone and focused on the mail survey. We selected respondents to represent a variety of sponsor sizes and industry types, including a law firm, an electronics company, a defense contractor, a bank, and a university medical center, among others. We conducted these pretests to determine if the questions were burdensome, understandable, and measured what we intended. On the basis of the feedback from the pretests, we modified the questions as appropriate.

Content Coding of Responses

In addition to the closed-ended questions, we provided an opportunity to provide responses to an open-ended question about the key challenges facing the future health of the single-employer DB system. The responses to this question were classified and coded for content by a GAO analyst, while a second analyst verified that the original analyst had coded the response appropriately. Two-hundred-seventeen respondents provided substantive comments to this item. Some comments were coded into more than one category since some respondents provided more than one topic or category. This means that the number of coded items does not equal the total number of respondents who commented. These comments cannot be generalized to our population of plan sponsors. See table 3 for a tally of the comments.

Table 3. Summary of Content Analysis, by General Category of Comment

General category of comment	Number of mentions
Affordability (i.e. cost of funding, administrative cost, cash flow)	108
Uncertainty/volatility of funding	59
Volatility of market forces	24
Non-cost administrative issues (i.e. complexity, reporting requirements, accounting rules)	46
Legislative issues	21
Regulatory issues	40
Workforce issues (i.e. demographics, recruitment/retention)	46
Disadvantageous compared to DC plans	7
Competition (i.e. industry, international)	13
Strong belief in DB system	5
Litigation	5
PBGC insurance (i.e. premiums, incentives for unhealthy plans)	17
Miscellaneous other	35

Source: GAO content analysis of survey of DB pension plan sponsors regarding frozen plans.

Sampling Error and Estimation

To produce the estimates from this survey, answers from each responding case were weighted in the analysis to account statistically for all the members of the population, including those that were not selected or did not respond to the survey. Estimates produced from this sample are from the population of sponsors represented in PBGC's 2004 Research Database that had at least 100 participants.

Because our results are based on a sample and different samples could provide different estimates, we express our confidence in the precision of our particular sample's results as a 95 percent confidence interval (for example, plus or minus 11 percentage points). We are 95 percent confident that each of the confidence intervals in this report include the true values in the study population. Unless we note otherwise, percentage estimates based on all sponsors (for example, percent of sponsors with at least one frozen plan) have 95 percent confidence intervals of within plus or minus 8 percentage points. All other percentage estimates in this report have 95 percent confidence intervals of within plus or minus 11 percentage points, unless otherwise noted. Confidence intervals for other estimates are presented along with the estimate where used in the report.

Nonsampling Error

In addition to the reported sampling errors, the practical difficulties of conducting any survey may introduce other types of errors, commonly referred to as nonsampling errors. For example, differences in how a particular question is interpreted, the sources of information available to respondents, or the types of people who do not respond can introduce unwanted variability into the survey results. We included steps in both the data collection and data analysis stages for the purpose of minimizing such nonsampling errors.

We took the following steps to increase the response rate: developing the questionnaire, pretesting the questionnaires with pension plan sponsors, conducting multiple follow-ups to encourage responses to the survey, contacting respondents to clarify unclear responses, and double keying and verifying all data during data entry.

Although the overall response rate was 78 percent, we performed an additional analysis to check whether our survey respondents had characteristics that were significantly different from all sponsors in the study population. To do this, we identified several sponsor characteristics[27] that were available for the entire study population and estimated these population values using the survey respondents. For each estimate tested, we found no significant difference between the estimate and the actual population value.[28]

We performed computer analyses of the sample data to identify inconsistencies and other indications of error and took steps to correct inconsistencies or errors. A second, independent analyst checked all computer analyses.

Comparability of Survey Results with 2006 PBGC Results

In July 2008 discussions with PBGC staff and in their comments on this report, PBGC indicated that it has calculated estimates of the number of hard frozen plans on the most recently available Form 5500 data. Based on Form 5500 filings received to date, PBGC currently estimates that 15.9 percent of plans were hard frozen in 2006. Our survey estimates are not directly comparable with PBGC's estimates for a number of reasons:

The GAO Survey is Based on a Statistical Sample - GAO survey estimates, including those involving hard freezes are based on a probability sample and is subject to sampling error. The PBGC calculations are based on Form 5500 data filings which must be completed by plan sponsors of PBGC-insured defined benefit plans.

The GAO Survey Focuses on Sponsors with Larger Plans - Our survey specifically excluded "smaller" sponsors—those with less than 100 total participants. Although leaving out such smaller sponsors excluded a majority of all plans on the 2004 Form 5000 file, it only excluded about 1 percent of participants, and allowed us to survey a smaller sample. However, if the rate of hard freezes was different for plans having fewer than 100 participants than for larger plans, then we would expect that our survey estimate would differ from an estimate developed from all plans.

The GAO Survey Focuses on Hard- and Soft-Freezes and Includes Post-2006 Freezes - Our survey questionnaire used a definition of a hard freeze that was intended to be substantively similar to the definition contained with the Form 5500 instructions. However, our questionnaire also included a broad range of plan freeze definitions as well as additional questions pertaining to a sponsor's largest frozen plan. The mode of data collection, topical focus, format, item wording or item interpretation of our questionnaire may influence respondents in different ways relative to the applicable hard freeze character code on the Form 5500. One critical difference that could lead to different estimates is that our survey captures freezes that occurred since 2006. The 2006 Form 5500 only includes information as of the end of the 2006 plan year.

Possible Differences in Actual Survey Respondents - While we generally directed our survey to the individual we identified as being most knowledgeable about the DB plans of a given sponsor, it may be the case that the individuals responding to our survey are not the very same individuals that also complete the Form 5500, possibly leading to different responses.

Despite these differences in approach and methodology, some may wish to compare PBGC's estimate of 15.9 percent of plans were hard frozen in 2006 and our study population estimate of 23.3 percent of plans as hard frozen among sponsors with 100 or more participants in all plans. Any comparisons should be made with extreme caution for all of the reasons noted above. Further, the 95 percent confidence interval for our estimate ranges from 18.3 to 28.3 percent.

PBGC also calculated that, based on Form 5500 filings for plan year 2006 received as of July 2008, 0.75 million active participants out of 2.39 million total participants were in frozen plans. As with the estimated percentage of hard frozen plans, our numbers are not completely comparable, due to differences in our methodologies Although our survey identified the active participants affected by the sponsor's largest frozen plan, we did not specifically ask about total participants in the largest frozen plan. Our questionnaire also asked sponsors to report the calendar year of freeze implementation, while the Form 5500 data is reported on a plan year basis, which can differ from the calendar year.

Another important difference is that PBGC data is not current and new hard frozen plans and active participants affected by such freezes may yet be identified. Some of these newly identified plans may be plans of sponsors that reported freezes in our survey in 2007 or later. When we removed hard frozen plans that occurred for a sponsor's largest plan since 2006 and recalculated the number of active participants affected by hard freezes, we estimate that 1.27 million active participants are affected by a hard freeze in the sponsor's largest frozen plan. As with all of our survey estimates, this result is subject to sampling error. The 95 percent confidence interval of active participants affected by the sponsors largest hard frozen plan (removing post-2006 freezes) ranges from 0.75 million to 1.78 million.

APPENDIX III. COMMENTS FROM THE PENSION BENEFIT GUARANTY CORPORATION

PBGC
Protecting America's Pensions

Pension Benefit Guaranty Corporation
1200 K Street, N.W., Washington, D.C. 20005-4026

Office of the Director

July 17, 2008

Ms. Barbara Bovbjerg, Director
Education, Workforce, and Income Security Issues
Government Accountability Office
441 G Street, N.W.
Washington, D.C. 20548

Dear Ms. Bovbjerg:

Thank you for the opportunity to review and comment on the draft report entitled, "DEFINED BENEFIT PENSIONS: Plan Freezes Affect Millions of Participants and May Pose Retirement Income Challenges" (GAO-08-817).

In many respects, the report's findings are consistent with what PBGC has found in its studies based on data from plans' Form 5500s—the number of newly frozen plans increased over the 2003-2005 period and then decreased; small plans (those with fewer than 1,000 participants) are more likely to be frozen that larger plans; and freezing plans has long-term implications for the health of the defined benefit system, PBGC, and current workers' future retirement incomes.

In other respects, the report's findings differ rather substantially from our own hard-frozen plan findings—the percentage of plans the report shows as being hard frozen is fifty percent larger than our most recent data indicate (based on 2006 Form 5500 filing information), and the number of active workers in hard-frozen plans is about 2.25 times as high as we found. These differences are, no doubt, due to differences in the studies' methodologies. PBGC's studies looked only at hard-frozen plans using data from the Form 5500, the annual report plans file with DOL, IRS, and PBGC. The GAO study uses survey data, is sponsor-based rather than plan-based, and covers a broader range of plan freeze types. We note that GAO's plan size category was determined in a manner that makes direct comparison with data from other sources difficult.

There are several reasons GAO's estimate of the percentage of hard-frozen plans could be 50 percent larger than ours:

- One reason the hard-frozen plan results are different is that GAO's data are more current than the data we used. GAO's sample includes plans that were hard frozen after 2006. These plans are only now beginning to report their hard-freeze status on the Form 5500. We know companies are continuing to freeze plans, so we would expect GAO to find a higher percentage of hard-frozen plans than we found. However, we would not expect it to find fifty percent more hard-frozen plans than were reported on the Form 5500 for 2006, especially since news reports seem to indicate that the number of companies announcing an immediate or future plan freeze declined after 2006. (This highlights the critical importance of PBGC receiving more current Form 5500 data, as discussed below.)
- A second reason for different results is the possibility of response bias in GAO's testing. It is possible that sponsors who have frozen one or more of their plans are more likely to have responded to GAO's survey than sponsors who did not freeze any of their plans. Comparing the GAO sample of plans against those reporting being hard frozen on the Form 5500 would indicate whether a higher percentage of responders than non-responders reported being hard frozen. If response bias is present, GAO's frozen plan estimates will likely be too high.
- As noted above and discussed in more detail below, GAO's size variable is unusual. Possibly, the weights, which apparently were based on this variable, had the unintended effect of increasing the estimates of the percentage of plans that were hard frozen and frozen to a lesser extent. The weights may have substantially increased the percentage of plans found to be hard frozen.
- One thing we noticed was that an attempt was made to remove from the universe plans that terminated after 2004, but no attempt was made to add plans that were newly covered after 2004. These newly insured plans are much less likely to have been frozen than plans we have insured for a longer period. Not including these newly insured plans reduces the apparent universe of PBGC-covered plans and would slightly increase the percentage of plans estimated to be frozen.
- Some plans that are hard-frozen may not report that fact on the Form 5500. Our studies are based solely on reported freezes, but we have noticed that some plans, that do not report being hard frozen, also do not report on the Schedule B to the Form 5500 any "expected increase in current liability due to benefits accruing during the plan year." If some or all of these plans are hard frozen, then the data we use underreport the true number of hard-frozen plans.

GAO estimates that 3.3 million active workers are in frozen plans, with just over half, 1.7 million, in hard-frozen plans. Form 5500 data indicate that about 2.4 million total participants were in hard-frozen plans at the end of the 2006 plan year and that just 750,000 of them were active workers. We realize that a number of large plans have been frozen recently, and that they have not yet reported being frozen on the Form 5500. This will explain some, but we doubt all of the difference between our numbers and GAO's. Some of the potential explanations listed above for the differences in our findings of the percentage of plans that have been hard frozen may also help explain the differences in the number of active participants who are in frozen plans. In addition, this part of GAO's analysis focuses on the largest frozen plan a sponsor has. Applying the study's weights to these "largest frozen plans" may cause an overestimate of the number of impacted active participants because many frozen plans will be smaller than the sponsors' "largest frozen plan."

GAO's size indicator appears to be atypical. GAO added the participants in all a sponsor's defined benefit plans to determine its size variable, but what this total represents is unclear. It is not a good estimator of the company's size--less than half of plan participants are active workers; there is no requirement that all of a company's workers be covered by a defined benefit plan; some participants may belong to more than one of the sponsor's plans; and, if the company is part of a controlled group, participants who never worked for the company could be included in this size total. Using this size variable is a concern if the weights GAO uses to adjust its results are based on this variable and not on actual plan size. It is unclear what the results would represent. Using this unusual size variable makes GAO's results not strictly comparable with results from studies that use other data and methodologies.

Despite our concerns about the magnitudes of the findings in the report, it advances our knowledge on the extent of freezes that are not hard freezes. GAO finds that about as many plans as are hard frozen are frozen to a lesser extent. While we are as concerned about the absolute magnitude of these findings as we are about the magnitude of the hard freeze findings, the relative magnitudes are probably close and provide important information not previously available.

GAO's finding that most active participants in plans being frozen are eligible for coverage under another employer-sponsored plan is also an important finding. Freezing a defined benefit plan does not generally end a sponsor's sense of responsibility for providing some retirement income for its workers. However, GAO did not determine how many active participants actually participate in the new, generally defined contribution plans nor whether the new plans will provide benefits comparable to the benefits that would have been earned had the participants' defined benefit plans not been frozen. This was beyond the scope of their study, but as GAO points out, the answer has implications for the adequacy of retirement income for these participants.

One issue that is made apparent in comparing the results of the draft report with our own work is the delay the PBGC faces in obtaining basic plan data. GAO recently highlighted this issue in its report "Private Pensions: Government Actions Could Improve the Timeliness and Content of Form 5500 Pension Information," (GAO-05-491, June 3, 2005). Some improvement in timeliness will ensue once the mandated electronic filing of the Form 5500 becomes operational for the 2009 filing year. Even then, however, the reported data will reflect the status of plans seven or more months prior to PBGC receiving the data. PBGC's awareness of changing trends among the plans it insures will continue to lag the actual changes, unless the data can be made available on a more timely basis. PBGC has consistently pressed for more current Form 5500 data in order to better perform the work that is required of the agency.

With nearly 44 million workers and retirees relying on PBGC's insurance programs, we appreciate GAO's work in highlighting issues that relate to pensions, including those that are the subject of this report. We look forward to working with GAO in the future. Again, thank you for the opportunity to comment on this report.

Sincerely,

Charles E.F. Millard

End Notes

[1] Employers may voluntarily sponsor DB plans, defined contribution (DC) plans, or both for their employees. DB plans promise to provide a benefit that is generally based on a formula that typically includes an employee's salary and years of service. Under a DC plan, such as a 40 1(k) plan, employees have individual accounts to which the employee, employer, or both make contributions, and benefits are based on contributions along with investment returns (gains and losses) on the accounts.

[2] The voluntary termination of a fully funded DB plan is called a standard termination. Plan sponsors may terminate fully funded plans by purchasing a group annuity contract from an insurance company, under which the insurance company agrees to pay all accrued benefits, or by paying lump-sum benefits to participants if permissible.

[3] GAO, *Private Pensions: Timely and Accurate Information Is Needed to Identify and Track Frozen Defined Benefit Plans*, GAO-04-200R (Washington, D.C.: Dec. 17, 2003).

[4] See Pension Benefit Guaranty Corporation, Pension Insurance *Data Book 2006*, p. 3-13 (Washington, D.C., Fall 2007) and Pension Benefit Guaranty Corporation, *An Analysis of Frozen Defined Benefit Plans* (Washington, D.C., Dec. 21, 2005).

[5] The Form 5500 Annual Return/Report of Employee Benefit Plan is jointly published by the Department of Labor, in conjunction with the Internal Revenue Service and Pension Benefit Guaranty Corporation, to be used by plan administrators and employers in order to satisfy their legally required annual reporting obligations.

[6] All estimates based on our sample are subject to sampling error. For example the 95 percent confidence interval of the total participant estimate ranges from 2.25 million to 4.34 million participants. Unless otherwise noted, all percentage estimates based on this survey have 95 percent confidence intervals of within +/- 11 percentage points of the estimate itself. Of the 3.3 million estimated participants affected by a freeze, 1.7 million are affected by a hard freeze, and 1.8 million are affected by a soft, partial, or other freeze. The 95 percent

confidence interval for participants affected by hard freeze is from 1.1 million to 2.3 million. The 95 percent confidence interval for participants affected by soft, partial, or other freezes is from 0.7 million to 2.5 million. See appendix II for additional information on sampling error of estimates.

[7] Active participants may continue to accrue benefits because they are currently employed by the sponsoring firm. Retirees are no longer employed by the firm and are collecting their retirement benefits. Separated vested participants are no longer employed by the sponsoring firm and no longer accrue benefits, but they are not yet collecting their retirement benefits.

[8] See appendix I, slide 5 for general freeze type definitions. Exact definitions used in the survey may be found in the special product supplement. See GAO, *Defined Benefit Pensions: Survey of Sponsors of Large Defined Benefit Pension Plans*, GAO-08-818SP (Washington, D.C.: July 21, 2008).

[9] Closed and unclassified plans are only included for this analysis (see app. I, slide 12). In other analyses, only those plans reporting a specific freeze type will be included in calculations of frozen plans. Of the 51 percent of all plans reported as closed to new entrants, 44 percent reported a specific freeze type. Another roughly 9 percent of plans were closed to new entrants but were not classified by their sponsors as being frozen. Those plans defining a freeze plus those that reported the plan as closed to new hires, but not defined as frozen, may not sum to the total number of closed plans. This occurs because, in certain instances, a partial freeze may not be closed to all new entrants. For example, a subset of new entrants may be part of the group unaffected by the partial freeze.

[10] An example of a tier might be if an employer were to offer certain participants the option to freeze certain accruals in one DB plan as a condition of participation and accruals in another, alternative plan (either DB or DC).

[11] The statistical significance of this finding applies only to hard frozen plans. Sponsors with some or all plans that were subject to CB did not freeze their plans overall at a statistically different rate from the general population of sponsors. Estimated percentages for sponsors with no CB or some CB have 95 percent confidence intervals of within +/- 11 percentage points of the estimates themselves. For sponsors with all plans subject to CB, the confidence intervals are within +/- 15 percentage points of the estimates themselves.

[12] For further information on how plan, demographic, and market factors generally influence larger sponsors with respect to plan freezes, see Alicia H. Munnell and Mauricio Soto, Center for Retirement Research, Boston College "*Why Are Companies Freezing Their Pensions*?" (Boston, 2007).

[13] For this survey, a replacement plan is defined as an addition to retirement plan offerings, either in the form of a new plan or an enhancement of an existing plan. Therefore, a sponsor that allows affected participants to join an existing and unchanged plan would not be considered to have replaced its frozen plan(s).

[14] These reasons were identified as the most prevalent among a list of 15 reasons given to survey respondents. The reasons were created and selected using a literature review and feedback from survey pretesters.

[15] To view the complete list of reasons and prevalence, see GAO-08-818SP.

[16] The 95 percent confidence intervals for percentage estimates by freeze type are within +/- 14 percent of the estimate itself.

[17] For a discussion on how plan freezes may affect expected retirement income, see Jack VanDerhei, *Defined Benefit Plan Freezes: Who's Affected, How Much, and Replacing Lost Accruals*," Employee Benefits Research Institute (EBRI) Issue Brief No. 291 (Washington D.C., March 2006). The EBRI study modeled the effect of a universal hard freeze to show how anticipated accruals were affected by key plan, participant, and market characteristics.

[18] Traditional formula is used to refer to pay based plans, which use formulas based on salary and service, such as final average pay plans. These types of plan formulas typically accrue increasingly larger benefits at the end of an employee's active working career.

[19] See GAO, *Private Pensions: Low Defined Contribution Plan Savings May Pose Challenges to Retirement Security, Especially for Many Low-Income Workers*, GAO-08-8 (Washington, D.C.: Nov. 7, 2007).

[20] Frozen plan sponsors must continue to pay premiums to PBGC for its participants even if those participants' future benefit accruals have been frozen. Frozen plan sponsors must also continue to maintain the plan in accordance with federal pension law, including funding the plan by making minimum required contributions. However, sponsors may find it somewhat easier to bring the frozen plan to full funding if future participant accruals are limited.

[21] PBGC has witnessed a steady decline in the percentage of single-employer participants that are active participants. PBGC has only recently seen a slight decrease in the number of total insured participants, but the large percentage of plans closed to new entrants seems to suggest possible further decline.

[22] The flat-rate premium is a per-participant premium that plans pay to PBGC each year. In 2008, the rate for the flat premium is $33 per participant in insured single-employer plans. This rate is adjusted annually by an average-national-wage index.

[23] The variable-rate premium applies only to insured single-employer plans that have unfunded vested benefits. The rate for the variable-rate premium is $9 per $1,000 of underfunding.

[24] We removed plans that terminated after 2004, which may also include plans that reported a final filing or merged into another plan. We also remove any sponsors whose total plans had fewer than 100 total participants. We

were unable to add any new plans or sponsors that may have been newly insured by PBGC after 2004 because complete data was not available at the time we constructed our survey sample. Although newly-insured plans may be considerably less likely to be frozen, we expect not including these plans would have an extremely small impact on our estimates. Likely, very few new plans would have qualified under our sponsor definition in relation to the number of plans represented in our survey. Further, any newly created plans will be represented to the extent that they are associated with sponsors already in our survey.

[25] These include the nine-digit employee identification number (EIN) found in the Form 5500 as well as the Committee on Uniform Securities Identification Procedures (CUSIP) number, which is contained in the PBGC Research Database. A CUSIP number identifies most North American securities, including stocks of all registered U.S. and Canadian companies and U.S. government and municipal bonds. The number consists of nine characters (including letters and numbers) that uniquely identify a company or issuer and the type of security. In addition to these two methods, we identified sponsors by visually inspecting plan names and sponsor names from the database to find common sponsors that were not identified by EINs or CUSIPs.

[26] Initially a sample of 480 sponsors was selected, but we found that some of the sponsors on our sponsor file were listed more than once. We then aggregated information to a unique sponsor and removed these additional sponsor listings from both the sample and the population. The above tables present totals by stratum after this removing duplicate sponsor listing.

[27] These sponsor characteristics were the number of plans, number of total participants, number of active participants, total sponsor liabilities for plans, and total retired participants.

[28] This analysis was repeated separately for the largest sponsors only (stratum 4), and for this group there were also no significant differences between the sample and the population of sponsors with 50,000 or more participants.

In: Pensions: Backgrounds, Trends and Issues
Editor: Henry J. Mullen
ISBN: 978-1-60876-840-0

Chapter 3

PENSION SPONSORSHIP AND PARTICIPATION: SUMMARY OF RECENT TRENDS

Patrick Purcell

SUMMARY

According to the Census Bureau's *Current Population Survey (CPS)*, the number of private-sector workers between the ages of 25 and 64 whose employer sponsored a retirement plan rose from 51.2 million in 2006 to 53.5 million in 2007. The number of private-sector workers who participated in employer-sponsored retirement plans rose from 42.0 million in 2006 to 44.1 million in 2007. The proportion of 25 to 64 year-old workers in the private sector who participated in employer-sponsored retirement plans increased from 43.2% in 2006 to 45.1% in 2007. Between 2000 and 2007, the number of private-sector workers between the ages of 25 and 64 who participated in employer-sponsored retirement plans fell from 46 million to 44 million. The percentage of workers who participated in an employer-sponsored plan fell from 50.3% in 2000 to 45.1% in 2007.

A CRS analysis of the *Current Population Survey* indicates that, among private-sector workers aged 25 to 64 who were employed *year-round, full-time*:

- The percentage of workers whose employer sponsored a retirement plan rose from 57.2% in 2006 to 59.9% in 2007.
- The percentage of workers who participated in employer-sponsored retirement plans rose from 49.2% in 2006 to 52.0% in 2007.
- Only 25.5% of workers at firms with fewer than 25 employees participated in an employer-sponsored retirement plan in 2007, compared to 45.5% of workers at firms with 25 to 99 employees and 65.4% of workers at firms with 100 or more employees.
- Among men and women who were employed year-round, full-time, 51.6% of men and 52.6% of women participated in an employer-sponsored retirement plan in 2007.
- Only 43.0% of private-sector workers aged 25 to 34 and employed year- round, full-time participated in an employer-sponsored retirement plan in 2007, compared to 5 1.8%

of workers aged 35 to 44, 57.4% of those aged 45 to 54, and 57.6% of those aged 55 to 64.

Black, Hispanic, and other non-white workers were less likely to have participated in an employer-sponsored retirement plan. Fifty-eight percent of white workers participated in a company-sponsored retirement plan in 2007, compared to 47.1% of black non-Hispanic workers, 30.6% of Hispanic workers, and 48.5% of other non-white workers (mainly Asian- American and Native American workers).

Only 27.7% of workers whose earnings were in the lowest quartile in 2007 (under $27,000) participated in a retirement plan at work, compared to 69.2% of workers whose earnings were in the top quartile (above $63,000).

The percentage of part-time workers in the private sector whose employer sponsored a retirement plan rose from 37.8% in 2006 to 38.3% in 2007. Twenty-three percent of part-year or part-time workers in the private sector participated in an employer sponsored retirement plan in 2007, essentially unchanged from 2006.

BACKGROUND: EMPLOYMENT AND AN AGING WORKFORCE

The aging of the American population has made retirement income an issue of increasing concern to the Congress and the public. Although Americans are living longer than ever before, most retire before age 65. Moreover, while the nation's population continues to grow, the decline in birth rates that followed the post-World War II "baby boom" and the continued lengthening of life spans will result in fewer workers relative to the number of retirees. These trends will affect the economic well-being of future retirees because pensions and Social Security benefits will be paid over longer periods of time; savings will have to be stretched over longer retirements; and Social Security benefits will have to be financed by a working population that is shrinking relative to the number of retirees.

Life Expectancy Continues to Increase

The average life expectancy of Americans born in 1960 was 69.7 years. It has been estimated that those who were born in 2005 will live for an average of 77.8 years. A man who reached age 65 in 1960 could expect to live another 13.0 years.[1] A man who reached age 65 in 1960 could expect to live another 13.0 years, while a woman who turned 65 in 1960 had a remaining life expectancy of 15.8 years. A man who reached age 65 in 2005 could expect to live another 16.8 years, while a woman who turned 65 in 2005 had a remaining life expectancy of 19.8 years. As more people live into old age, the age-profile of the population will shift. In 1960, 16.7 million people in the United States — 9.2% of the population — were age 65 or older. In 2005, there were 36.7 million Americans age 65 or older, representing 12.4% of the population. By 2025, according to projections made by the Bureau of the Census, there will be 63.5 million people age 65 or older, comprising 18.2% of the U.S. population.

Table 1. Labor Force Participation Rates in 2007

Age	Total Number of People (thousands)	Number in the Labor Force (thousands)	Labor Force Participation Rate (percent)
Men			
Age 25 to 54	62,081	56,408	**90.9**
Age 45 to 54	21,313	18,801	**88.2**
Age 55 to 64	15,658	10,904	**69.6**
Age 65 and up	15,525	3,188	**20.5**
Women			
Age 25 to 54	63,615	47,945	**75.4**
Age 45 to 54	22,231	16,896	**76.0**
Age 55 to 64	16,876	9,846	**58.3**
Age 65 and up	20,703	2,615	**12.6**

Source: U.S. Department of Labor, Bureau of Labor Statistics, *Employment and Earnings* (January 2008).

Labor Force Participation Begins to Drop after Age 55

The proportion of the population that is either working or looking for work is called the "labor force participation rate." As indicated by the data in **Table 1**, the labor force participation rate starts to drop significantly after age 55. When income is no longer derived from earnings, individuals depend more on pensions, interest and dividends, withdrawals from their savings, and — when they become eligible through age or disability — Social Security. The aging of the U.S. population will place strains on the components of the traditional "three-legged stool" of retirement income: Social Security, pensions, and personal saving.

Congress and Retirement Income Policies

The Internal Revenue Code was first amended to provide favorable tax treatment for qualified pension and retirement plans in the 1920s. These provisions have been expanded and modified many times since then. Among the tax exemptions that apply to traditional "defined benefit" pension plans are the deduction of pension contributions from employer income, exclusion of employer contributions to pension plans from employee income, and tax exemption of the earnings of pension trusts.[2] In "defined contribution" plans such as those authorized under section 401(k) of the tax code, income taxes are deferred until retirement on employer and employee contributions to the plan and on the investment earnings of the plan.

By establishing the tax-favored status of pension programs and defining the terms under which tax exemptions and deductions are granted, federal tax law has both encouraged the growth of retirement plan coverage among workers and shaped the development of pensions and retirement savings plans. Congress also has sought to protect the pension benefits earned by workers through direct regulation of pension plans, most notably through the *Employee Retirement Income Security Act of 1974* (ERISA, P.L. 93-406). ERISA, too, may have influenced the development of employer-sponsored retirement plans. Since its enactment, defined contribution (DC) plans have proliferated while the number of defined benefit (DB) plans has fallen.

Two Kinds of Retirement Plans: Defined Benefit and Defined Contribution

Retirement programs are legally classified as either *defined benefit* plans or *defined contribution* plans. In *defined benefit* or "DB" plans, the retirement benefit usually is based on an employee's salary and number of years of service. With each year of service, a worker accrues a benefit equal to either a fixed dollar amount per month or year of service or a percentage of his or her final pay or average pay.

A *defined contribution* or "DC" plan is much like a savings account maintained by the employer on behalf of each participating employee. The employer contributes a specific dollar amount or percentage of pay into the account, which is usually invested in stocks and bonds. In some plans, the size of the employer's contribution depends on the amount the employee contributes to the plan. When the worker retires, the amount of the retirement benefit that he or she receives will depend on the balance in the account, which is the sum of all the contributions that have been made plus interest, dividends, and capital gains (or losses). The worker usually has the choice of receiving these funds as a lump sum, a series of fixed payments over a period of years, or in the form of a life annuity.

In recent years, many employers have converted their traditional pensions to *hybrid plans* that have characteristics of both DB and DC plans. The most popular of these hybrids has been the *cash balance plan*. A cash balance plan looks like a DC plan in that the accrued benefit is defined in terms of an account balance. The employer makes contributions to the plan and pays interest on the accumulated balance. However, in a cash balance plan, the account balances are merely bookkeeping devices. They are not *individual accounts* that are owned by the participants. At retirement, the employee must receive a benefit that is equal to the amount contributed to the plan plus the interest that has been credited to those contributions. Legally, therefore, a cash balance plan is a defined benefit plan.

Who Bears the Investment Risk?

In a defined benefit plan, it is the *employer* who bears the investment risk of the plan, while in a defined contribution plan it is the *employee* who bears the investment risk. In a defined benefit plan, the employer promises to provide retirement benefits equal to a certain dollar amount or a specific percentage of the employee's pay. The employer contributes money to a pension trust that is invested in stocks, bonds, real estate, or other assets. Retirement benefits are paid from this trust fund. The employer is *at risk* for the amount of the retirement benefits that have been promised to employees and their survivors. If there are insufficient funds in the pension trust to pay the accrued benefits, the firm that sponsors the pension plan is legally obligated to make up the difference by paying more money into the pension fund. This can be done over a period of years.

In a defined contribution plan, the employer bears no risk beyond an obligation to make contributions to each employee's retirement account. In these plans, it is the *employee* who bears the risk that his or her retirement account will increase in value by an amount sufficient to provide adequate income during retirement. If the contributions made to the account by the employer and the employee are insufficient, or if the securities in which the account is invested lose value or increase in value too slowly, the employee risks having an income in retirement that is not sufficient to maintain his or her desired standard of living. If this situation occurs, the worker might choose to delay retirement.

Many factors affect a firm's decision to sponsor a retirement plan and a worker's decision to participate in the plan. In any given year, changes in the business climate — inflation, interest rates, wage increases, the cost of other benefits (such as health insurance), trends in business revenues and profits — could weigh more heavily in a firm's decision to establish or continue a retirement plan than the potential tax advantages it could gain by sponsoring a plan. Likewise, an employee's decision to participate or not to participate in a retirement plan may be affected by such variables as the rate of growth of wages, the rising cost of employee health insurance premiums, his or her confidence in the financial status of Social Security, and whether another family member already participates in a retirement plan.

Encouraging sponsorship of retirement plans by small firms is an important issue to the Congress in part because of the large number of people employed by small businesses. In 2007, for example, more than 36 million wage and salary workers were employed by firms with fewer than 25 employees.[3] The relatively low rates of employer sponsorship and employee participation in retirement plans at small businesses have prompted Congress to look for ways to make it easier for small employers to establish and maintain retirement plans for their employees. Because small employers may be reluctant to take on the financial risk and administrative burden of establishing a defined-benefit pension plan, Congress has sought to encourage greater retirement plan sponsorship among small businesses mainly by easing the financial and reporting requirements associated with certain types of defined contribution pension plans. The *Revenue Act of 1978* (P.L. 95-600) authorized a defined contribution plan called the Simplified Employee Pension (SEP).[4] The *Small Business Job Protection Act of 1996* (P.L. 104-188) authorized another type of defined contribution plan called the Savings Incentive Match Plan for Employees (SIMPLE). Nevertheless, rates of retirement plan sponsorship and participation in small firms continue to lag behind the rates achieved in larger firms.

The Number of Defined Benefit Plans Is Declining

According to the Pension Benefit Guaranty Corporation (PBGC), the number of PBGC-insured defined benefit plans fell from 114,396 in 1985 to 30,328 in 2006.[5] The decline in the number of DB plans resulted mainly from the termination of a large number of small plans. Between 1985 and 2006, the number of single- employer defined benefit pension plans with fewer than 100 participants fell from 90,061 to 18,199, a decline of 80%. The number of large DB plans fell from 22,147 to 10,585, a decline of 52.2%. In recent years, however, several large pension plans have been terminated, and others have been "frozen" so that participants no longer accrue pension benefits.

RECENT TRENDS IN RETIREMENT PLAN SPONSORSHIP AND PARTICIPATION

Every month, the Bureau of the Census conducts the *Current Population Survey* (CPS) among a nationally representative sample of approximately 100,000 households, primarily for the purpose of estimating the rates of employment and unemployment. During March of each year, the survey includes supplemental questions about employment, income, health insurance, retirement plan participation, and receipt of government benefits during the previous calendar year. This information allows analysts and researchers to calculate the number and percentage of workers who reported whether their employer offered a retirement plan and whether they participated in the plan. Responses can then be categorized by demographic and economic characteristics, such as the worker's age, race, sex, income, and the size of firm at which they worked. Unfortunately, however, because the CPS asks only two pension-related questions — if the worker's employer offered a retirement plan and if the worker was included in the plan — we cannot ascertain whether the plan is a defined benefit plan or a defined contribution plan.

PLAN PARTICIPATION BY FULL-TIME VS. PART-TIME EMPLOYMENT

Table 2 compares retirement plan participation among year-round, full-time wage and salary workers in the private sector with participation among workers who were employed part-year or part-time. Workers with part-year or part-time employment are much less likely to be employed by a firm that sponsors a retirement plan. Part-time and part-year workers also are less likely to participate if their employer sponsors a plan.

The proportion of year-round, full-time workers employed at firms that sponsored a retirement plan increased from 57.2% in 2006 to 5 9.9% in 2007. The participation rate among these workers rose from 49.2% in 2006 to 52.0% in 2007. Between 1990 and 2000, plan participation among full-time workers increased from 54.6% to 57.4%. It has since fallen by about five percentage points. Between 2006 and 2007, the proportion of part-time or part-year workers employed by firms that sponsored a retirement plan rose from 37.8% to 38.3%. The participation rate among part-year and part-time workers whose employer sponsored a retirement plan was essentially unchanged from 2006 to 2007, at approximately 23% in both years..

The lower rate of retirement plan participation among part-year and part-time workers is one of the reasons that women are less likely than men to participate in a company-sponsored retirement plan. There is little difference in retirement plan participation between men and women who work *year-round, full-time*. (See **Table 4**.) Women, however, are more likely than men to work part-year or part-time. In 2007, 82.7% of working men between the ages of 25 and 64 were employed year-round, full-time compared to 68.7% of working women in this age-group. Consequently, while women who worked *full-time* in 2007 were as likely as their male counterparts to have participated in a retirement plan (52.6% of women vs. 51.6% of men), the retirement plan participation rate among *all* women 25 to 64 years old in the private sector in 2007 was lower than the participation rate among all working men in that age group.[6] (43% of women participated vs. 47% of men.)

Table 2. Participation in Retirement Plans by Full-Time vs. Part-Time Employment (Private-Sector Wage and Salary Workers, Ages 25 to 64)

	Workers (thousands)	Employer Sponsors Plan		Employees Participating	
		Workers	Percent	Participant	Percent
Full-time					
1990	53,026	33,323	62.8	28,955	54.6
1995	60,687	38,344	63.2	33,298	54.9
2000	70,177	46,499	66.3	40,304	57.4
2001	69,265	45,097	65.1	38,678	55.8
2002	69,093	42,805	62.0	36,973	53.5
2003	69,306	43,450	62.7	37,464	54.1
2004	70,402	43,488	61.8	37,588	53.4
2005	72,331	43,195	59.7	37,347	51.6
2006	74,542	42,601	57.2	36,676	49.2
2007	74,588	44,645	59.9	38,756	52.0
Part-time					
1990	23,608	8,838	37.4	5,273	22.3
1995	23,790	9,348	39.3	5,508	23.2
2000	21,420	9,708	45.3	5,756	26.9
2001	23,449	10,535	44.9	6,444	27.5
2002	24,104	10,353	43.0	6,192	25.7
2003	23,714	9,868	41.6	5,991	25.3
2004	23,137	9,597	41.5	5,748	24.8
2005	23,394	9,337	39.9	5,707	24.4
2006	22,660	8,566	37.8	5,287	23.3
2007	23,187	8,891	38.3	5,322	23.0
All workers					
1990	76,633	42,161	55.0	34,228	44.7
1995	84,477	47,692	56.5	38,806	45.9
2000	91,597	56,207	61.4	46,060	50.3
2001	92,714	55,632	60.0	45,122	48.7
2002	93,197	53,158	57.0	43,165	46.3
2003	93,020	53,318	57.3	43,455	46.7
2004	93,539	53,085	56.8	43,337	46.3
2005	95,725	52,532	54.9	43,053	45.0
2006	97,201	51,167	52.6	41,963	43.2
2007	97,775	53,536	54.8	44,078	45.1

Source: Congressional Research Service analysis of the *Current Population Survey*, various years.

Retirement Plans and Employer Size

Data from the CPS show that retirement plan participation in small firms rose between 1990 and 2000, but has recently declined. The CPS data also indicate that access to a company-sponsored retirement plan remains substantially lower in small firms than in firms with 100 or more employees. The data displayed in **Table 3** show that from 1990 to 2007, the number of workers between the ages of 25 and 64 who were employed in the private sector and worked year-round, full-time at firms of all sizes increased from 53.0 million to 74.6 million. At the same time, the number of such workers whose employer offered a retirement plan increased from 33.3 million to 44.6 million. The proportion of year-round, full-time workers who were employed at firms that offered a retirement plan rose from 62.8% in 1990 to 66.3% in 2000. It has since fallen to 5 9.9%.

The data displayed in **Table 3** show that since 2000, the proportion of workers in firms with 100 or more workers whose employer sponsors a retirement plan has fallen from 80.5% to 75.2%. Nevertheless, workers at large firms remain substantially more likely than employees of small businesses to work for an employer that sponsors a retirement plan. In 2007, 29.3% of full-time workers in businesses with fewer than 25 employees were employed at firms that sponsored a retirement plan, down from 34.2% in 2000. This was still higher than the 25.4% of workers at small firms whose employer sponsored a retirement plan in 1995. Among workers in firms with 25 to 99 employees, 53.1% were employed at firms that sponsored a retirement plan in 2007, compared to 58.5% in 2000 and 54.1% in 1995.

Table 3 also shows the percentage of year-round, full-time employees in the private sector who *participated* in an employer-sponsored retirement plan.[7] This statistic takes into account the impact of employers that do not sponsor a plan on overall retirement plan participation rates. Among firms of all sizes, the proportion of year-round, full-time employees between the ages of 25 and 64 who participated in a retirement plan rose from 49.2% in 2006 to 52.0% in 2007. This was lower than the participation rates of 57.4% in 2000 and 54.9% in 1995. In firms with fewer than 25 employees, just 25.5% of full-time employees between the ages of 25 and 64 participated in a retirement plan in 2007, down from 29.3% in 2000, but higher than the 21.3% who participated in a plan in 1995. In firms with 25 to 99 employees, retirement plan participation rose from 42.6% in 2006 to 45.5% in 2007. This was lower than the participation rates of 49.4% in 2000 and 46.0% in 1995. Participation in retirement plans among workers in firms with 100 or more employees also rose between 2006 and 2007, increasing from 62.7% to 65.4%. This was about five percentage points lower than the participation rates of 70.2% in 2000 and 70.4% in 1995.

Plan Participation among Men and Women

Table 4 shows the rates of participation in employer-sponsored retirement plans by men and women between the ages 25 and 64 who were employed in the private sector and worked year-round, full-time. Between 1990 and 2000, the proportion of men whose employer sponsored a retirement plan rose from 63.3% to 66.2%. Since then, it has dropped to 59.1%. The proportion of women who worked at firms that sponsored a retirement plan increased from 62.1% in 1990 to 66.4% in 2000. In 2007, 61.0% of women who worked year-round, full-time were employed at firms that sponsored a retirement plan. Thus, in 2007 women who were employed year-round, full-time were more likely than men to have worked for an employer that sponsored a retirement plan. Men and women, however, were almost equally likely to have *participated* in an employer-sponsored retirement plan. In 2007, 51.6% of men who were employed year-round, full-time participated in a company-sponsored retirement plan, compared to 52.6% of women. Both of these participation rates were lower than the 2000 participation rates of 58.3% for men and 56.1% for women. The participation rate for men was 6.7 percentage points lower in 2007 than in 2000. The participation rate for women was 3.5 percentage points lower in 2007 than in 2000.

Table 3. Participation in Retirement Plans by Size of Firm (Private-Sector Wage and Salary Workers, Ages 25 to 64, Employed Year-Round, Full-Time)

Size of firm	Workers (thousands)	Employer Sponsors Plan		Employees Participating	
		Workers	Percent	Participants	Percent
Under 25 employees					
1990	12,119	3,042	25.1	2,619	21.6
1995	14,627	3,715	25.4	3,109	21.3
2000	16,591	5,575	34.2	4,857	29.3
2001	17,061	5,788	33.9	4,965	29.1
2002	17,878	5,658	31.7	4,880	27.3
2003	18,616	5,850	31.4	5,064	27.2
2004	18,906	5,795	30.7	5,016	26.5
2005	19,200	5,569	29.0	4,851	25.3
2006	19,406	5,160	26.6	4,434	22.9
2007	19,449	5,702	29.3	4,954	25.5
25 to 99 employees					
1990	7,892	3,904	49.5	3,291	41.7
1995	9,108	4,923	54.1	4,188	46.0
2000	10,492	6,139	58.5	5,186	49.4
2001	10,466	6,086	58.2	5,067	48.4
2002	10,719	6,030	56.3	5,126	47.8
2003	10,540	6,133	58.2	5,254	49.9
2004	10,532	5,969	56.7	5,121	48.6
2005	11,214	5,975	53.3	5,070	45.2
2006	11,489	5,829	50.7	4,889	42.6
2007	11,367	6,041	53.1	5,166	45.5
100 or more employees					
1990	33,014	26,378	79.9	23,045	69.8
1995	36,951	29,706	80.4	26,000	70.4
2000	43,094	34,692	80.5	30,262	70.2
2001	41,739	33,223	79.6	28,645	68.6
2002	40,496	31,116	76.8	26,967	66.6
2003	40,149	31,466	78.4	27,146	67.6
2004	40,964	31,724	77.4	27,452	67.0
2005	41,917	31,562	75.5	27,425	65.4
2006	43,646	31,612	72.4	27,353	62.7
2007	43,772	32,903	75.2	28,636	65.4
All firms					

Table 3. (Continued)

Size of firm	Workers (thousands)	Employer Sponsors Plan		Employees Participating	
		Workers	Percent	Workers	Percent
1990	53,026	33,323	62.8	28,955	54.6
1995	60,687	38,344	63.2	33,298	54.9
2000	70,177	46,499	66.3	40,304	57.4
2001	69,265	45,097	65.1	38,678	55.8
2002	69,093	42,805	62.0	36,973	53.5
2003	69,306	43,450	62.7	37,464	54.1
2004	70,402	43,488	61.8	37,588	53.4
2005	72,331	43,195	59.7	37,347	51.6
2006	74,542	42,601	57.2	36,676	49.2
2007	74,588	44,645	59.9	38,756	52.0

Source: CRS analysis of the *Current Population Survey*, various years.

Table 4. Employee Participation in Retirement Plans, by Sex (Private-Sector Wage and Salary Workers, Ages 25 to 64, Employed Year-Round, Full-Time).

	Workers (thousands)	Employer Sponsors Plan		Employees Participating	
		Workers	Percent	Participants	Percent
Men					
1990	32,208	20,389	63.3	18,242	56.6
1995	36,504	23,008	63.0	20,359	55.8
2000	41,516	27,463	66.2	24,220	58.3
2001	40,976	26,539	64.8	23,164	56.5
2002	40,851	25,100	61.4	22,033	53.9
2003	40,963	25,306	61.8	22,083	53.9
2004	41,732	25,190	60.4	22,079	52.9
2005	42,881	25,136	58.6	22,021	51.4
2006	44,210	24,898	56.3	21,616	48.9
2007	43,844	25,897	59.1	22,600	51.6
Women					
1990	20,817	12,934	62.1	10,713	51.5
1995	24,182	15,336	63.4	12,939	53.5
2000	28,661	19,036	66.4	16,083	56.1
2001	28,290	18,558	65.6	15,513	54.8
2002	28,242	17,704	62.7	14,939	52.9
2003	28,342	18,144	64.0	15,381	54.3
2004	28,670	18,298	63.8	15,509	54.1
2005	29,450	18,059	61.3	15,326	52.0
2006	30,332	17,703	58.4	15,060	49.7
2007	30.744	18,749	61.0	16,156	52.6

Source: Congressional Research Service analysis of the *Current Population Survey*, various years.

Plan Participation by Employee Age

Table 5 displays rates of participation in employer-sponsored retirement plans among workers who were employed in the private sector and worked year-round, full-time, according to their age. Young workers — ages 25 to 34 — were less likely than middle-aged and older workers to be employed at a firm that sponsored a retirement plan in 2007. They also were less likely to participate in retirement plans than are older workers. In 2007, 54.3% of workers 25 to 34 years old worked for an employer that sponsored a retirement plan, and 43.0% of workers in this age group participated in a company-sponsored plan. Thus, 79.2% of those aged 25 to 34 who worked for a firm that sponsored a plan participated in the plan (0.430/0.543 = 0.792). In contrast, among workers 55 to 64 years old, 63.5% worked at firms that sponsored a retirement plan, and 57.6% participated in a company-sponsored plan. Thus, among workers aged 55 to 64 who worked for a firm that sponsored a retirement plan, 90.7% participated in the plan (0.576/0.63 5 = 0.907).[8]

Table 5. Employee Participation in Retirement Plans, by Age (Private-Sector Wage and Salary Workers, Ages 25 to 64, Employed Year-Round, Full-Time).

Employee Age	Workers (thousands)	Employer Sponsors Plan		Employees Participating	
		Workers	Percent	Participants	Percent
25 to 34					
1990	19,344	11,489	59.4	9,135	47.2
1995	19,759	11,673	59.1	9,337	47.3
2000	20,398	12,803	62.8	10,173	49.9
2001	19,542	11,908	60.9	9,330	47.7
2002	19,389	11,090	57.2	8,638	44.6
2003	19,288	11,221	58.2	8,822	45.7
2004	19,122	10,878	56.9	8,584	44.9
2005	19,677	10,577	53.8	8,268	42.0
2006	20,359	10,648	52.3	8,371	41.1
2007	20,053	10,895	54.3	8,625	43.0
35 to 44					
1990	16,989	11,042	65.0	9,871	58.1
1995	20,439	13,235	64.8	11,742	57.5
2000	23,362	15,479	66.3	13,559	58.0
2001	22,445	14,841	66.1	12,882	57.4
2002	21,826	13,681	62.7	11,879	54.4
2003	21,328	13,428	63.0	11,609	54.4
2004	21,587	13,314	61.7	11,564	53.6
2005	21,688	12,893	59.5	11,289	52.1
2006	21,875	12,313	56.3	10,781	49.3
2007	21,448	12,793	59.7	11,119	51.8
45 to 54					
1990	10,922	7,148	65.5	6,586	60.3
1995	14,042	9,240	65.8	8,381	59.7

Table 5. (Continued)

Employee Age	Workers (thousands)	Employer Sponsors Plan		Employees Participating	
		Workers	Percent	Workers	Percent
2000	18,489	12,951	70.1	11,787	63.8
2001	18,625	12,650	67.9	11,324	60.8
2002	18,796	12,308	65.5	11,204	59.6
2003	19,227	12,752	66.3	11,521	59.9
2004	19,763	12,827	64.9	11,531	58.4
2005	20,466	12,995	63.5	11,686	57.1
2006	21,188	12,959	61.2	11,542	54.5
2007	21,265	13,449	63.2	12,200	57.4
55 to 64					
1990	5,771	3,644	63.1	3,363	58.3
1995	6,446	4,196	65.1	3,838	59.5
2000	7,929	5,267	66.4	4,785	60.3
2001	8,653	5,698	65.9	5,141	59.4
2002	9,082	5,725	63.0	5,252	57.8
2003	9,463	6,045	63.9	5,512	58.3
2004	9,930	6,470	65.2	5,910	59.5
2005	10,500	6,730	64.1	6,104	58.1
2006	11,120	6,681	60.1	5,981	53.8
2007	11,821	7,508	63.5	6,812	57.6

Source: CRS analysis of the *Current Population Survey*, various years.

Plan Participation by Employee Race

The March 2003 CPS introduced newly expanded categories of race and ethnicity, making comparisons with prior years problematic. In **Table 6,** race and ethnicity are categorized as white non-Hispanic, black non-Hispanic, Hispanic, and other. The "other"category includes mainly persons whose heritage is Asian, Native American, Eskimo, or Pacific Islander. In 2007, the likelihood of being employed at a firm that sponsored a retirement plan was highest for white non-Hispanic workers and lowest for Hispanic workers. Black non-Hispanic workers and "Asian/Other" workers were about equally likely to have worked for an employer that sponsored a retirement plan. Among white non-Hispanic workers, 65.4% worked for an employer that sponsored a retirement plan, and 57.6% participated in an employer- sponsored plan. Among Hispanic workers, just 37.5% worked for an employer that sponsored a retirement plan and only 30.6% participated in an employer-sponsored retirement plan. Of workers who classified their race and ethnicity as black non-Hispanic, 57.6% worked for an employer that sponsored a plan and 47.1% participated in a plan, while among Asian-American and other workers, 55.4% worked for an employer that sponsored a retirement plan and 48.5% participated in a plan.

Table 6. Employee Participation in Retirement Plans, by Race (Private Sector Wage and Salary Workers, Ages 25 to 64, Employed Year-Round, Full-Time)

Employee Race	Workers (thousands)	Employer Sponsors Plan		Employees Participating	
		Workers	Percent	Participants	Percent
White, non-Hispanic					
2002	49,012	32,711	66.7	28,836	58.8
2003	48,524	32,800	67.6	28,759	59.3
2004	48,618	32,427	66.7	28,522	58.7
2005	49,952	32,490	65.0	28,618	57.3
2006	50,627	31,740	62.7	27,817	55.0
2007	50,835	33,251	65.4	29,291	57.6
Black, non-Hispanic					
2002	7,078	4,156	58.7	3,363	47.5
2003	7,241	4,311	59.5	3,555	49.1
2004	7,556	4,570	60.5	3,753	49.7
2005	7,511	4,295	57.2	3,491	46.5
2006	7,927	4,224	53.3	3,468	43.8
2007	7,805	4,499	57.6	3,675	47.1
Hispanic					
2002	8,942	3,582	40.1	2,777	31.1
2003	9,073	3,750	41.3	2,956	32.6
2004	9,651	3,802	39.4	2,987	31.0
2005	10,208	3,775	37.0	2,964	29.0
2006	10,982	3,843	35.0	3,032	27.6
2007	10,834	4,065	37.5	3,310	30.6
Other					
2002	4,062	2,356	58.0	1,996	49.2
2003	4,468	2,588	57.9	2,193	49.1
2004	4,578	2,689	58.7	2,326	50.8
2005	4,660	2,636	56.6	2,274	48.8
2006	5,007	2,794	55.9	2,358	47.1
2007	5,114	2,830	55.4	2,481	48.5

Source: Congressional Research Service analysis of the *Current Population Survey*, various years.

Plan Participation by Employee Earnings

Table 7 shows the relationship between earnings and participation in an employer-sponsored retirement plan. In **Table 7**, workers' annual earnings from wages and salaries — as reported on the Current Population Survey — are ranked by quartile. In 2007, one-quarter of private-sector wage and salary workers between the ages of 25 and 64 who were employed year-round, full-time earned more than $63,000. Another quarter had earnings between $40,000 and $63,000. The next quarter had earnings between $27,000 and $40,000, and those in the lowest quartile earned less than $27,000.

Table 7. Participation in Retirement Plans by Annual Earnings (Private-Sector Wage and Salary Workers, Ages 25 to 64, Employed Year-Round, Full-Time)

Worker's Annual Earnings	Employer Sponsors Plan	Employee Participates
	Percentage of Workers	Percentage of Workers
Highest Earnings Quartile		
1990	77.9	73.7
1995	77.1	73.0
2000	80.2	75.5
2001	78.2	73.3
2002	75.3	71.0
2003	77.0	72.5
2004	75.8	71.4
2005	74.4	70.3
2006	70.9	66.7
2007	73.8	69.2
Second-highest Earnings Quartile		
1990	72.0	64.2
1995	72.4	65.1
2000	74.3	67.1
2001	74.2	66.7
2002	70.9	63.3
2003	71.0	63.6
2004	71.3	64.1
2005	68.6	61.5
2006	66.8	59.9
2007	69.4	62.8
Third-highest Earnings Quartile		
1990	61.3	51.4
1995	61.0	51.3
2000	66.0	55.5
2001	63.9	52.9
2002	61.3	51.6
2003	61.6	51.7
2004	60.9	51.0
2005	59.0	49.8
2006	56.2	46.3
2007	59.1	49.7
Lowest Earnings Quartile		
1990	41.2	30.3
1995	42.4	30.4
2000	44.9	32.1
2001	44.9	31.5
2002	41.4	29.5
2003	41.2	28.4
2004	41.6	29.9
2005	39.0	27.5
2006	36.6	26.2
2007	38.4	27.7

Source: CRS analysis of the *Current Population Survey*, various years.

In 2007, 73.8% of year-round, full-time workers in the private sector with annual earnings in the top quartile were employed by firms that sponsored a retirement plan, and 69.2% of workers in the top earnings quartile participated in a retirement plan. Both of these percentages were lower than the rates in 2000 and 1995. In 2000, 80.2% of year-round, full-time workers in the private sector with annual earnings in the top quartile were employed by firms that sponsored a retirement plan, and 75.5% of workers in the top earnings quartile participated in a retirement plan. The equivalent sponsorship and participation rates in 1995 were 77.1% and 73.0%, respectively.

The percentage of workers employed at firms that sponsored a retirement plan and the percentage who participated in these plans were progressively lower in each of three lowest earnings quartiles. For example, among workers in the lowest earnings quartile in 2007, 38.4% were employed at firms that sponsored a retirement plan, and 27.7% of workers in the bottom quartile participated in a retirement plan. Both of these percentages were lower than the comparable rates in 2000 and 1995. In 2000, 44.9% of year-round, full-time workers in the private sector with annual earnings in the bottom quartile were employed by firms that sponsored a retirement plan, and 32.1% of workers in the bottom earnings quartile participated in a retirement plan. The equivalent sponsorship and participation rates in 1995 were 42.4% and 30.4%, respectively.

Low-wage workers are not only less likely to work for an employer that sponsors a retirement plan; they also are less likely to participate if a plan is offered. Among employees whose earnings in 2007 were in the top quartile, 73.8% worked for an employer that sponsored a retirement plan and 69.2% participated in a retirement plan. Therefore, the participation rate among employees in the top earnings quartile whose employer sponsored a retirement plan was 93.8% (0.692/0.738 = 0.938). Among workers whose 2007 earnings were in the bottom quartile, only 3 8.4% worked for an employer that sponsored a retirement plan and just 27.7% participated in a retirement plan. Thus, the participation rate among low- wage employees whose employer sponsored a retirement plan was 72.1% (0.277/0.3 84 = 0.721).

ANOTHER MEASURE OF RETIREMENT PLAN PARTICIPATION: THE NATIONAL COMPENSATION SURVEY

The Bureau of Labor Statistics collects data from employers about paid leave, health insurance, retirement plan participation, flexible spending accounts, and other employee benefits as part of the *National Compensation Survey* (NCS). This survey is conducted among a nationally representative sample of private-sector business establishments.[9] The term *establishment* usually refers to a single place of business at a particular location or all branches of a business in a particular metropolitan area or county. An establishment might be a branch or small operating unit of a larger firm. In contrast, a *firm* comprises *all* of the establishments that together form a corporation, partnership, or other business entity.[10]

According to the data collected from employers through the National Compensation Survey, 51% of workers in the private sector participated in employer- sponsored retirement plans in March 2007. (See **Table 8.**) Twenty percent of private- sector workers participated in defined benefit plans and 43% participated in defined contribution plans. Approximately 12% of private-sector workers participated in both types of plan. The NCS indicates that 66% of employees in establishments with 100 or more workers participated in an employer-sponsored retirement plan in March 2007, while only 37% of employees at establishments with fewer than 100 employees participated in an employer-sponsored retirement plan. The data from the NCS also indicate that among full-time workers, 60% participated in an employer-sponsored retirement plan in March 2007, compared to just 23% of part-time workers.

Table 8. Percentage of Private-Sector Employees Participating in Employer-Sponsored Retirement Plans

	Type of Retirement Plan		
	All Types	Defined Benefit	Defined Contribution
Establishment Size			
1-99 workers			
March 2003	35	8	31
March 2004	37	9	32
March 2005	37	9	32
March 2006	37	9	33
March 2007	37	9	33
100 or more workers			
March 2003	65	33	51
March 2004	67	34	53
March 2005	67	36	53
March 2006	67	33	54
March 2007	66	32	53
Work Schedule			
Full-time workers			
March 2003	58	24	48
March 2004	60	24	50
March 2005	60	25	50
March 2006	60	23	51
March 2007	60	23	50
Part-time workers			
March 2003	18	8	14
March 2004	20	9	14
March 2005	19	9	14
March 2006	21	8	16
March 2007	23	9	18
All workers			
March 2003	49	20	40
March 2004	50	21	42
March 2005	50	21	42
March 2006	51	20	43
March 2007	51	20	43

Source: U.S. Department of Labor, National Compensation Survey.

Note: Data represent 102 million workers employed in the private sector in 2003 and 108 million workers employed in the private sector in 2007.

While it is not necessarily surprising that the results of the NCS differ from those of the CPS, nor that the NCS shows higher rates of participation, it is important to note that in recent years the difference in the results shown by the two surveys has increased because the NCS has indicated a generally steady rate of retirement plan participation whereas the CPS data indicate that retirement plan participation has been falling. As recently as 2003, the NCS indicated that 49% of private-sector workers participated in a retirement plan whereas the CPS data showed a participation rate of 47%. This two percentage point difference was small enough to be inconsequential for most analytical purposes. The slightly higher rate of participation indicated by the NCS might partly be due to the fact that the business owners and benefits specialists who are interviewed for the NCS could be expected to have greater knowledge of employer-provided benefits than the household members interviewed for the CPS. By March 2007, however, the NCS indicated that the proportion of private-sector workers participating in employer-sponsored retirement plans was 51%, whereas the March 2008 CPS (which asks about pension participation in 2007) showed that participation in retirement plans among private sector workers had fallen to 45%. The difference in the results shown by the two surveys can no longer be considered inconsequential, leaving analysts to question whether one or both surveys have problems related to sample selection or survey methodology.

End Notes

[1] U.S. National Center for Health Statistics, *Vital Statistics of the United States.*

[2] Defined benefit pensions are taxed when the employee receives benefits during retirement.

[3] Full-time and part-time wage and salary workers. (Source: *Current Population Survey.*)

[4] P.L. 95-600 authorized tax exemption only for employer contributions to a SEP. The *Tax Reform Act of 1986* (P.L. 99-514) allowed workers in firms with fewer than 25 employees to contribute to a SEP on a tax-deferred basis through salary reduction (SARSEP). P.L. 104-188 authorized SIMPLE plans to replace SARSEPs. Firms may continue to establish SEPs funded exclusively by employer contributions, but new SARSEPs were prohibited after December 31, 1996. Previously existing SARSEPs may continue as before.

[5] Pension Benefit Guaranty Corporation, *Pension Insurance Data Book 2006.*

[6] CRS estimates based on the March 2008 CPS (not shown in accompanying tables).

[7] Not all employees whose employer sponsors a retirement plan are eligible to participate. For example, employees under age 21, those who have been employed for less than one year, and those who work fewer than 1,000 hours in a year can be excluded from the plan.

[8] Some of the difference in participation rates is because workers under 35 are somewhat more likely to be in their first year with an employer and can be excluded from participating in the plan. Employees who work fewer than 1,000 hours in a year and those under age 21 also can be excluded from participating, but neither group is represented in Table 5.

[9] For more information on the National Compensation Survey, see U.S. Department of Labor, *National Compensation Survey: Employee Benefits in Private Industry in the United States, March 2007*, available online at [http://www.bls.gov/ncs/ebs/sp/ebsm0006.pdf].

[10] In the Census Bureau's *Current Population Survey*, employer characteristics are reported at the level of the *firm*, which may include more than one establishment.

In: Pensions: Backgrounds, Trends and Issues
Editor: Henry J. Mullen

ISBN: 978-1-60876-840-0

Chapter 4

CONFLICTS OF INTEREST CAN AFFECT DEFINED BENEFIT AND DEFINED CONTRIBUTION PLANS

Charles A. Jeszeck

WHY GAO DID THIS STUDY

Conflicts of interest typically exist when someone in a position of trust, such as a pension consultant, has competing professional or personal issues. Such competing interests can make it difficult for pension plan fiduciaries and others, in general, to fulfill their duties impartially and could cause them to breach their duty to act solely in the interest of plan participants and beneficiaries. The proliferation of consulting work and the complexity of business arrangements among investment advisors, plan consultants, and others have increased the likelihood of conflicts of interests for both defined benefit (DB) plans, where investment risk is largely borne by the plan sponsor and defined contribution (DC) plans, where such risk is largely borne by the participant. Given the potential financial harm conflicts of interest may pose to DB and DC plans, GAO was asked to report on (1) the effects undisclosed conflicts of interest may have on the financial performance of DB plans, and (2) the vulnerabilities that conflicts of interest may pose for DC plan participants. GAO interviewed a variety of experts, reviewed the Department of Labor's (Labor) legal and regulatory authority and analyzed government and industry data associated with terminated plans.

WHAT GAO RECOMMENDS

GAO is not making recommendations at this time but has ongoing work.

View GAO-09-503T or key components. For more information, contact Charles Jeszeckat (202) 512-7215 or jeszeckc@gao.gov.

WHAT GAO FOUND

GAO's analysis of available data on pension consultants and plans revealed a statistical association between inadequate disclosure and lower investment returns for ongoing plans, suggesting the possible adverse financial effect of such nondisclosure. Specifically, our econometric analysis using ongoing defined benefit (DB) plans and Securities and Exchange Commission (SEC) study data on pension consultants registered as investment advisers, who adequately disclosed their conflicts of interest and those who did not, detected lower annual rates of return for those ongoing plans associated with consultants that had failed to disclose significant conflicts of interest. These lower rates generally ranged from a statistically significant 1.2 to 1.3 percentage points over the 2000 to 2004 period. Since the average return for the ongoing plans that used consultants who did not have significant disclosure violations was about 4.5 percent, the model implies that the average returns for ongoing plans that used consultants who failed to disclose significant conflicts was 3.2 to 3.3 percent for the period. Because many factors can affect returns, and data as well as modeling limitations limit the ability to generalize and interpret the results, this finding should not be considered as proof of causality between conflicts and lower rates of return, although it suggests the importance of detecting the presence of conflicts among pension plan consultants. GAO's analysis of data from a 2005 SEC staff report examining 24 registered pension consultants, including 13 that failed to disclose significant conflicts in conjunction with other sources of data also showed that, in 2006, these 13 consultants had over $4.5 trillion in U.S. assets under advisement, which included private DB and DC plan assets.

Conflicts of interest can have adverse effects on both DB and DC plans. Our study focused exclusively on DB plans and less information exists on the extent or nature of conflicts of interest in the DC plan environment. However, because the risk of investment is largely borne by the individual participant in DC plans, participants are vulnerable to any decision, including those involving conflicts of interest, that could result in higher fees or other outcomes that can lower investment returns for participants. Given the multiplicity of parties involved in today's 401(k) plan arena, many opportunities exist for business arrangements to go undisclosed. Problems may occur when pension consultants or other companies providing services to a plan also receive compensation from other service providers. Without disclosing these arrangements, service providers may be steering plan sponsors toward investment products or services that may not be in the best interest of participants. Labor has published proposed regulations to improve the information disclosed about the various business arrangements among service providers. However, those proposed regulations are currently awaiting review and approval by the new Secretary of Labor. We are currently conducting a review of Labor's revisions to the Form 5500 Schedule C, which could provide some information to Labor about previously undisclosed business arrangements.

Mr. Chairman and Members of the Committee:

I am pleased to be here today to discuss how conflicts of interest can affect participants in private pension plans. As you know, a conflict of interest in a pension context typically exists when someone in a position of trust, such as a pension consultant, has competing professional or personal interests. Competing interests can make it difficult for a plan's fiduciaries, in general, to fulfill their duties impartially and could cause them to breach their duty to act solely in the interest of plan participants and beneficiaries. The degree of challenge to sound pension sponsorship posed by financial conflicts of interest is largely a consequence of the changes experienced by financial markets over the last 30 years. In fact, the pre-ERISA world of 1974 never anticipated the multiplicity and complexity of financial instruments that have expanded both investment opportunities and risks for plan fiduciaries.

Regulators and others have analyzed how conflicts of interest have affected defined benefit (DB) plan performance. Congressional interest in how fees affect 401(k) plans has focused attention on business arrangements or conflicts of interest between plan sponsors and third party providers that can increase the fees charged to 401(k) participants. DB and defined contribution (DC) plan fiduciaries use the variety of service providers that have become available to help them assess choices. While conflicts of interest are not necessarily inherent in the provision of such financial services, the prevalence and the proliferation of consulting work and the complexity of business arrangements among investment advisers, plan consultants, and others have increased the potential for such conflicts to occur.

My comments today are based on findings from several recent reports[1]. My remarks focus on (1) the effects undisclosed conflicts of interest may have on the financial performance of DB plans and (2) vulnerabilities that conflicts of interest may pose for DC plan participants.

Before I discuss our key findings, some background on the U.S. pension landscape would be useful. Today, roughly half of all American workers participate in employer-sponsored pension plans. Private sector pension plans are classified as either DB or DC plans. DB plans provide, generally, a monthly retirement income for the life of the participant that is based on salary, years of service, and age at retirement, regardless of how the plan's investments perform. With DB plans, the risk of poor investing or low rates of return fall largely on the plan sponsor. In contrast, benefits from DC plans are based on the contributions to and the performance of the investments in individual accounts, which may fluctuate in value. One type of DC, or individual account, plan is the 401(k) plan. Unlike DB plans, the risk of low rates of return under DC plans falls largely on the individual participant.

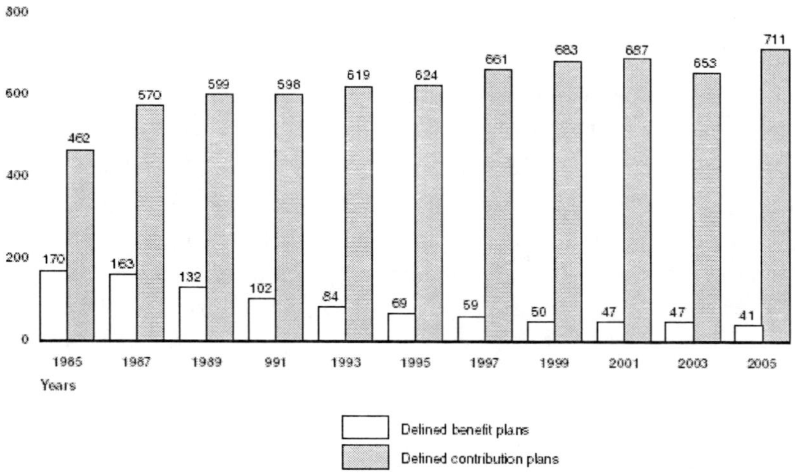

Source: U.S. Department of Labor (1985-2003 data); Investment Company Institute (2005 estimates).

Figure 1. Comparison of Defined Benefit Plans with Defined Contribution Plans, 1985 and 2005.

Over the last several decades the number of DC plans has continued to increase, while the number of traditional DB plans has declined. Today, DC plans account for the majority of private sector retirement plans and participants.

Meanwhile, the financial services industry and the DB pension system have also changed significantly since the 1970s. The globalization of financial markets, as well as technological and international regulatory changes, has facilitated the development of new financial instruments and the complexity of investment opportunities.[2] Consequently, the financial services industry has responded to the growing need for assistance with managing, investing, transferring, settling, valuing, and holding pension assets. In 2005, over 81 percent of large public/government plans used an investment consultant and 42 percent of private pension plans did so.[3] As of October 31, 2005, there were more than 1,800 SEC-registered investment advisers that indicated on their Securities and Exchange Commission (SEC) registration forms that they provide pension consulting services.[4] These firms vary widely from small one-person operations to large organizations employing hundreds. Some firms only provide pension consulting, while others may have started as pension consultants, but then added additional business operations such as brokerage and money management.

A conflict of interest is typically a situation in which someone in a position of trust, such as a pension plan trustee or investment adviser, has competing professional or personal interests. Such competing interests can make it difficult for a plan's fiduciaries, in general, to fulfill their duties impartially and could cause them to breach their duty to act solely in the interest of plan participants and beneficiaries. Having a conflict in and of itself does not constitute a breach of fiduciary duty. However, given the potential of financial harm to plan sponsors and participants, questions have been raised about the extent and nature of these conflicts of interest.

Inadequate Disclosure of Conflicts of Interest by Pension Consultants are Associated with Rates of Return for DB Plans

Although no complete information is available on the prevalence of conflicts of interest, pension plan consultants assisting significant numbers of pension plan sponsors may have such conflicts as a result of their affiliations or business arrangements with other firms which could affect the advice they provide to these sponsors. SEC, through its examination and enforcement, has identified potential conflicts of interest among money managers that could result in harm to clients, including pension plans. A May 2005 study by SEC staff on conflicts of interest among pension consultants registered as investment advisers revealed that 13 out of the 24 consultants examined that had provided services to sponsors of pension plans, including ongoing DB and Pension Benefit Guaranty Corporation (PBGC)-trusteed DB plans, had failed to disclose significant ongoing conflicts of interest to their pension fund clients.[5]

These ongoing conflicts took a number of different forms. For example, SEC found that 13 pension consultants or their affiliates had conflicts of interest because they provided products and services to pension plan advisory clients, money managers, and mutual funds on an ongoing basis without adequately disclosing these conflicts. SEC staff also found that the majority of pension consultants examined had business relationships with broker-dealers that raised a number of concerns about potential harm to pension plans. For example, in certain directed brokerage arrangements, a pension consultant may convince a pension plan client to direct their money manager to place plan trades through a broker-dealer that was affiliated with the consultant as a means for paying advisor fees a plan owed to its consultant using a portion of the brokerage commission paid on such trades. These arrangements raised concerns that plans might not have received the best price for each trade—or "best execution"—because the directions given to a plan's money manager by the plan may have restricted the money manager's ability to select a broker-dealer that was the best able to execute a trade. These arrangements raised the additional concern that consultants might be overpaid because the plan did not always know when the fee had been paid in full, as brokerage commissions were being used to pay the fee rather than checks drawn on the plan's checking account.

These consultants also had extensive relationships with DB pension funds. In particular, they:

- had over $4.5 trillion in U.S. assets under advisement, including private DB and DC plan assets, as well as public pension plan and other types of assets as of 2006;[6]
- provided advisory services to 36 percent (9 out of 25) of the largest plan sponsors, in terms of claims, currently trusteed by PBGC since 2000;[7]
- provided advisory services to 14 percent (12 out of 86) of the plan sponsors that were trusteed by the Pension Benefit Guaranty Corporation (PBGC) in 2005; and
- provided advisory services to 24 percent (1,009 out of 4,203) of the sponsors of ongoing DB plans between the years 2000 and 2004.

Association between Inadequate Disclosure of Conflicts and Lower Rates of Return

Using data from the SEC conflicts of interest study and ongoing DB pension data, we conducted an analysis that revealed a statistical association between inadequate disclosure and lower investment returns for ongoing plans, suggesting the possible adverse financial effect of undisclosed conflicts. Specifically, we conducted an econometric analysis on pension consultants in the SEC study, both those that adequately disclosed their conflicts of interest and those who did not.[8] We found lower annual rates of return for those ongoing plans associated with consultants who had failed to disclose significant conflicts of interest, with lower rates generally ranging from a statistically significant 1.2 to 1.3 percentage points over the 2000 to 2004 period, depending on the different model specifications tested.[9] Since the average return for the ongoing plans that used consultants who did not have significant disclosure violations was about 4.5 percent, the model implies that the average returns for ongoing plans that used consultants who failed to disclose significant conflicts was 3.2 to 3.3 percent for the period. We did not find significant differences in returns for those plans that had associations with both types of consultants. As of year-end 2004, our sample of ongoing plans represented assets of $183.5 billion for these plans, and average assets were $155.3 million.

While the results suggest a negative association between returns and plans that are associated exclusively with pension consultants with significant undisclosed conflicts of interest, they should not be viewed necessarily as evidence of a causal relationship. These results, like those of most studies, should be understood in of the context of their modeling and data limitations. Although the analysis controlled for plan size, funding level, performance of asset markets, differences in plan fiscal years, and other key variables, other unknown, omitted factors could have influenced the results of our analysis. While this result gives an indication of the potential harm conflicts of interest may cause in the aggregate, these results cannot be generalized to the population of pension consultants since the consultants examined by the SEC were not selected randomly. In addition, while these findings are consistent with the views of the experts we interviewed concerning the adverse effect that complex service–providerrelated conflicts of interest can have on pension plans, we cannot rule out the possibility that some other differences between the plans could explain the differences in estimated returns.

Regardless of any global statistical relationships, a detailed audit would be needed to uncover a conflict of interest in any one plan. Independent experts and officials stated that though a typical first step to identify harm related to a conflict of interest is to examine a plan's investment returns, determining whether any financial harm is caused to an individual pension plan by a conflict of interest requires a detailed forensic audit to identify any accrued harm from a conflict of interest. Such audits are fairly elaborate requiring at a minimum, 5 years worth of service-providerspecific documents including contracts with the plan sponsor, fees charged, payment and other financial transactions between service providers and those involving plan fiduciaries.

Financially costly as conflicts of interest might be in the DB plan context, their risk is largely borne by the plan sponsor and not the participant. In most instances, the benefits of DB plan participants are not affected by fluctuations or even long term declines in a fund's rate of return. Plan sponsors must pay for the benefits they have promised to their employees, increasing contributions to the plan as necessary to cover those benefits. In the event that a plan sponsor of an underfunded plan goes bankrupt, insurance provided by the PBGC will pay most benefits promised to participants.[10]

Participants Could Be More Vulnerable to Potential Adverse Effects of Conflicts of Interest in DC Plans such as 401(k) Plans

While our study focused on DB plans, conflicts of interest can affect DC plans. Because the risk of investment is largely borne by the individual participant in DC plans, participants are vulnerable to any decision, including those involving conflicts of interest which could result in higher fees that can lower investment returns for participants. For example, research by one industry group showed that 36 percent of responding sponsors either did not know the fees being charged to participants or mistakenly thought no fees were charged at all. A registered investment advisor (RIA) told us that if a "free" 401(k) plan has been selected by the sponsor, it was unlikely that sponsor used an RIA to examine the underlying fee structure, and, as a result, a sponsor may select an arrangement that reduces an employer's fees at the expense of the higher embedded fees paid by participants, which we were told may involve a fiduciary breach under certain circumstances.

In prior work,[11] we also found that some plan sponsors do not understand their service providers' revenue sharing arrangements or may be unaware of potential conflicts of interest. For example, a service provider that assists a plan sponsor in selecting investment options for the plan may also be receiving compensation from mutual fund companies for recommending their funds. The service provider may not disclose this business arrangement to the plan sponsor, and as a result, participants may have more limited investment options and pay higher fees for these options than they otherwise would. These limitations and higher fees could translate into lower rates of return on participants' accounts and ultimately could result in reduced retirement income.

Given the multiplicity of parties involved in today's 401(k) arena, many opportunities exist for business arrangements to go undisclosed. Problems may occur when pension consultants or other companies providing services to a plan also receive compensation from other service providers. Without disclosing these arrangements, service providers may be steering plan sponsors toward investment products or services that may not be in the best interest of participants. In addition, plan sponsors, being unaware, are often unable to report information about these arrangements to Labor on Form 5500 Schedule C.

SEC also identified certain undisclosed arrangements or conflicts of interest in the business practices of pension consultants in its study. Plan sponsors pay pension consultants to give them advice on matters such as selecting investment options for the plan and monitoring their performance and selecting other service providers, such as custodians, administrators, and broker-dealers.[12] In its report, SEC highlighted concerns that these arrangements may provide incentives for pension consultants to recommend certain mutual funds to a 40 1(k) plan sponsor and create conflicts of interest that are not adequately disclosed to plan sponsors. Plan sponsors may not be aware of these arrangements and thus could select mutual funds recommended by the pension consultant over lower-cost alternatives. As a result, participants may again have more limited investment options and may pay higher fees for these options than they otherwise would.

Finally, significant differences in ways that advisers and other providers are compensated may have important implications for the sponsor's oversight, including identifying potential conflicts of interest. Experts noted that a sponsor may opt for what appears to be a "free" 401(k) plan (with no record keeping fees for the employer) without understanding that the providers' compensation may be passed on to participants by embedding fees in the plan's investment options. In other cases, specific fees that are considered to be "hidden" may mask the existence of a conflict of interest. Hidden fees are usually related to business arrangements where one service provider to a 401(k) plan pays a third-party provider for services, such as record keeping, but does not disclose this compensation to the plan sponsor. For example, a mutual fund normally provides record-keeping services for its retail investors, i.e., those who invest outside of a 401(k) plan. The same mutual fund, when associated with a plan, might compensate the plan's record keeper for performing the services that it would otherwise perform, such as maintaining individual participants' account records and consolidating their requests to buy or sell.[13]

Without disclosing these business arrangements, service providers may be steering plan sponsors toward investment products or services that may not be in the best interest of participants. In addition, plan sponsors may not know what entity is receiving the compensation and whether or not the compensation fairly represents the value of the service being rendered. If a plan sponsor does not know that a third party is receiving these fees, they cannot monitor them, evaluate the compensation in view of services rendered, and take action as needed to protect the interest of plan participants.

Labor Has Proposed Regulations to Address Conflicts of Interest Issues but the Regulations Have Not Been Finalized

Labor has proposed regulations to improve the information disclosed to plan fiduciaries about the various business arrangements among service providers.[14] Labor's proposal would provide (in order to qualify for the contracting or reasonable arrangements exemption to ERISA's prohibited transactions provisions) that any contract or arrangement to provide services to an employee benefit plan would have to require the service provider to disclose the compensation it will receive, directly or indirectly, and any conflicts of interest that may arise in connection with its services to the plan.[15] Labor believes that in order to satisfy their ERISA obligations, plan fiduciaries need information on all compensation to be received by the service provider and any conflicts of interest that may adversely affect the service provider's performance under the contract or arrangement.

Labor's proposal would also require that service providers specify whether they will provide services to the plan as a fiduciary, either as a fiduciary under ERISA or as a fiduciary under the Investment Advisers Act of 1940.[16] Service providers would have to disclose any financial or other interest in transactions involving the plan in connection with the contract or arrangement. The proposal also defines a reasonable contract or arrangement as one that would require the service provider to disclose its relationships with other parties that may give rise to conflicts of interest.[17] If the relationship between the service provider and this third party is one that a reasonable plan fiduciary would consider to be significant in its evaluation of whether an actual or potential conflict of interest exists, then the service provider would have to disclose the relationship.

Finally, Labor recognizes that service providers may have policies or procedures in place to manage real or potential conflicts of interest. For example, a fiduciary service provider may have procedures for offsetting fees received from third parties (through revenue sharing or other indirect payment arrangements) against the amount that it otherwise would charge a plan client. Accordingly, the proposed regulation would provide that a reasonable contract or arrangement would require service providers to state whether or not any such policies or procedures exist and, if so, to provide an explanation of these policies or procedures and how they address conflicts of interest. Labor views this requirement as an opportunity for service providers to educate plan fiduciaries about how they address potential conflicts of interest.

At this time, Labor's proposed regulations are awaiting review and approval by the new Secretary of Labor. We are currently conducting a review of Labor's revisions to the Form 5500 Schedule C, which could provide some information to Labor about previously undisclosed business arrangements.

CONCLUDING OBSERVATIONS

Conflicts of interest can adversely affect both DB and DC plan designs, with the primary difference being in who bears the cost of their potentially adverse effects on their rate of return. The threat posed to participants in account based retirement plans like 401(k)s, now the primary plan design in the United States, is quite direct. Since workers largely bear the risk of investment under this plan design, any factor, any decision that reduces the account's rate of return can have potentially irreversible consequences for the participant's retirement income, depending on her age and personal circumstances.

The recent national and worldwide economic turmoil has amplified the enormous complexity risk workers face with respect to their retirement security. In this uncertain environment, fiduciaries of all plan types must utilize a variety of service providers to help themselves and plan participants assess choices. While conflicts of interest are not necessarily inherent in engaging service providers, the likelihood that conflicts of interest exist has significantly increased over the years given the complexity and nature of business arrangements among investment advisers, plan consultants, and others. To the extent that financially harmful conflicts of interest exist, they pose a potential threat to the investment confidence of sponsors and participants and to the retirement security of employees.

As we have noted in past reports, updating regulations to better reflect the potential impact of undisclosed business arrangements among 401(k) service providers will help Labor provide more effective oversight of 401(k) plans and likely result in reduced fees for 401(k) plan participants. Without such changes, Labor will continue to lack comprehensive information on all fees being charged directly or indirectly to 401(k) plans and 401(k) plan participants' returns are likely to be potentially affected by some conflicts of interest.

Mr. Chairman, this completes my prepared statement. I would be happy to respond to any questions you or other members of the subcommittee may have at this time.

End Notes

[1] *Defined Benefit Pensions: Conflicts of Interest Involving High Risk or Terminated Plans Pose Enforcement Challenges*, GAO-07-703 (Washington, D.C.: June 28, 2007); *Private Pensions: Changes Needed to Provide 401(k) Plan Participants and the Department of Labor Better Information on Fees* GAO-07-21, (Washington, D.C.: November 16, 2006); and *Private Pensions: Fulfilling Fiduciary Obligations Can Present Challenges for 401(k) Plan Sponsors*, GAO-08-774 (Washington, D.C.: July 16, 2008).

[2] GAO, *Financial Regulation: Industry Changes Prompt Need to Reconsider U.S. Regulatory Structure*, GAO-05-61 (Washington, D.C.: Oct. 6, 2004).

[3] For consultant usage information, see Thomson Nelson, *Annual Report of Pension Fund Consultants* 2006 (New York, N.Y.: 2006).

[4] For information on SEC's pension consultant examination, see SEC, Speech by SEC Staff: Conflicts of Interest in Pension Consulting, (Washington, D.C.: Dec. 5, 2005), http://www.sec.gov/news/speech (accessed 2007).

[5] See U.S. Securities and Exchange Commission, Office of Compliance Inspections and Examinations, *Staff Report Concerning Examination of Select Pension Consultants* (Washington, D.C.: May 16, 2005.) The report's findings were based on a 2002 to 2003 examination of 24 pension consultants. See http://www.sec.gov/news/speech (accessed 2007).

[6] Pensions and Investments periodical's list of Top 25 consultants ranked by U.S. institutional, tax exempt assets, 2006. 9 of the 13 consultants made the list of Top 25 consultants.

[7] We constructed this analysis so that we looked at plan sponsors rather than plans. For example, PBGC's 25 largest trusteed sponsors since fiscal year 2000 had a total of 67 plans and comprised 70 percent of the total claims against the agency between 1975 and 2006.

[8] Our analysis is based on a data set we constructed by matching SEC consultant data with financial information compiled from the Form 5500 database on 1,111 plans over 5 years. Of those, 983 were associated with the 13 consultants identified by the SEC as having provided services to DB plans that had serious disclosure problems, while 39 were associated with 11 consultants that either were in compliance or had minor inadequacies with disclosure and another 89 that were associated with both types of consultants. A complete discussion of our econometric approach, including model specification, variables used, data sources, estimation techniques, and limitations, is provided in appendix II in GAO-07-703.

[9] These include an ordinary least squares specification with time-fixed effects and various random-effect and fixed-effect model specifications. "Fixed-effects" helps to control for the potentially large number of unmeasured forces that can explain the difference in plan returns. See appendix II in GAO-07-703.

[10] PBGC also faces long term financial challenges. GAO, *Pension Benefit Guaranty Corporation: Long-Term Financing Risks to Single-Employer Insurance Program Highlight Need for Comprehensive Reform*, GAO-04-150T (Washington, D.C.: Oct. 14, 2003), GAO, *Defined Benefit Pensions: Plan Freezes Affect Millions of Participants and May Pose Retirement Income Challenges*, GAO-08-817 (Washington, D.C.: July 2008).

[11] GAO, Private Pensions: Fulfilling Fiduciary Obligations Can Present Challenges for 40 1(k) Plan Sponsors, GAO-08-774, (Washington, D.C. July 2008).

[12] Office of Compliance Inspections and Examinations, Staff Report Concerning Examinations of Select Pension Consultants (U.S. Securities and Exchange Commission: May 16, 2005)

[13] These fees are known as subtransfer agent fees.

[14] 72 Fed. Reg. 70,988-71,005 (Dec. 13, 2007).

[15] 29 U.S.C. §§ 1001-1461. ERISA is the primary federal law governing the sponsorship and operation of private sector employee pension plans, including DB plans. Among various statutory exemptions to ERISA's prohibited transactions is one for contracting or making reasonable arrangements for services necessary for the operation of the plan if no more than reasonable compensation is paid for those services. 29 U.S.C. § 1108(b)(2).

[16] 15 U.S.C. §§ 80b-1 – 80b-21. SEC regulates certain money managers and pension consultants under the Investment Advisers Act of 1940 (Advisers Act), which requires those firms meeting certain criteria to register with the commission as investment advisers. Regulations under the act permit pension consultants to plans having an aggregate value of at least $50,000,000 to register with SEC. 17 C.F.R. § 275.203A-2(b) (2008). According to SEC, investment advisers have a fiduciary obligation under the Advisers Act to provide disinterested advice and disclose any material conflicts of interest to their clients. When an adviser fails to disclose information regarding material conflicts of interest, clients are unable to make informed decisions about entering into or continuing the advisory relationship.

[17] Specifically, service providers would be obligated to describe any material financial, referral, or other relationship it has with various parties (such as investment professionals, other service providers, or clients) that creates or may create a conflict of interest for the service provider in performing services pursuant to the contract or arrangement put cite in. 72 Fed. Reg. 71,005.

In: Pensions: Backgrounds, Trends and Issues
Editor: Henry J. Mullen

ISBN: 978-1-60876-840-0

Chapter 5

FULFILLING FIDUCIARY OBLIGATIONS CAN PRESENT CHALLENGES FOR 401(K) PLAN SPONSORS

United States Government Accountability Office

WHY GAO DID THIS STUDY

American workers increasingly rely on 401(k) plans for their retirement security, and sponsors of 401(k) plans—typically employers—have critical obligations under the Employee Retirement Income Security Act of 1974 (ERISA). When acting as fiduciaries, they must act prudently and solely in the interest of plan participants and beneficiaries. The Department of Labor (Labor) is responsible for protecting private pension plan participants and beneficiaries by enforcing ERISA. GAO examined: (1) common 401(k) plan features, which typically have important fiduciary implications, and factors affecting these decisions; (2) challenges sponsors face in fulfilling their fiduciary obligations when overseeing plan operations; and (3) actions Labor takes to ensure that sponsors fulfill their fiduciary obligations, and the progress Labor has made on its regulatory initiatives. To address these objectives, GAO administered a survey asking sponsors how they select plan features and oversee operations, reviewed industry research, conducted interviews, and reviewed related documents.

WHAT GAO RECOMMENDS

GAO is not making any additional recommendations in this report, but GAO has previously suggested that Congress consider changes to ERISA addressing fiduciary roles.

To view the full product, including the scope and methodology, click on GAO-08-774. To view the survey results, click on GAO-08-870SP. For more information, contact Barbara Bovbjerg at (202) 512-7215 or bovbjergb@gao.gov.

What GAO Found

Plan sponsors commonly select certain noninvestment and investment features, and their decisions about which investment features to select generally have important fiduciary implications. According to industry research, most 40 1(k) plans offer a number of common features, such as employer contributions and loans for employees. Some of these decisions seldom involve fiduciary obligations set by ERISA because they are mainly business decisions related to establishing the plan. However, a sponsor's decisions about investment features, like the menu of investment options, entail important fiduciary obligations under ERISA. ERISA and its regulations stipulate certain requirements for these investment decisions, like offering diversified funds and prudently selecting and monitoring investment options. Various other factors also affect a sponsor's menu decisions, including the size of the plan and the role of external advisers and other providers.

Plan sponsors face challenges in fulfilling their obligations when fiduciary roles are not clearly defined or when sponsors lack important information about arrangements between service providers. Fiduciary roles that are not clearly defined can lead to gaps in plan oversight. For example, several industry professionals noted situations when sponsors assumed they had delegated fiduciary investment advice for the selection and monitoring of investment funds to a service provider, but the service provider did not acknowledge that fiduciary role. Sponsors also have fiduciary obligations when selecting and monitoring one or more service providers. To fulfill these obligations, Labor's guidance indicates that sponsors should obtain information about service providers' compensation arrangements and potential conflicts of interest that could affect the service provider's performance. Labor and various industry practitioners have proposed new ways to improve fiduciary oversight that may address some of the challenges of unclear fiduciary roles and providers' arrangements.

Labor takes various actions to monitor sponsors' fiduciary oversight of 401(k) plans and has made some progress on its regulatory initiatives. Labor's actions include investigating reports of questionable 401(k) plan practices, collecting information from plan sponsors, and conducting outreach to educate plan sponsors about their responsibilities. Labor is also proceeding with several initiatives to improve disclosures to participants, plan sponsors, government agencies and the public. For example, Labor recently published a proposed rule on the information that service providers must disclose to plan sponsors but is trying to resolve several questions before issuing a final rule. In addition, certain matters that GAO has asked Congress to consider would help Labor in its efforts to improve sponsors' fiduciary oversight. We previously suggested that Congress amend ERISA to (1) explicitly require 401(k) service providers to disclose to plan sponsors the compensation they receive from other service providers and (2) give Labor authority to recover plan losses against certain types of service providers even if they are not currently considered fiduciaries under ERISA.

Abbreviations

CAP	Consultant/Adviser Project
EBSA	Employee Benefits Security Administration
ERISA	Employee Retirement Income Security Act of 1974

IPS	investment policy statement
Labor	Department of Labor
OPA	Office of Participant Assistance
Plansponsor	*Plansponsor Magazine*
PSCA	Profit Sharing/401(k) Council of America
RFI	request for information
RIA	Registered Investment Adviser
VFCP	Voluntary Fiduciary Correction Program

July 16, 2008

The Honorable George Miller
Chairman
Committee on Education and Labor
House of Representatives

Dear Mr. Chairman:

Over the past two decades, American workers have become increasingly reliant on 401(k) plans for their retirement security. These employer- sponsored pension plans typically allow workers to divert a portion of their pretax income, often with employer contributions, into an investment account that can grow tax free until withdrawn in retirement. According to the Department of Labor (Labor), in 2005, there were about 436,000 401(k) plans that held about $2.4 trillion in assets for the retirement savings of more than 54 million plan participants—more than any other type of employer-sponsored pension plan in the United States. To administer these plans, the sponsor—typically the employer offering the 401(k) plan—selects plan features and other characteristics, including the types of investment options offered to participants, and monitors the performance of one or more service providers, such as investment advisers and record keepers. The Employee Retirement Income Security Act of 1974 (ERISA) imposes significant fiduciary obligations on plan sponsors and other plan fiduciaries, requiring them to act prudently and in the interests of the plan's participants and beneficiaries.[1] Labor is responsible for ensuring that plan sponsors and other plan fiduciaries fulfill these obligations.

In two recent reports, we asked Congress to consider amending ERISA to expand Labor's statutory authority over plan service providers and help ensure that sponsors are properly overseeing plan services.[2] While Congress continues to consider new legislation, Labor has also tried to address some of these underlying issues through regulatory initiatives. As Congress considers changes to the law that governs how these plans are designed, managed, and overseen, GAO was asked to identify the following:

- common 401(k) plan features, those that typically have important fiduciary implications, and what factors affect these decisions;
- challenges sponsors face in fulfilling their fiduciary obligations when overseeing plan operations; and
- actions Labor takes to ensure that sponsors fulfill their fiduciary obligations, and the progress Labor has made on its regulatory initiatives.

To determine common plan features and which decisions typically have fiduciary implications and related factors, and the challenges sponsors face in fulfilling their fiduciary obligations, we collected and analyzed the results of published industry research. We also collected information on sponsor practices from a range of plan sponsors, service providers, industry associations, and other industry professionals—including fiduciary advisers—through interviews and reviews of documents, such as materials on fiduciary obligations given by service providers to sponsors. In addition, we administered a survey in coordination with *Plansponsor Magazine (Plansponsor*) asking sponsors how they select plan features and oversee plan operations. The survey and a more complete tabulation of the results can be viewed at GAO-08-870SP. The survey respondents were members of *Plansponsor's* subscription list, and their responses cannot be considered representative of the overall population of 401(k) plan sponsors. We received a total of 448 completed survey responses after distributing the survey to a population of about 22,000. Because of the methodological limitations of this survey, information from this survey is anecdotal and represents only the views of the 448 survey respondents. To determine the actions that Labor takes to ensure that sponsors fulfill their fiduciary obligations, we interviewed Labor officials and reviewed Labor's legal and regulatory authority and its procedures for assuring that plans are meeting the overall requirements. See appendix I for more details regarding our scope and methodology. We conducted our review from January 2007 through June 2008 in accordance with generally accepted government auditing standards.

RESULTS IN BRIEF

Plan sponsors determine a number of common noninvestment plan features, but they also make decisions about investment features with important fiduciary implications. Industry research indicates that most 401(k) plans offer a number of common features, including an employer contribution, a loan program, eligibility of employees, and vesting of benefits. Some selections are primarily business decisions, similar to whether or not to establish the plan, that seldom involve fiduciary obligations. About one-half of sponsors responding to our survey said that a committee of the sponsor and about one-half said that employer management was the primary decision maker on various noninvestment features, but this information cannot be considered representative of all 401(k) plan sponsors.[3] However, when a sponsor makes decisions about investment features—like selecting the menu of investment options—it acts as a fiduciary and is subject to fiduciary obligations under ERISA, including the duties to act prudently and solely in the interest of participants and beneficiaries. In our survey, most responding sponsors said that a committee of the sponsor was the primary decision maker for areas like the investment menu or investment goals. While sponsors that act as a fiduciary for investment functions must satisfy their fiduciary obligations, they have considerable latitude in selecting investment options, such as the number and types of options. Besides ERISA and its regulations, various other factors affect a sponsor's decision regarding the selection of the investment menu, including the size of the plan and the role of external advisers and providers. For example, many sponsors responding to our survey used a third-party investment adviser.

Plan sponsors face challenges in fulfilling their obligations when fiduciary roles are not clearly defined or when sponsors lack important information about arrangements between service providers. Sponsors often hire outside professionals to manage some or all of a 40 1(k) plan's day-to-day operations. Some of these service providers provide investment advice for a fee, or exercise sufficient control or discretion over the plan or its assets, thereby becoming fiduciaries under ERISA. However, fiduciary roles that are not clearly defined between the sponsor and other plan fiduciaries can lead to gaps in plan oversight. For example, several industry professionals noted situations when sponsors assumed they had delegated fiduciary investment advice for the selection and monitoring of investment funds to a service provider, but the service provider did not acknowledge that fiduciary role. Sponsors also have fiduciary obligations when they select and monitor one or multiple service providers. To fulfill these obligations, Labor's guidance indicates that sponsors should obtain information about service providers' compensation arrangements and potential conflicts of interest that could affect the service provider's performance. To improve fiduciary oversight in these areas, Labor has proposed a rule to require pension plan service contracts to disclose additional information, including the extent to which service providers will become fiduciaries for the functions they will perform.[4] If finalized, compliance with this rule could eliminate some of the confusion surrounding the sharing of fiduciary duties between sponsors and their service providers and help sponsors provide better oversight of plan services.

Labor takes various actions to monitor sponsors' fiduciary oversight of 401(k) plans and has made some progress on its regulatory initiatives. Labor investigates reports of questionable 401(k) plan practices, collects information from plan sponsors, and conducts outreach to educate plan sponsors about their responsibilities. Labor is also pursuing several regulatory initiatives to improve disclosures provided to participants, plan sponsors and fiduciaries, government agencies and the public. Labor has recently issued proposed regulations to specify the information that service providers must disclose to plan sponsors. However, Labor is in the process of resolving several questions before it can issue final regulations, such as the extent to which providers within a bundled arrangement—a package of plan services—would be bound by the disclosure requirements of the regulations. Some of the matters that GAO has asked Congress to consider, if addressed, would also help Labor in its efforts to improve sponsors' fiduciary oversight. For example, we previously suggested that Congress amend ERISA to explicitly require 401(k) service providers to disclose to plan sponsors the compensation they receive from other service providers.[5] Furthermore, we found that undisclosed business arrangements or conflicts of interest may have resulted in financial harm to some plans.[6] Given this risk, we asked that Congress consider amending ERISA to give Labor greater authority to recover plan losses against certain types of service providers even if they are not currently considered fiduciaries under ERISA. These changes would provide Labor with greater statutory authority over plan service providers and help ensure that sponsors are properly overseeing plan services.

BACKGROUND

Roughly half of all workers participate in an employer-sponsored retirement, or pension, plan. Private sector pension plans are classified as either defined benefit or defined contribution plans. Defined benefit plans promise to provide, generally, a fixed level of monthly retirement income that is based on salary, years of service, and age at retirement, regardless of how the plan's investments perform. In contrast, benefits from defined contribution plans are based on the contributions to and the performance of the investments in individual accounts, which may fluctuate in value. These accounts are tax-advantaged in that contributions are typically excluded from current income, and earnings on balances grow tax-deferred until they are withdrawn.[7] One type of defined contribution, or individual account, plan is the 401(k) plan.

Fiduciary Obligations under ERISA

In accordance with ERISA and related Labor regulations and guidance, plan sponsors and other fiduciaries must exercise an appropriate level of care and diligence given the scope of the plan and act for the exclusive benefit of plan participants and beneficiaries, rather than for their own or another party's gain. Responsibilities of fiduciaries include:

- selecting and monitoring any service providers to the plan;
- reporting plan information to the government and to participants;
- adhering to the plan documents, including any investment policy statement;
- identifying parties-in-interest to the plan and taking steps to monitor transactions with them;
- selecting and monitoring investment options the plan will offer and diversifying plan investments; and
- ensuring that the services provided to their plan are necessary and that the cost of those services is reasonable.

ERISA allows plan sponsors to hire companies that will provide services necessary to operate their 401(k) plan if certain conditions are met. In general, ERISA prohibits parties-in-interest—such as service providers, plan fiduciaries, the employer, the union, owners, officers, and relatives of parties-in-interest—from doing business with the plan, but provides various exemptions to these prohibited transactions.[8] Some of the exemptions provide for dealings with banks, insurance companies, and other financial institutions essential to the ongoing operations of the plan. The Internal Revenue Code sets forth parallel prohibited transaction provisions with respect to "disqualified persons," such as service providers, and provides a parallel conditional exemption for the provision of services. The exemption requires that: (1) the contract or arrangement must be reasonable, (2) the services must be necessary to operate the plan, and (3) the compensation can not exceed what is reasonable for the services provided.[9] Some other prohibited transactions relate solely to fiduciaries using plan assets in their own interest or acting on both sides of a transaction involving a plan.

Fiduciaries cannot receive money or any other consideration for their personal account from any party doing business with the plan related to that business.

In the course of providing services, a service provider may become a fiduciary by reason of providing investment advice for a fee, or exercising sufficient control over, or discretion with respect to, the administration or assets of the plan.[10] For example, holding plan assets in trust to assure that they are used solely to benefit the participants and their beneficiaries would make the trustee a fiduciary. An outside professional that provides advice for a fee to plan sponsors about the selection of funds to be included in the menu of options made available to participants would also be a fiduciary. Providers of many other necessary services—such as keeping the record of participants' individual accounts and providing the investment funds being made available to plan participants—are typically not fiduciaries.

The Department of Labor's Role

Labor's Employee Benefits Security Administration (EBSA) is the primary agency responsible for protecting private pension plan participants and beneficiaries from the misuse or theft of their pension assets by enforcing ERISA, which defines and sets certain standards for employee benefit plans sponsored by private sector employers. EBSA oversees 401(k) plans because they are considered employee benefit plans under ERISA. Enacted before the 401(k) provision was added to the Internal Revenue Code, ERISA establishes the responsibilities of employee benefit plan decision makers.

EBSA conducts civil and criminal investigations to determine whether the provisions of ERISA or other federal laws related to employee benefit plans have been violated. EBSA regularly works in coordination with other federal and state enforcement agencies, including Labor's Office of the Inspector General, the Pension Benefit Guaranty Corporation, the Internal Revenue Service, the Department of Justice (including the Federal Bureau of Investigation), the Securities and Exchange Commission, the federal banking agencies, state insurance commissioners, and state attorneys general.

In addition to its investigations, Benefits Advisors in the field and in EBSA's Office of Participant Assistance (OPA), help workers get the information they need to protect their benefit rights and obtain benefits that have been improperly denied. In fiscal year 2007, Benefits Advisors recovered over $96 million on behalf of participants and beneficiaries through informal resolution of participant complaints. Benefits Advisors also refer cases for investigation. There were 611 enforcement cases closed in fiscal year 2007 whose original source was a Benefit Advisor referral. Of these, 451 were 401(k) plan investigations, including 389 that were closed with monetary results of over $46 million.[11]

EBSA's policy is to resolve 401(k) participant complaints involving late or unremitted employee contributions at the earliest possible opportunity. Benefits Advisors are provided with guidance on how to handle these 401(k) contribution-related complaints. While Benefits Advisors do not have investigative authority and cannot make formal demands on employers or plan sponsors, they are authorized to request that the employer, plan sponsor, or other appropriate third-party official provide documents or information related to a participant's complaint on an individual or plan-wide basis. EBSA's Benefits Advisors may also attempt to resolve the complaints and correct any violations on a plan-wide basis through informal dispute resolution. If the complaint involves unremitted or untimely employee contributions, Benefits Advisors can request information from the plan sponsor and, after review, advise the plan on the amount of contributions due. In fiscal year 2007, $5.8 million in pension benefits were restored to plans by Benefits Advisors as a result of this procedure.

EBSA also has regional initiatives focused on fiduciary oversight. Several of them have produced results related to 401(k) fiduciary issues. Even with an initiative focused on settlor fees,[12] one regional office still obtained results related to fiduciary issues under the project. According to an EBSA official, 401(k) plans have obtained monetary results related to fiduciary issues in three cases under the project, totaling more than $8 million.[13]

Labor's ERISA Advisory Council, created by ERISA to provide advice to the U.S. Secretary of Labor, is another resource for Labor. For example, in 2007, this council formed the Working Group on Fiduciary Responsibilities and Revenue Sharing Practices to study numerous issues regarding fiduciary responsibilities arising from the enactment of the Pension Protection Act of 2006[14] and to address issues relative to the practice of revenue sharing, a now-common practice used to offset plan expenses with respect to defined contribution 401(k) plans. The working group's report concluded that there is a role for Labor to take the lead in formally defining 401(k) terms, such as "revenue sharing," and that Labor should compile appropriate terminology in connection with that definition. According to the report, the provision of concise definitions would be a considerable step in reducing the confusion about the flows of revenues, fees, and costs, and could only benefit the plan sponsors, fiduciaries, and service providers in fulfilling their role to participants.

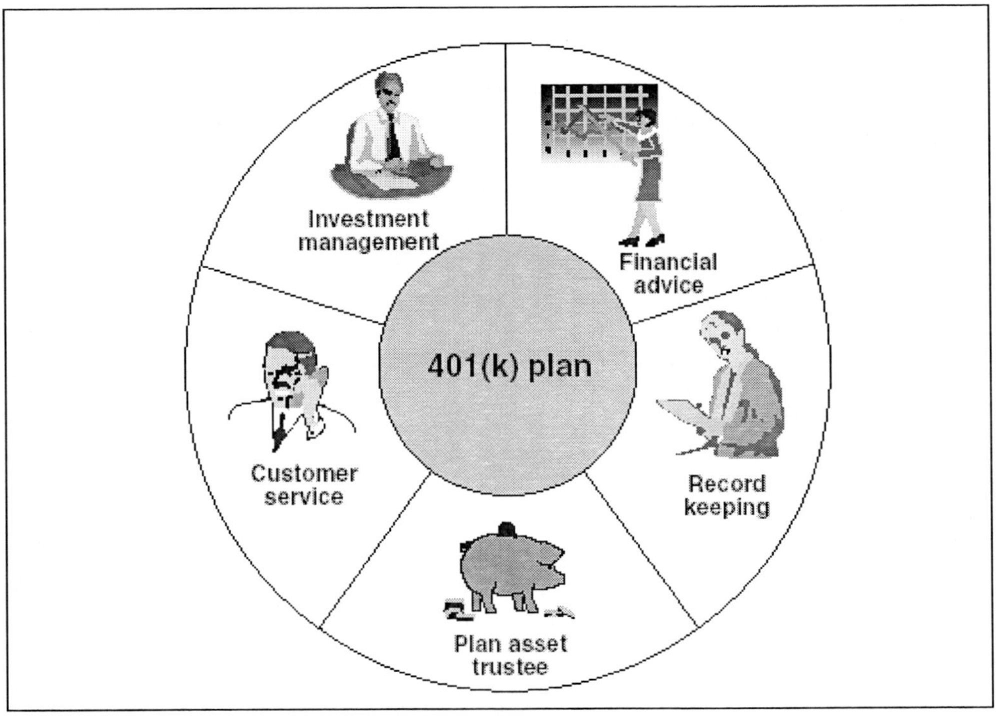

Sources: GAO and Art Explosion (clip art).

Figure 1. Services That 401(k) Plan Sponsors May Hire Various Outside Companies to Provide

Plan Services

Plan sponsors of 401(k) plans often hire various outside companies to provide a number of services necessary to operate a 401(k) plan. As shown in figure 1, these services can include investment management (e.g., selecting and managing the securities included in a bank collective trust fund); consulting and providing financial advice (e.g., selecting vendors for investment options or other services); record keeping (e.g., tracking individual account contributions); custodial or trustee services for plan assets (e.g., holding the plan assets in a bank); and telephone or Web-based customer services for participants.

The delivery structure for providing plan services can vary. Generally, there are two structures: "bundled" (the sponsor hires one company that provides the full range of services directly or through subcontracts) and "unbundled" (the sponsor uses a combination of service providers), as shown in Figure 2.

In a bundled arrangement, a sponsor might delegate the oversight for the selection and monitoring of plan services, except for the selection and monitoring of the bundled provider itself. In contrast, in an unbundled arrangement, the sponsor might retain oversight of the selection and monitoring for some or all other service providers.

SPONSORS DETERMINE A NUMBER OF COMMON PLAN FEATURES, AND THEIR DECISIONS ABOUT INVESTMENT FEATURES HAVE IMPORTANT FIDUCIARY IMPLICATIONS

Although, when determining a number of common, noninvestment features and other plan characteristics, plan sponsors are frequently acting as settlors,[15] their decisions about investment features have important fiduciary implications. Industry research finds that most 401(k) plans offer a number of common noninvestment features such as employer contributions and loan programs. For example, industry research shows that at least 94 percent of sponsors offered some type of employer contribution.[16] Like whether or not to establish a plan, these determinations are primarily business decisions that seldom involve fiduciary duties. However, when a sponsor makes decisions about investment features—like selecting the menu of investment options—it acts as a fiduciary and is subject to fiduciary obligations under ERISA. While sponsors must act prudently and solely in the interest of participants and beneficiaries when acting as a fiduciary for investment functions, they have considerable latitude in selecting fund options, such as the number and types of options. Besides ERISA and its regulations, various other factors affect a sponsor when it makes investment decisions regarding the selection of the investment menu, including the size of the plan and the role of external advisers and providers.

Plan Sponsors Determine Some Common Plan Features to Establish the Plan

Some common plan features and other characteristics include an employer contribution, a loan program, eligibility of employees, and vesting of benefits. While an employer contribution and a loan program are optional, a 401(k) plan is required to have eligibility and vesting rules.

- An employer contribution can take different forms, such as a matching contribution and/or nonmatching contribution made regardless of participant contributions. In industry research we reviewed, at least 94 percent of sponsors indicated that they offer some type of employer contribution, while 6 percent or fewer do not offer such contributions.[17] Research by the Bureau of Labor Statistics and industry groups shows the different methods to determine any employer contribution, such as formulas based on participant contributions, years of service, company profits, or other means.[18]
- A loan program enables participants to take one or more loans from the contributions in their account. In industry research we reviewed, at least 84 percent of sponsors include a loan program.[19]
- Eligibility of employees refers to the requirements for employees to become eligible to participate in the plan, such as an age or service requirement. Sponsors can choose less restrictive requirements for eligibility than required by law. For example, in industry research GAO reviewed, about half of respondents to industry research offer immediate eligibility with no age or service requirements.[20]
- Vesting of benefits refers to the length of time before a plan participant has a nonforfeitable right to an accrued benefit. For 401(k) plans, participant contributions are required to be vested immediately, but employer contributions may be vested over time according to plan terms. As with employee eligibility, the law sets the maximum amounts of time before an employee is vested, but sponsors can decide on less restrictive vesting provisions. For example, in industry research GAO reviewed, about 40 percent of respondents have immediate vesting in employer matching contributions.[21]

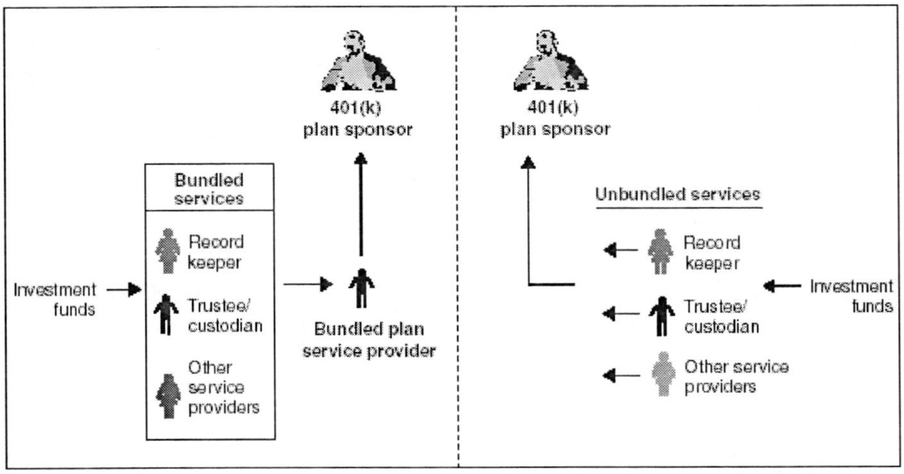

Sources: GAO analysis of information from industry practitioners and Art Explosion (clip art).

Note: This figure depicts a simplified example of one possible arrangement and is not intended to depict all arrangements.

Figure 2. Flow of Bundled and Unbundled Plan Services.

When making decisions about some noninvestment plan features, sponsors act as settlors rather than fiduciaries. According to our survey, 186 of 441 sponsors said the sponsor's committee was the primary decision maker for various noninvestment, settlor decisions, while 205 sponsors said that company management was.[22] Sponsors make many settlor function decisions, such as those related to establishing, amending, or terminating a plan. They are considered business decisions and include the decision to offer a particular type of plan, the levels of benefits to provide, and the termination of the plan. The fiduciary obligations under ERISA, including the overarching duties to act prudently and solely in participants' interest, are seldom involved in many of these decisions.[23]

Sponsors' Decisions about Investment Features Have Important Fiduciary Implications

When making decisions about investment features, ERISA's fiduciary duties apply. As a result, when plan sponsors acting as a fiduciary for investment functions make such decisions, they must offer prudent, diversified choices for participants to fulfill the duties of acting prudently and diversifying plan investments. Several pension professionals told us, in fact, that the main plan feature with important fiduciary implications is the investment menu.[24] When developing that menu, sponsors must act for the sole benefit of participants and beneficiaries, rather than that of their own or another party. According to our survey, 349 of 440 responding sponsors said that the sponsor committee or management was the primary decision maker for selecting the menu of investment options. Industry research shows that the median number of options was in the range of 11 to 15, with as many as 24 percent of responding plans offering 20 or more funds.[25]

When acting as fiduciaries for investment functions, sponsors have considerable latitude in selecting fund options, including the number and types of funds, from which participants choose. Table 1 shows funds available for participant contributions, according to research from one industry group. These funds involve different categories of investments.

ERISA's fiduciary obligations require that fees paid by the plan are reasonable and that services provided to the plan are necessary. Thus, sponsors must consider the fees and other characteristics of the funds, including potential returns and risk. For example, index funds are passively managed funds with lower management fees than actively managed funds, for which the investment provider pursues particular investments in an attempt to obtain higher than average returns. Similarly, sponsors must prudently select the service providers to the plan, such as the providers of record keeping services and service providers that make investment options available to the plan. In our survey, the primary decision maker for selecting service providers for investment options was the sponsor committee for 283 of 445 respondents and sponsor management for 108 respondents. For selecting providers of record keeping, the primary decision maker was the sponsor committee for 256 of 445 respondents and sponsor management for 135 respondents. As with selecting funds, fees are one of many issues—such as providers' qualifications and quality of services—to consider when selecting providers.

Table 1. Investment Funds Available for Participant Contributions, Expressed as a Percentage of Respondents

Fund type	Plan size, by number of participants					
	1-49	50-199	200-999	1,000-4,999	5,000+	All plans
Balanced stock/bond fund	52.0	62.8	66.1	75.3	65.0	64.8
Bond-actively managed, domestic	50.0	62.0	58.8	69.8	60.2	60.5
Bond-indexed, domestic	25.3	30.2	26.1	28.0	43.9	30.0
Cash equivalents (CD/money market)	53.3	48.8	41.8	39.6	48.8	45.9
Company stock	4.7	0.8	10.3	28.6	56.9	19.6
Equity-actively managed, domestic	70.7	78.3	76.4	87.4	79.7	78.8
Equity-actively managed, international	62.0	76.7	74.5	85.2	79.7	75.8
Equity-indexed, domestic	53.3	69.8	72.1	78.0	87.0	71.8
Equity-indexed, international	18.7	14.0	19.4	14.3	35.8	19.8
Real estate fund	29.3	25.6	15.8	14.8	10.6	19.1
Other sector fund	12.7	11.6	10.9	7.7	4.1	9.5
Self-directed (brokerage window)[a]	12.0	9.3	12.1	14.8	20.3	13.6
Self-directed (mutual fund window)[a]	8.0	5.4	4.8	3.8	6.5	5.6
Stable value fund	34.0	55.8	58.8	69.2	68.3	57.4
Target retirement date	22.0	24.8	37.0	41.8	39.0	33.4
Other lifestyle fund(s)	20.7	24.8	25.5	22.0	26.0	23.6
Other	18.0	11.6	10.3	9.3	11.4	12.0

[a] self-directed window allows participants to invest in individual stocks or mutual funds.
Source: Profit Sharing/401(k) Council of America.

ERISA's fiduciary duties also apply to a sponsor including a default option for participants not making an investment choice. These duties include prudently selecting and monitoring the option based on an objective, thorough, and analytical process that involves careful consideration of the quality of competing providers and investment products, as appropriate. A recent Labor regulation provides certain fiduciary relief when participants' contributions are invested in qualified default investment alternatives that include lifecycle funds, balanced funds, or managed accounts.[26] Labor decided on these alternatives, which combine stocks and fixed income securities like bonds, based on considerations that included diversification and adequacy of savings for retirement. Thus, if participants do not provide instructions on how to invest their contributions, sponsors may place contributions into a default investment. For example, participants may not provide investment instructions when automatically enrolled in a plan by their sponsor.

Once the investment menu is selected, sponsors must monitor the fund options as part of their fiduciary obligations. Several pension professionals noted that monitoring funds may involve quantitative criteria that include investment returns as compared to benchmarks, risk, and fees, along with qualitative criteria such as the stability of the provider. In our survey, 362 of 448 sponsors said they benchmark the investment performance of the 401(k) plan.[27] Of those who do benchmarking, 297 respondents said they benchmark each option to the performance of a peer group as one way of monitoring performance. As part of this monitoring of fund options, efforts of sponsors may include reviewing reports about the performance of the funds, holding meetings, placing poorly performing funds on a watch list, ultimately removing funds or replacing them with better options, and documenting their decisions. Some pension professionals told us that investment monitoring efforts generally were of good quality overall but that certain fund characteristics, such as risk, or particular plan sizes, such as some small plans, were not always monitored adequately.

Some pension professionals are concerned that sponsors may rely on the investment provider or record keeper to monitor the funds. For example, one fiduciary adviser noted that research by an industry group showed that the provider may conduct investment monitoring for as many as 38 percent of respondents. According to this fiduciary adviser, if a sponsor relies on the provider for fund monitoring and lacks an independent adviser, an objective analysis of the funds may not occur, which could result in a prohibited transaction under certain circumstances. According to our survey, the entity primarily responsible for monitoring the performance of the plan investments as compared to investment goals or policy was frequently the plan sponsor committee (214 of 443 respondents) or an external investment/financial adviser (107 respondents).

Sponsors may also set investment goals and policies for the 401(k) plan. Before selecting funds for the menu, sponsors may set investment goals and policies that affect which particular categories of funds it can include in the menu. Many pension professionals noted that such planning by the sponsor should take into account the needs of its workforce, such as its age profile or level of knowledge about investments.[28] This planning may be documented in a written investment policy statement (IPS), which 339 of 440 sponsors responding to our survey have. An IPS is a document that can guide future decisions by documenting the intended goals and performance of the plan, as well as the guidelines for selecting, monitoring, and altering investments.[29] According to our survey, 208 of 339 respondents said the sponsor's committee was the primary decision maker for establishing a written IPS. Despite the advantages of an IPS, the policy statement may present difficulties for certain sponsors, such as greater risks of fiduciary breaches and potential liability if the sponsor does not follow it. Regardless of a plan's goals and policies, Labor's regulation on investment duties specifies factors for sponsors to consider for prudent investment decisions, including diversification, liquidity, return, and risk in relation to the overall portfolio.[30]

The asset size of the plan may affect the investment menu, as sponsors of larger plans generally have greater internal expertise and/or capacity for committees to aid in overseeing the plan, as well as more leverage to negotiate the menu and fees. Of 447 sponsors answering this question in our survey, 396 had one or more plan committees with typically three to seven members, while research by an industry group found 72 percent had committees. For plans with $200 million or more in assets, 60 of 90 sponsors reported that they have exactly one committee, and 29 reported having more than one committee. However, for some employers, particularly smaller businesses, the owner of the company acts as the fiduciary to decide about the plan investments and providers but may have less time, knowledge, and resources to make those decisions. In addition, larger plans typically have more leverage as they negotiate with providers about fund options and the fees to operate the plan. Several professionals stated that large and sometimes medium-sized sponsors have greater ability to prescribe the investment menu than small sponsors who are more likely to face restricted choices with requirements to include the investment provider's own funds. For example, one adviser noted that plans with over $100 million in assets can generally offer the funds they want in the menu. Plans with more assets are also better positioned to negotiate lower fees, given the competition among providers to manage sponsors' pension assets.[31]

Furthermore, advisers assisting sponsors may affect decisions about the investment menu. While ERISA allows the hiring of external advisers and other providers, they must be prudently selected and monitored for the quality of their services and conflicts of interest, among other things. Of 445 sponsors responding to this survey question, 308 said they use a third- party investment adviser. According to Labor's guidance, a plan fiduciary should hire and monitor external experts if the sponsor lacks the expertise internally. Several types of advisers are available to assist the sponsor, such as registered investment advisers, consultants, and insurance or securities brokers. However, advisers differ in a number of ways, including by the services they provide, the extent to which they are willing to serve as a fiduciary, how they are compensated, and whether they are affiliated with a larger company like an insurance company or a broker-dealer. As a result, some of these advisers may have incentives not to act solely in the interest of participants, which may shape the investment menu. In our survey, for 170 of 438 sponsors, a sponsor committee monitors plan investment decisions for such potential conflicts of interest, while an external investment/financial adviser does so for 94 of the sponsors.

As with advisers, other service providers—such as the investment provider or the record keeper—may shape the menu of investments in different ways. For example, sponsors or providers can limit the menu largely or entirely to the provider's own proprietary funds, which tend to have greater profit margins or may not always perform as well as funds offered by other investment providers. Also, a number of pension professionals indicated that sponsors may defer to the provider about the menu, and thus about fund performance and fees.[32] However, according to our survey, most sponsors said that the sponsor's committee was the primary decision maker for the investment goals, menu, and any investment policy statement, with relatively few saying the primary decision maker was the 401(k) provider.

Plan Sponsors Can Face Challenges in Fulfilling Their Fiduciary Obligations When Business Arrangements Are Unclear or Undisclosed

Plan sponsors face challenges in fulfilling their obligations when fiduciary roles are not clearly defined or when sponsors lack important information about arrangements between service providers. Fiduciary roles that are not clearly defined between the sponsor and other plan fiduciaries can lead to gaps in plan oversight. Sponsors also have fiduciary obligations when they select and monitor one or multiple service providers. To fulfill these obligations, Labor's guidance indicates that sponsors should obtain information about service providers' compensation arrangements and potential conflicts of interest that could affect the service provider's performance. To improve fiduciary oversight in these areas, Labor has proposed a rule to require pension plan service contracts to disclose additional information, including the extent to which service providers will become fiduciaries for the functions they will perform.[33] If finalized, compliance with this rule could eliminate some of the confusion surrounding the sharing of fiduciary duties between sponsors and their service providers and help sponsors provide better oversight of plan services.

A Sponsor's Failure to Clearly Define Fiduciary Relationships Can Lead to Gaps in Oversight

Plans may have one or multiple plan fiduciaries, but who is and who is not a fiduciary is not always apparent. ERISA requires that at least one fiduciary be named in the plan documents, although others may be identified voluntarily.[34] Depending on how the delivery of plan services is structured, the sponsor may retain, share, or delegate certain fiduciary roles with the advisers or other providers it hires. For example, sponsors may use an officer or company manager, one or more internal committees, or an outside professional—sometimes called a third-party service provider—as a fiduciary to manage some or all of a plan's day-to-day operations. These services can include investment management, consulting and providing financial advice, record keeping, custodial or trustee services for plan assets, and telephone or Web-based customer services for participants. Providers may also assist sponsors to fulfill their fiduciary obligations by educating sponsors or helping them comply with ERISA requirements. For example, one provider we met has informational materials for its clients, including checklists about fiduciary obligations, sample documents, and newsletters on regulatory updates.

While ERISA allows a plan sponsor to hire outside professionals to manage some or all of their plan's day-to-day operations, this does not relieve the sponsor of all fiduciary obligation. The hiring of any service provider is itself a fiduciary act, and under ERISA, a sponsor must act prudently when selecting one or multiple service providers and monitor their performance. To comply with ERISA, the plan sponsor must have sufficient information to make informed decisions about the services, costs and the qualifications of the service providers, and the quality of the services being provided. The sponsor must ensure that expenses paid out of plan assets, including fees paid to service providers, are and continue to be reasonable in light of the level and quality of services provided. The sponsor must also determine whether there are conflicts of interest related to service provider compensation. Conflicts of interest can occur, for example, when a service provider steers a plan sponsor toward offering investment options that benefit the service provider but may not be in the best interest of the plan participants.

Rather than prescribing the specific actions that a sponsor needs to take when selecting and monitoring one or multiple service providers, ERISA requires that a prudent process be followed to ensure that the sponsor's fiduciary obligations are met. According to Labor, prudence requires expertise in a variety of areas, such as investments. Lacking that expertise, a fiduciary will want to hire someone with that professional knowledge to carry out the investment and other functions. Prudence focuses on the process for making fiduciary decisions. For instance, in hiring a plan service provider, a fiduciary may decide to survey a number of potential providers, asking for the same information and providing the same requirements. By so doing, a fiduciary can make a meaningful comparison and selection. According to Labor, however, many of the specific actions that sponsors may take to meet these duties can vary. Labor recommends that sponsors establish and follow a formal review process at reasonable intervals.

Sponsors may assume that they have delegated all their fiduciary duties to an outside professional hired to run the plan, but the sponsor always retains some fiduciary obligation. While plan sponsors may hire various advisers and consultants to provide advice on the selection and monitoring of investment funds, fiduciary duties may be distributed differently depending on the service arrangement. For example, an investment adviser who recommends investment funds to a plan sponsor for a fee, may be a fiduciary under ERISA.[35] In contrast, if the sponsor is selecting funds from a broker and the broker provides no investment advice, the fiduciary obligations may lie entirely with the sponsor under ERISA, as shown in figure 3.

Sharing or delegating fiduciary duties among service providers can contribute to indistinct fiduciary roles if their respective roles are not well defined. Some sponsors may be more concerned with hiring a provider to perform a particular service than about determining whether or not the provider will be acting as a plan fiduciary. For example, several industry professionals noted situations when sponsors assumed they had delegated fiduciary investment advice for the selection and monitoring of investment funds to a service provider, but the service provider did not acknowledge that fiduciary role. Several pension practitioners observed that most sponsors, especially sponsors of small plans, have very little fiduciary knowledge. For example, one attorney with an employee benefits firm stated that while sponsors may know they are fiduciaries, without understanding the concept and extra duties of being responsible for plan assets, they primarily see their function as hiring service providers who they may view as the "real" fiduciaries. A number of practitioners have stated that some service providers understand fiduciary roles better than plan sponsors do but may wish to avoid the liability associated with certain fiduciary duties, even though their actions may define them as fiduciaries under the law. This can lead some sponsors to assume that they have delegated certain fiduciary duties to a service provider, although the provider may not acknowledge any fiduciary role. When the service provider is not a fiduciary, it is not bound by the fiduciary duties to act prudently and solely in the plan's best interest. For example, according to several practitioners, Registered Investment Advisers (RIA) are generally fiduciaries, while some other advisers describe themselves as consultants in an attempt to avoid fiduciary responsibility.

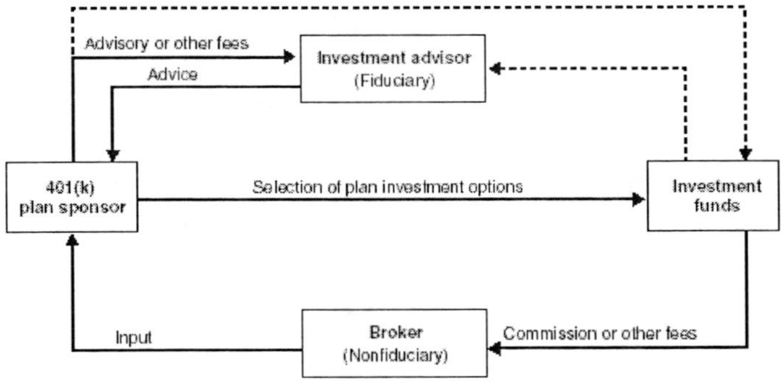

------ Optional advisory or other fees

Source: GAO analysis of information from industry practitioners.

Figure 3. Differences in Fiduciary Role and Possible Fee and Service Arrangements Using an Investment Adviser versus a Broker.

Because ERISA generally does not require that additional fiduciaries be named, determinations may not be made unless a lawsuit is filed claiming that the plan has been harmed. Misunderstanding can also occur because many large providers offer a range of services that a sponsor can choose from, including some that involve fiduciary duties and others that may not.

Sponsors Cannot Fulfill Their Fiduciary Obligations without Disclosures about Compensation Arrangements and Potential Conflicts of Interest

Labor's guidance indicates that to fulfill their fiduciary obligations sponsors should obtain certain information about service providers' compensation arrangements and potential conflicts of interest. However, some sponsors do not understand their service providers' revenue sharing arrangements or may be unaware of potential conflicts of interest. Research by one industry group found that about 60 percent of responding sponsors said that providers fully disclosed revenue sharing. According to pension practitioners, sponsors of large plans, helped by advisers or consultants, may have a better understanding of revenue sharing and are negotiating lower fees than in the past, but sponsors of medium-sized plans generally do not understand how undisclosed compensation flows between service providers behind the scenes, even if they understand mutual fund expense ratios.

Significant differences in ways that advisers and other providers are compensated may have important implications for the sponsor's oversight, including identifying potential conflicts of interest. According to an RIA that we spoke with, if the adviser is an RIA hired by a plan sponsor on a fee-for-service basis, his allegiance may be different than an adviser who is a broker and receives a commission based on the value of the investment product that is selected. Furthermore, other experts noted that a sponsor may opt for what appears to be a "free" 401(k) plan (with no record keeping fees for the employer) without understanding that the providers' compensation may be passed on to participants by embedding fees in the plan's investment options. "Hidden" fees may also mask the existence of a conflict of interest. Hidden fees are usually related to business arrangements where one service provider to a 401(k) plan pays a third-party provider for services, such as record keeping, but does not disclose this compensation to the plan sponsor. Without disclosing these arrangements, service providers may be steering plan sponsors toward investment products or services that may not be in the best interest of participants. Research by one industry group showed that 36 percent of responding sponsors either did not know the fees being charged to participants or thought no fees were charged at all. An RIA told us that if a "free" 401(k) plan has been selected by the sponsor, it is unlikely that the sponsor used an RIA to examine the underlying fee structure. In a situation like this, one practitioner said that it is more likely that the human resources department, rather than the finance department, selected the free plan option. In addition to failing to understand the fee structure, some less knowledgeable staff may act out of loyalty to their employer without fully understanding ERISA's fiduciary duty to act in the best interests of the plan. Consequently, they may select an arrangement that reduces the employer's fees at the expense of the higher embedded fees paid by participants, which may involve a fiduciary breach under certain circumstances.

Various Ways to Improve Fiduciary Oversight Have Been Proposed

Labor officials and various industry practitioners have proposed new ways to improve fiduciary oversight. A regulation recently proposed by Labor could eliminate some of the confusion surrounding fiduciary obligations. In December 2007, Labor proposed a regulation that would require, among other things, a service provider of an employee benefit plan, including 401(k) plans, to state whether it will provide services to the plan as a fiduciary.[36] Labor believes that plan fiduciaries, including sponsors and service providers, would benefit from regulatory guidance in this area. According to Labor, the increased complexity of administering services and benefits for these plans has made it more difficult for plan sponsors to understand compensation arrangements between service providers. The proposed regulation would amend the current regulations under ERISA to clarify the meaning of a reasonable contract or arrangement between sponsors (or other fiduciaries) and service providers to include the disclosure of information concerning all compensation to be received by the service providers and any conflicts of interest that may have adverse effects on the cost and quality of plan services. Among the information that would be required under the proposed provision on conflicts of interest, is a requirement to determine whether the entity will provide services to the plan as a fiduciary.

If finalized, compliance with this rule could eliminate some of the confusion surrounding the sharing of fiduciary duties between sponsors and their service providers and help sponsors provide better oversight of plan services. Labor is in the process of analyzing the information from the public comments it received earlier this year and the hearings it held regarding this regulation. Labor officials anticipate issuing a final regulation by the end of this year.

In addition, consulting organizations have suggested other measures to improve accountability for fulfilling fiduciary obligations, such as fiduciary training for plan sponsors and auditing plans for fiduciary compliance.

Labor Monitors Sponsors' Operation of 401(k) Plans and Has Made Progress on Recent Regulatory Initiatives

Labor takes various actions to monitor sponsors' fiduciary oversight of 401(k) plans and has made some progress on its regulatory initiatives. Labor investigates reports of questionable 401(k) plan practices, collects information from plan sponsors, and conducts outreach to educate plan sponsors about their responsibilities. Labor is also pursuing several initiatives to improve disclosures provided to participants, plan sponsors and fiduciaries, government agencies and the public. Recently, Labor issued proposed regulations to clarify the information that service providers must disclose to plan sponsors.[37] However, Labor is in the process of resolving several questions before it can issue a clear set of final regulations. In previous reports, we asked Congress to consider certain matters that, if addressed, could provide Labor with greater statutory authority over plan service providers and help ensure that sponsors are properly overseeing plan services.[38]

Labor Investigates Fiduciary Breaches and Conducts Outreach to Educate Plan Sponsors

Labor uses a variety of methods to ensure that sponsors fulfill their fiduciary obligations. These include enforcement efforts, such as investigations of employee benefit plans, and outreach efforts to educate plan sponsors about their responsibilities.

EBSA's regional offices seek to detect, correct, and deter violations, such as excessive fees and expenses, and failure by fiduciaries to monitor ongoing fee structure arrangements. EBSA opened 3,746 civil investigations and obtained nearly $1.3 billion monetary results in fiscal year 2007. Over $245 million of those monetary results were related to 401(k) investigations. These investigations cited violations, such as failure to act prudently, payment of excessive administrative expenses, and failure to monitor ongoing arrangements.

We reported in 2007 that EBSA does not conduct routine compliance examinations, such as evaluations of a company's books, records, and internal controls. Instead, EBSA uses participant complaints and other agency referrals as sources of investigative leads and to detect potential violations. EBSA also identifies leads through informal targeting efforts by investigators, primarily using data reported by plan sponsors on their Form 5500 annual returns. During our 2007 review, EBSA officials raised concerns that conducting such examinations would divert resources from EBSA's current enforcement practices.[39]

When EBSA uncovers a fiduciary breach, it can take several actions against the fiduciary. These actions can result in a monetary result for the plan (such as restored plan assets), or an action taken by EBSA that results in the fiduciary or a service provider being enjoined or removed (these commonly include compelling the fiduciary to fulfill its obligations, enjoining the fiduciary from committing a further violation, compelling the fiduciary to make restitution for the violation, removing the fiduciary, and/or disallowing the fiduciary from ever serving in another fiduciary capacity, to name a few).

Labor receives complaints regarding fiduciary breaches in several areas, such as

- fees or expenses charged for plan services. This can include the plan having paid unreasonable/excessive fees or settlor fees.
- situations where the employer has filed for or may file for bankruptcy. This includes alleged mismanagement and/or misuse of plan assets combined with the fact that the employer has filed bankruptcy.
- how long an employer may take to deposit participant contributions into the plan (including participant's loan repayments). This includes inquiries regarding possible fiduciary violations and missing or delinquent contributions. Contributions are delinquent when an employer fails to transmit employee contributions as soon as reasonably possible.[40]
- investment of funds. This includes imprudent investments, those prohibited by the plan document or failure of the plan administrator to offer a diversified menu of investment options in a 401(k) plan.
- loans or sales to parties in interest and/or the use of plan assets for personal or company use. This includes prohibited transactions related to self-dealing (a fiduciary acting in its own interest); dual loyalties (representing adverse parties); or receipt of consideration from a third party, also known as kickbacks.

EBSA also focuses some of its enforcement efforts on compensation arrangements between pension plan sponsors and service providers hired to assist in the investment of plan assets. EBSA's Consultant/Adviser Project (CAP), created in October 2006, is focused on identifying conflicts of interest and the receipt of indirect, undisclosed compensation by pension consultants and other investment advisers. Its investigations determine whether the receipt of such compensation violates ERISA because the adviser or consultant used its status with respect to a benefit plan to generate additional fees for itself or its affiliates.[41] According to an EBSA official, the agency has not yet taken enforcement action against consultants or advisers or 401(k) plan fiduciaries. However, the official told us that by implementing this initiative, EBSA has demonstrated its concern about the receipt of indirect, undisclosed compensation by fiduciary consultants and advisers doing business with 401(k) plans. CAP also seeks to identify potential criminal violations, such as kickbacks or fraud.

In addition to its enforcement efforts, EBSA works to educate and assist employers (particularly small employers), auditors and other service providers in understanding and complying with their obligations under the law and related regulations and procedures, including those related to 401(k) plans.[42] EBSA also has a program called the Voluntary Fiduciary Correction Program (VFCP), which allows plan officials to disclose and correct certain violations without penalty. In fiscal year 2007, 1,303 40 1(k) VFCP applications were received by EBSA's regional offices, and over $20.7 million was restored to 40 1(k) plans as a result of this program. According to EBSA, virtually all transactions under the VFCP program are related to fiduciary issues.

Labor Has Made Some Progress on Relevant Regulatory Initiatives but Legislation Could Also Promote Fiduciary Oversight

Since our November 2006 report, EBSA has made progress on three regulatory initiatives to improve the transparency of fee and expense information to participants, plan sponsors and fiduciaries, government agencies and the public. It began these initiatives, in part, amid concerns that participants were not receiving information in a format useful to them when making investment decisions and that plan fiduciaries were having difficulty getting needed fee and compensation arrangement information from service providers to fully satisfy their fiduciary obligations.

EBSA's regulatory initiatives to expand disclosure requirements cover three distinct areas, (1) disclosures by plan sponsors to participants to assist in making informed investment decisions; (2) disclosures by service providers to plan fiduciaries to assist in assessing the reasonableness of provider compensation and potential conflicts of interest; and (3) more efficient, expanded fee and compensation disclosures to the government and the public through a substantially revised, electronically filed Form 5500 Annual Report.[43] At the time of our last review, EBSA had a proposed rule for its initiative on disclosures to the government and the public. Table 2 shows the progress EBSA has made since our November 2006 report.

Table 2. Summary of Labor's Disclosure Initiatives.

Disclosure by plan sponsors to participants	
Information gathering 72 Fed. Reg. 20,457	In April 2007, Labor published a request for information (RFI) to solicit the views, suggestions, and comments from plan participants, plan sponsors, plan service providers, and members of the financial community, as well as the general public, on the extent to which rules should be adopted or modified, or other actions taken, to ensure that participants and beneficiaries have the information they need to make informed decisions about the management of their individual accounts and the investment of their retirement savings. Labor officials have stated that they soon plan to publish a proposed regulation that will govern disclosure by plans to plan participants.
Disclosures by service providers to plan sponsors	
Proposed rule 72 Fed. Reg. 70,988	On December 13, 2007, EBSA published a proposed rule to amend its current regulations under section 408(b)(2) of ERISA to clarify the information fiduciaries must receive and service providers must disclose for purposes of determining whether a contract or arrangement is "reasonable," as required by ERISA's statutory exemption for service arrangements.[a] The regulation would require service providers to disclose, in writing, to plan fiduciaries of 401(k) plans, all services to be furnished; all direct and indirect compensation to be received; and any potential conflict of interest, such as certain third-party relationships, that could affect their objectivity under a service contract or arrangement. The information provided must be sufficient for fiduciaries to make informed decisions about the services that will be provided, the costs of those services, and potential conflicts of interest. Labor believes that such disclosures are critical to ensuring that contracts and arrangements are "reasonable" within the meaning of the statute.
Disclosure by plan sponsors to Labor and the public	
Final rule 72 Fed. Reg. 64,710	On November 16, 2007, EBSA published a final rule revising the annual reporting requirements of plans concerning service provider compensation. For the most part, the reporting changes, including the requirement to file forms electronically, go into effect for plan years beginning on or after January 1, 2009. The new regulations expanded Schedule C of the Form 5500 so that, in addition to compensation paid directly by a plan to a service provider, it requires the reporting of "indirect compensation" paid to those who directly or indirectly provide services to the plan. All persons receiving $5,000 or more of total compensation must be identified on Schedule C. In general, the Schedule requires additional information for any service provider who is a fiduciary or provides contract administrator, consulting, custodial, investment advisory, investment management, broker, or record keeping services. It is expected that existing regulatory disclosures may be used to meet these requirements, e.g., prospectus, SEC Form ADV, if they meet certain requirements. Labor's intent is to ensure that revenue sharing payments and other forms of indirect compensation, such as float, are reported at least to the plan administrators if not to Labor.[b]

Source: GAO analysis.

[a] Labor's December 2007, notice of proposed rule making also proposed a class exemption that would provide relief from certain prohibited transaction restrictions of ERISA. The proposed class exemption would relieve the responsible plan fiduciary from any liability for a prohibited transaction that would result from entering into a contract or arrangement for the provision of services when the service provider failed to comply with the proposed regulation.

[b] Float revenue is revenue earned from the short-term investment of plan assets.

Status of Initiative on Disclosure by Plan Sponsors to Participants

Labor's request for information (RFI) requested comments on fee and expense disclosure issues affecting participants and beneficiaries of 401(k)-type plans governed by ERISA. Specifically, Labor sought information on what administrative and investment-related fee and expense information participants should consider when investing their retirement savings, the manner in which the information should be furnished to participants, and who should provide that information. The RFI cited our November 2006 report on fees as part of the impetus for issuing the RFI. However, while we did suggest that Congress consider amending ERISA to require all sponsors to disclose fee information to participants in a way that facilitates comparison among the options, our recommendation to the Secretary of Labor was to require plan sponsors to report a summary of all fees that are paid out of plan assets or by participants to Labor. Labor has not yet published a proposed regulation related to the RFI.

Status of Initiative on Disclosures by Service Providers to Plan Sponsors

According to Labor officials, they are in the process of resolving several questions before Labor can issue final regulations, such as the extent to which providers within a bundled arrangement—a package of plan services—would be bound by the disclosure requirements of the regulations. Labor held a hearing on March 31, 2008, to further develop the public record regarding the regulation and the class exemption and to assist the department in understanding the issues involved. Labor heard testimony from a variety of interested parties, including plan service providers, industry and participant associations, plan sponsors, and law firms. According to Labor officials, they are still reviewing the comments and testimony received.

The Assistant Secretary for the Employee Benefits Security Administration told Congress that EBSA will work to ensure that the benefits of the proposed regulation—which may include lower fees, increased efficiencies, and some reduced costs—will outweigh the costs of compliance. According to the Assistant Secretary, plan fiduciaries could be provided an exemption if they enter into contracts that are not "reasonable" because, unbeknownst to them, the service provider failed to comply with its disclosure obligations.[44] Several members of Congress sent a letter to Labor expressing their displeasure over the proposed regulation.

Among other things, the letter stated that Labor, rather than excusing failures with class exemptions for fiduciaries who fail to receive required disclosures, should update its guidance on fiduciary responsibility and provide model documents and explanations of key terms to pension plan officials.

Several members of Congress have introduced bills that would require various additional disclosures related to individual account plans, including information from service providers.[45] One bill, as introduced, would require service providers to disclose to the plan sponsor all fees that workers will pay, including such things as sales commissions, trading costs, and termination or surrender charges. The bill would require service providers to outline any financial or other conflicts of interest to plan sponsors.

Some sponsors, however, have expressed concern about the introduction of fee disclosure legislation. For example, in our survey, sponsors expressed concern about the amount and manner in which information is disclosed to plan participants. Given the complexity of the information being provided, sponsors felt that disclosures should be simple and easy to understand. In our survey, sponsors also stated that fees should be disclosed in a transparent manner and should be readily identifiable by the plan sponsor and participants. In addition to concerns about fee disclosures, several sponsors suggested that disclosures would work best if standardized and that legislation may help providers be consistent in their data preparation and allow "apples to apples" comparisons of fee information.

While the Assistant Secretary of Labor for the Employee Benefits Security Administration has stated that a statutory amendment is not necessary for the department to complete its work, we continue to believe that a statutory change is necessary to ensure that these matters are fully addressed and that the matters that GAO has recently asked Congress to consider, if addressed, would help Labor in its efforts to improve sponsors' fiduciary oversight.[46] For example,

- We previously asked that Congress consider amending ERISA to explicitly require 401(k) service providers to disclose to plan sponsors the compensation they receive from other service providers. This change would provide Labor with explicit statutory authority over plan service providers for this purpose and help sponsors properly oversee plan services.
- In addition, in our 2007 report on conflicts of interest in defined benefit plans, we found that undisclosed business arrangements or conflicts of interest may have resulted in financial harm to some plans.[47] Given this risk, we asked that Congress consider amending ERISA to give Labor authority to recover plan losses against certain types of service providers even if they are not currently considered fiduciaries under ERISA. These findings may have similar implications for defined contribution plans, especially 401(k) plans.

Concluding Observations

As the retirement security of American workers increasingly depends on 401(k) plans, it is important that plan sponsors fulfill their fiduciary responsibilities in connection with such plans. Sponsors make decisions about the investment features of a 401(k) plan that carry significant fiduciary implications. Some, particularly those with small plans, may have limited time, specialization, knowledge, and ability to negotiate about service providers or investment funds. Absent a greater understanding of how sharing plan functions with their service providers or delegating functions to them may lead to confusion about fiduciary roles, some sponsors are likely to remain vulnerable to advisers or other providers whose compensation and affiliation may promote interests besides those of the plan, such as higher plan fees.

Since our 2006 report, Labor has made progress on its disclosure initiatives but some important fiduciary issues have yet to be fully addressed. In our previous reports, we asked Congress to consider amending ERISA to (1) explicitly require 401(k) service providers to disclose to plan sponsors the compensation they receive from other service providers and (2) give Labor authority to recover plan losses against certain types of service providers, even if they are not currently considered fiduciaries to that plan under ERISA. While Labor has proposed a regulatory change that could eliminate some of the confusion surrounding certain fiduciary obligations, it is unclear how closely the final regulation will follow the proposed rule. We continue to believe that changes to ERISA would help Labor in its efforts to promote sponsors' fiduciary oversight and be in the best interest of participants.

Agency Comments and Our Evaluation

We provided a draft of this report to the Department of Labor (Labor). Labor provided technical comments, which we have incorporated where appropriate.

As agreed with your staff, unless you publicly announce its contents earlier, we plan no further distribution of this report until 30 days after its issue date. At that time, we will send copies of this report to the Secretary of Labor, as well as to other interested parties. We will also make copies available to others upon request. In addition, the report will be available at no charge on the GAO Web site at http://www.gao.gov. If you or your staff have any questions concerning this report, please contact me at (202) 512-7215 or bovbjergb@gao.gov. Contact points for our Offices of Congressional Relations and Public Affairs may be found on the last page of this report. GAO staff who made key contributions to this report are listed in appendix II.

Sincerely yours,

Barbara D. Bovbjerg
Director, Education, Workforce, and Income Security Issues

Appendix I. Scope and Methodology

To determine common 401(k) plan features and which typically have important fiduciary implications as well as challenges sponsors face in fulfilling their fiduciary obligations, we collected and analyzed industry research and information from the Department of Labor (Labor), such as Bureau of Labor Statistics information, as well as previous GAO work. Although comprehensive data on 401(k) features is limited, industry research provides some indication of the prevalence of these features. The industry research that we reviewed has limitations, such as the lack of random sampling that prevents results generalizable to the universe of 401(k) plan sponsors. Thus, we used the following three sources of industry research that reached different audiences to corroborate one another, where possible. We also checked the reliability of the data by interviewing the surveyors about their methodology.

Profit Sharing/401(k) Council of America's (PSCA) survey results are based on responses from 1,000 plan sponsors that have profit-sharing plans, 401(k) plans, or a combination of both and represent 1 to 5,000-plus employees. Thirty-nine of 1000 respondents had profit-sharing plans without a 401(k) component. The survey was mailed, faxed, or made available online to respondents and conducted from April to

June 2007. The survey provides a snapshot as of the end of 2006. The survey response rate was 13 percent. PSCA is a national, nonprofit association of 1,200 companies and their 6 million plan participants. According to PSCA, it represents the interests of its members to federal policy makers and offers assistance with profit sharing and 401(k) plan design, administration, investment, compliance, and communication.

Hewitt Associates' survey results are based on responses from 302 employers with mostly 1,000 employees or more. Twenty-nine percent represented Fortune 500 companies. The survey was conducted from March through June 2007. The survey was online, and paper copies of the questionnaire that included the survey Web site were also mailed out. Most respondents completed the survey online. The survey had a 6 percent response rate. Hewitt Associates is a human resources outsourcing and consulting firm.

Deloitte Consulting received responses from 830 employers for its survey that was initially sent to over 3,000 contacts. The survey was sent by email and made available online to a wide array of sponsors based on the contacts of Deloitte and partnering organizations, along with other interested sponsors who became aware of the survey. It is possible that contacts beyond the initial mailing completed the survey, so a response rate was not calculated. As with other industry surveys, Deloitte's survey covers a range of plan sizes but under-represents small plans, as measured by number of participants. Deloitte is a professional services organization that provides pension consulting services.

In addition to analysis of industry research, we conducted a Web-based survey to learn more about how sponsors select plan features and oversee plan operations. In conducting our design work, we determined that a representative survey of sponsors would not be feasible for this study, given the methodological and administrative challenges associated with (1) establishing a sampling frame using Labor's Form 5500 data, (2) identifying appropriate points of contact for sponsors from the universe of over 400,000 plans, and (3) the perceived sensitivity of the survey's content and the willingness of sponsors to provide candid responses about their fiduciary obligations. To overcome the methodological and administrative challenges, we administered our survey in coordination with *Plansponsor Magazine* (*Plansponsor*). The sponsors who responded to our survey were members of *Plansponsor's* subscription list – which contains approximately 41,000 members who receive the organization's electronic newsletters and magazine.

Plansponsor used two methods for soliciting survey responses from their subscription list. These methods included the distribution of notices in their daily newsletter and a more targeted electronic mailing sent to the sponsors who responded to *Plansponsor's* 2007 Defined Contributions Survey. While there is some overlap between the sponsors that receive the daily newsletter and those who responded to *Plansponsor's* 2007 Defined Contributions Survey, *Plansponsor* estimates that the daily newsletter was distributed to approximately 41,000 subscribers. The targeted electronic mailing was sent to approximately 5,500 sponsors. Using *Plansponsor's* distribution estimates, we estimate the number of 40 1(k) sponsors that received our survey notification to be approximately 22,000. We received 448 usable responses to our survey, representing 594 plans. Labor's *Abstract of 2005 Form 5500 Annual Reports* shows that there are over 400,000 plans in the United States.

We do not have evidence to determine the extent to which our survey respondents are representative of the general sponsor population. Our respondent population excludes sponsors who do not belong to *Plansponsor's* subscriber list. Therefore, the extent to which our survey results provide useful information about the general population depends on whether or not there are differences between the excluded sponsors and those belonging to *Plansponsor's* subscriber list. For example, as members of *Plansponsor's* subscriber list, our survey respondents are self-selected recipients of a publication that provides information to managers of pensions and 401(k) retirement plans. Because of their affiliation with *Plansponsor,* our survey respondents are likely to be more informed than the average sponsor, given that they are actively engaged in learning through the magazine. Although our survey respondents may be more informed than the average sponsor, *Plansponsor* affirms that their membership represents the overall sponsor demographic.

To minimize the variability of survey results, we took steps in the development of the questionnaire, the data collection, and data analysis to minimize nonsampling errors. For example, prior to administering the survey, the questionnaire was reviewed by an independent survey expert in our methodology group, as well as an official from *Plansponsor.* In addition, we conducted six pretests by telephone to determine the extent to which (1) the survey questions were clear, (2) the terms used were precise, (3) respondents were able to provide the information we were seeking, and (4) the questions were unbiased. We identified sponsors for the pretest through a series of questions posted in a survey that *Plansponsor* administers weekly to its subscribers. Sponsors were selected for the pretest based upon the total number of participants and the total amount of assets in the plan. We made changes to the content and format of the questionnaire based on the feedback we received.

The Web-based questionnaire was accessible through a secure GAO server. Sponsors completing the survey created usernames and passwords to access the survey. *Plansponsor* notified its subscribers of the survey's availability in its daily newsletter over a period of several weeks between March 2008 and May 2008. To solicit additional responses, *Plansponsor* sent a targeted electronic mailing to sponsors who responded to *Plansponsor's* 2007 Defined Contribution Survey, within the same period. No follow-up discussions with survey respondents were conducted for this study.

To further determine which features typically have important fiduciary implications and factors when making such decisions, as well as challenges sponsors face in fulfilling their fiduciary obligations when overseeing plan operations, we identified the relevant laws and regulations for 401(k) plans under ERISA. We interviewed and collected documentation from a variety of stakeholders, including plan sponsors, service providers, fiduciary advisers, industry and consumer associations, attorneys, and Labor. We also obtained their views on sponsors' awareness of fiduciary responsibilities and identified any challenges sponsors might face. We also collected and analyzed information on plan sponsor oversight from other sources, such as the reports and testimonies from ERISA Advisory Council working groups.

To determine the actions that Labor takes to ensure that sponsors are fulfilling their fiduciary obligations and the progress Labor has made on its regulatory initiatives, we reviewed ERISA and Labor's regulations to clearly define Labor's authority to oversee the conduct of 401(k) plan sponsors in fulfilling their key fiduciary obligations. We reviewed Labor's enforcement strategies for overseeing plan sponsors (e.g., reviewing the types of complaints about fiduciary breaches). We reviewed the actions Labor has taken against plan sponsors and the reasons for such actions. We also reviewed the recent work of other GAO staff in order to provide an update on Labor's compliance assistance and outreach efforts; participated in certain fiduciary education seminars; and conducted follow-up interviews with agency officials about their current initiatives.

We conducted our review from January 2007 through June 2008 in accordance with generally accepted government auditing standards.

End Notes

[1] Under ERISA, a fiduciary is anyone, such as a sponsor, trustee, investment adviser, or other service provider, to the extent they exercise any discretionary authority or control over plan management or any authority or control over the management or disposition of plan assets, render investment advice respecting plan money or property for a fee or other compensation, or have discretionary authority or responsibility for plan administration. 29 U.S.C. § 1002(21)(a).

[2] GAO, *Private Pensions: Changes Needed to Provide 401(k) Plan Participants and the Department of Labor Better Information on Fees*, GAO-07-21 (Washington, D.C.: Nov. 16, 2006) and GAO, *Defined Benefit Plans: Conflicts of Interest Involving High Risk or Terminated Plans Pose Enforcement Challenges*, GAO-07-703 (Washington, D.C. June 28, 2007).

[3] Respondents to the survey as a whole exclude sponsors who are not part of *Plansponsor's* subscription list and recipients of the survey who chose not to complete it. These other sponsors may differ from our respondents, such as their knowledge and practices about deciding plan features or monitoring operations. Thus, the results of our survey may not represent and cannot be generalized to the population of all 401(k) sponsors.

[4] 72 Fed. Reg. 70,988 (Dec. 13, 2007).

[5] GAO-07-21.

[6] GAO-07-703.

[7] Beginning in 2006, plans were permitted to allow employees to designate some or all of their elective contributions to Roth 401(k) plans, which are not excluded from current income but allow for tax-free withdrawals after 5 years of participation and if certain other conditions related to age, death or disability have been met. Economic Growth and Tax Relief Reconciliation Act of 2001, Pub. L. No. 107-16, § 617, 115 Stat. 38, 103-06 (codified at 26 U.S.C. § 402A). According to the industry research that we reviewed, 18 percent or fewer of sponsors of 401(k) plans also offered a Roth 401(k) opportunity.

[8] 29 U.S.C. § 1106. Prohibited transactions under ERISA included a sale, exchange, or lease between the plan and party-in-interest; lending money or other extension of credit between the plan and party-in-interest; and furnishing goods, services, or facilities between the plan and party-in-interest. Labor may grant, by regulation, exemptions to certain prohibited transactions.

[9] 26 U.S.C. § 4975(c) and (d)(2). The Internal Revenue Code imposes a significant tax on disqualified persons involved in such prohibited transactions unless they fit within this or various other exemptions. 26 U.S.C. § 4975(a), (b) and (d).

[10] A person is deemed to be providing investment advice only if such person (1) provides advice as to the value of, or makes recommendations as to the advisability of investing in, purchasing or selling, securities or other property, and (2) has direct or indirect discretionary authority or control over the purchase or sell of securities or other property for the plan, or regularly provides advice as to the value of securities or other property, pursuant to a mutual agreement, arrangement, or understanding, that will serve as a primary basis for plan investment decisions and is based on the particular needs of the plan. 29 C.F.R. § 2510.3-21(c) (2007).

[11] Benefits Advisors also provided assistance to 62,000 inquirers with questions about their pension plans. In fiscal year 2007, fiduciary related pension issues were discussed 5,980 times with participants and 1,612 times with employers and other plan officials. Topics discussed included administrative charges, bankruptcy, employee contributions, fund investments, abandoned plans, and prohibited transactions.

[12] Labor has taken the position that there is a class of activities which relates to the formation, rather than the management, of plans. These activities, generally referred to as settlor functions, include decisions relating to the formation, design, and termination of plans and, with few exceptions, are generally not activities subject to Title I of ERISA. Expenses incurred in connection with settlor functions would not be reasonable expenses of a plan.

[13] In two cases the plan fiduciaries selected the plan sponsor to provide administrative services to its employee benefit plans. As a result, the sponsor was reimbursed for more than direct and indirect expenses. In the third case, the plan fiduciaries used plan assets to settle a legal claim made by former plan participants who alleged the sponsor failed to make timely distributions of their accounts upon termination of employment.

[14] Pub. L. No. 109-280, 120 Stat. 780.

[15] Plan sponsors are often characterized as wearing two hats under ERISA: As the creator of a plan and the trust to fund it, they are referred to as settlors. As the entity responsible for the administration of a plan and management of its trust, depending on the function performed, they often fall within the definition of a fiduciary under ERISA. Only in the latter capacity are plan sponsors obligated to make decisions solely in the interest of plan participants and beneficiaries. *Lockheed Corp. v. Spink*, 517 U.S. 882, 890-91 (1996).

[16] The 50th Annual Survey of Profit Sharing and 401(k) Plans for 2006 by the ProfitSharing/401(k) Council of America (PSCA), Trends and Experience in 401(k) Plans 2007 by Hewitt Associates, and the Annual 40 1(k) Benchmarking Survey 2005/2006 edition by Deloitte Consulting.

[17] We drew on the following industry research: the 50th Annual Survey of Profit Sharing and 401(k) Plans for 2006 by the Profit-Sharing/401(k) Council of America (PSCA), Trends and Experience in 401(k) Plans 2007 by Hewitt Associates, and the Annual 401(k) Benchmarking Survey 2005/2006 edition by Deloitte Consulting. While a new Deloitte survey is to be issued soon, it was not available at the time of our review. Where possible, we compared their results for convergence. For more information, see appendix I.

[18] See, for example, Keenan Dworak-Fisher, "Employer Generosity in Employer-Matched 401(k) Plans, 2002-03," Bureau of Labor Statistics *Monthly Labor Review* (Washington, D.C., July/August 2007).

[19] The 50th Annual Survey of Profit Sharing and 401(k) Plans, Trends and Experience in 401(k) Plans 2007, and the Annual 401(k) Benchmarking Survey 2005/2006 edition.

[20] Trends and Experience in 401(k) Plans 2007 and the Annual 401(k) Benchmarking Survey 2005/2006 edition.

[21] The 50th Annual Survey of Profit Sharing and 401(k) Plans, Trends and Experience in 401(k) Plans 2007, and the Annual 401(k) Benchmarking Survey 2005/2006 edition.

[22] Our respondents represent a nonrandom sample of sponsors from the subscription list of an industry publication. While 448 sponsors completed our survey, the number of sponsors answering particular questions varies. Survey responses represent the views of the 448 respondents to our survey and cannot be generalized to the population of 401(k) plan sponsors. See appendix I for more information about our survey methodology.

[23] However, once sponsors make these settlor decisions, then the fiduciary obligations may apply when implementing these decisions.

[24] Sponsors may include other features with fiduciary implications, such as providing employer stock as a fund option or offering investment advice to participants. These features have their own distinct considerations, such as the undiversified nature of employer stock or differences between education versus advice for plan participants. Industry research indicates that about half of responding 401(k) sponsors or less offered these features. Also, areas of plan operations other than investments, such as administration or communication with participants, may have fiduciary implications. For example, the sponsor must ensure the timely deposit of employee contributions to comply with ERISA and related Labor regulations.

[25] The 50th Annual Survey of Profit Sharing and 401(k) Plans, Trends and Experience in 401(k) Plans 2007, and the Annual 401(k) Benchmarking Survey 2005/2006 edition.

[26] 72 Fed. Reg. 60,452 (Oct. 24, 2007). According to the regulation, lifecycle, or target-date, funds combine different funds and automatically rebalance asset allocations toward more conservative investments as the participant nears retirement. Balanced funds are pooled accounts for different risk levels. Managed accounts resemble lifecycle funds but differ by the potential funds composing the portfolio and how they are provided. Besides these three alternatives, the regulation included grandfathered and short-term principal preservation funds.

[27] Our survey provides anecdotal information that represents the views of the 448 respondents and cannot be generalized to the population of 401(k) plan sponsors. See appendix I for more information about our survey methodology.

[28] For example, some professionals noted that a workforce with limited knowledge of investments may not be well served by a complex plan with dozens of funds, including less diversified funds specializing in particular economic sectors or a self-directed brokerage allowing investment in individual mutual funds or stocks.

[29] An investment policy statement (IPS) has fiduciary implications and can help demonstrate the execution of fiduciary obligations, including following a prudent process and offering diversified funds. Part of an ERISA fiduciary's duty is to follow plan documents, including any IPS. 29 U.S.C. § 1104(a)(1)(D). Labor's regulation on this issue states that a written statement of investment policy is consistent with ERISA's provisions to have a funding policy but does not say that one is required. 29 C.F.R. § 2509.94-2 (2007).

[30] 29 C.F.R. § 2550.404a-1 (2007).

[31] In light of the fiduciary obligation to act for the sole benefit of participants and to pay only reasonable fees, plans over a certain size may pursue nonretail investment vehicles, including separate accounts or collective trusts, which typically have lower fees than retail investment vehicles. However, some professionals noted that these vehicles with lower fees may not have listings in financial news for participants or obvious benchmarks for sponsors to monitor fund performance.

[32] For example, investment providers or record keepers may try to steer sponsors to funds which result in higher hidden fees for themselves or other providers, while sponsors have a fiduciary obligation to pay only reasonable plan expenses.

[33] 72 Fed. Reg. 70,988 (Dec. 13, 2007).

[34] 29 U.S.C. § 1102(a).

[35] A person is deemed to be providing investment advice only if such person (1) provides advice as to the value of, or makes recommendations as to the advisability of investing in, purchasing or selling, securities or other property, and (2) has direct or indirect discretionary authority or control over the purchase or sell of securities or other property for the plan, or regularly provides advice as to the value of securities or other property, pursuant to a mutual agreement, arrangement, or understanding, that will serve as a primary basis for plan investment decisions and is based on the particular needs of the plan. 29 C.F.R. § 2510.3-21(c) (2007).

[36] On December 13, 2007, Labor published a notice of proposed rulemaking to amend its regulations under section 408(b)(2) of ERISA, 29 C.F.R. § 2550.408b-2, relating to the provision of services to employee benefit plans. 72 Fed. Reg. 70,988.

[37] 72 Fed. Reg. 70,988 (Dec. 13, 2007).

[38] GAO-07-21 and GAO-07-703.

[39] GAO, *Employee Benefits Security Administration: Enforcement Improvements Made but Additional Actions Could Further Enhance Pension Plan Oversight*, GAO-07-22 (Washington, D.C.: Jan. 18, 2007).

[40] In no event is "as soon as reasonably possible" later than the 15th business day of the month following the month in which the participant contribution amounts are received by the employer (in the case of amounts that a participant or beneficiary pays to an employer) or the 15th business day of the month following the month in which such amounts would have been payable to the participant in cash (in the case of amounts withheld by an employer from a participant's wages). 29 C.F.R. § 2510.3-102(b).

[41] A related objective is to determine whether plan sponsors and fiduciaries understand the compensation and fee arrangements they enter into in order to prudently select, retain, and monitor pension consultants and investment advisers.

[42] One example of EBSA's efforts is its Fiduciary Education Campaign. Since the campaign was launched in May 2004, EBSA has conducted 24 seminars attended by 2,720 plan sponsors and practitioners. EBSA also provides a number of tools— such as its interactive ERISA Fiduciary Advisor on EBSA's Web site—as well as tips for employers on selecting and monitoring plan service providers. The ERISA Fiduciary Advisor was launched on October 9, 2007. From the launch date until April 30, 2008, the site was visited by 16,723 unique visitors.

[43] The Form 5500 includes information on the plan's sponsor and the number of participants, among other things. The form also provides more specific information, such as plan assets, liabilities, insurance, and financial transactions. Filing this form satisfies the requirement for the plan administrator to file annual reports concerning, among other things, the financial condition and operation of plans. Labor uses this form as a tool to monitor and enforce plan sponsors' responsibilities under ERISA.

[44] Statement of Bradford P. Campbell, Assistant Secretary of Labor, Before the Committee on Education and Labor, U.S. House of Representatives, Oct. 4, 2007. Statement of Bradford P. Campbell, Assistant Secretary of Labor, Before the Special Committee on Aging, U.S. Senate, Oct. 24, 2007.

[45] H.R. 3185, the 401(k) Fair Disclosure for Retirement Security Act of 2007, was introduced in Congress on July 26, 2007; H.R. 3765, the Defined Contribution Plan Fee Transparency Act of 2007, was introduced on October 4, 2007; and S. 2473, the Defined Contribution Fee Disclosure Act of 2007, was introduced on December 13, 2007.

[46] Statement of Bradford P. Campbell, Assistant Secretary of Labor, Before the Committee on Education and Labor, U.S. House of Representatives, Oct. 4, 2007.

[47] GAO-07-703.

CHAPTER SOURCES

The following chapters have been previously published:

Chapter 1 – This is an edited, excerpted and augmented edition of a United States Government Accountability Office (GAO), Report to Congressional Requesters. Publication GAO-08-692, dated August 2008.

Chapter 2 – This is an edited, excerpted and augmented edition of a United States Government Accountability Office (GAO), Report to Congressional Addressees. Publication GAO-08-817, dated July 2008.

Chapter 3 – This is an edited, excerpted and augmented edition of a United States Congressional Research Service publication, Report Order Code RL30122, dated September 8, 2008.

Chapter 4 - These remarks were delivered as Statement of Charles A. Jeszeck, Acting Director, Education, Workforce, and Income Security, before the Subcommittee on Health Employment, Labor and Pensions, Education and Labor Committee, U.S. House of Representatives, GAO-09-503T, dated March 24, 2009.

Chapter 5 – This is an edited, excerpted and augmented edition of a United States Government Accountability Office (GAO), Report to the Chairman, Committee on Education and Labor, House of Representatives. Publication GAO-08-774, dated July 2008.

Index

D

E